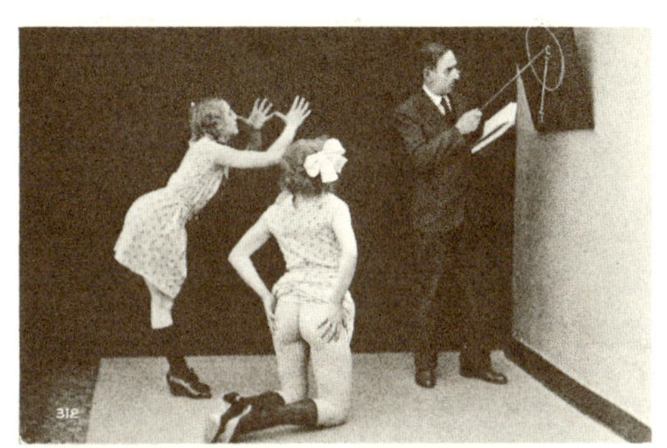
318

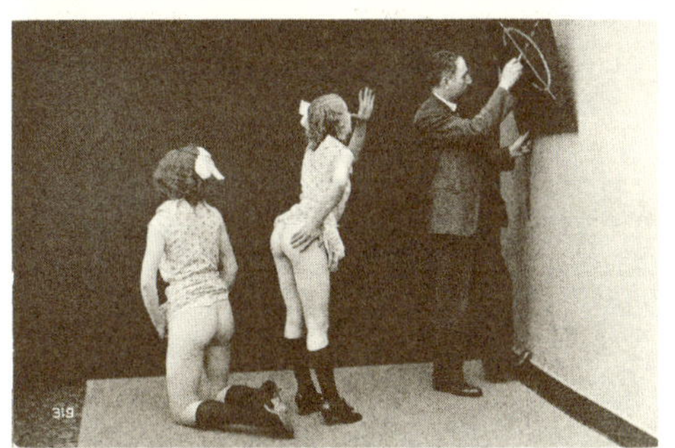
319

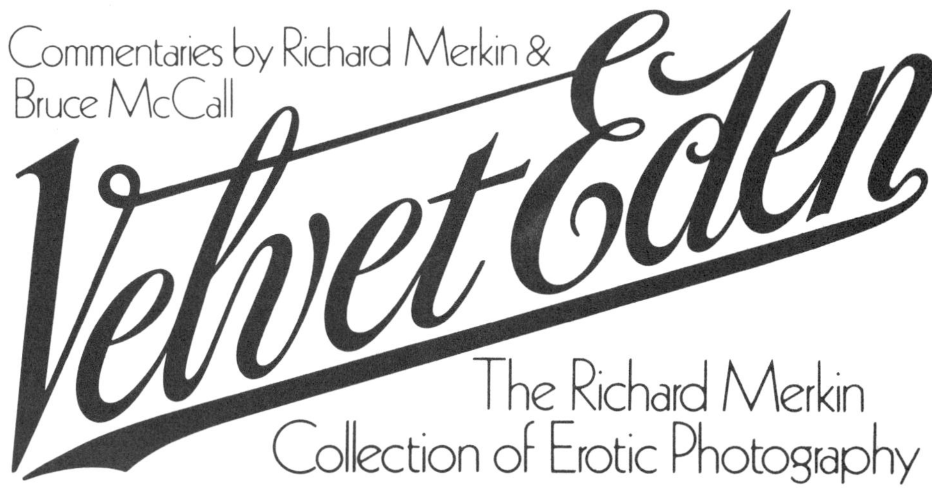

Commentaries by Richard Merkin &
Bruce McCall

Velvet Eden

The Richard Merkin Collection of Erotic Photography

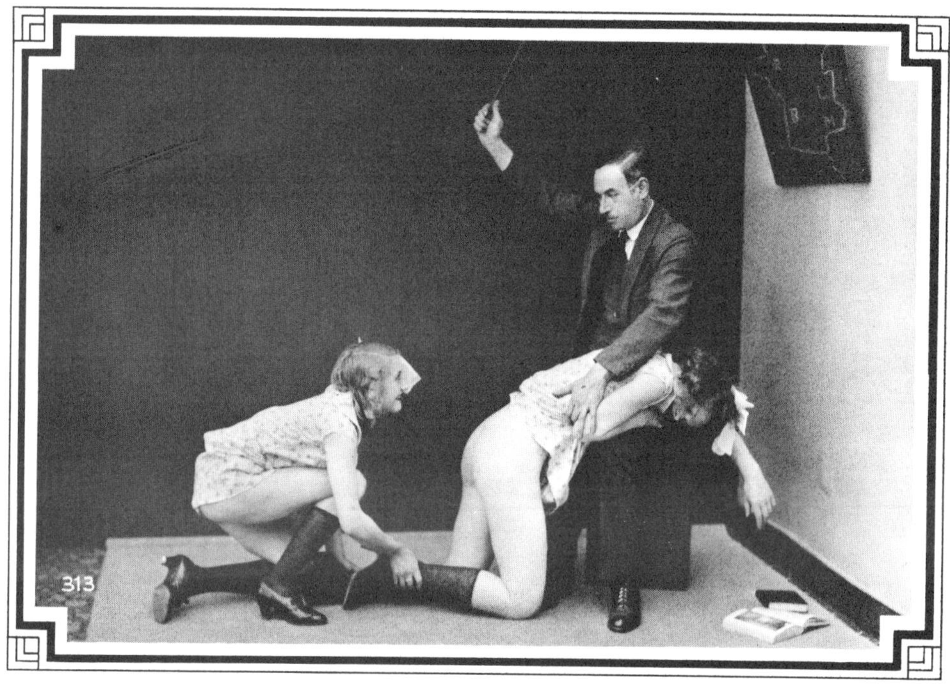

Produced and art directed by Harris Lewine

BELL PUBLISHING COMPANY
New York

This 1985 edition is published by
Bell Publishing Company,
by arrangement with Hilltown Press.

Printed and bound in the United States of America

Library of Congress Cataloging in Publication Data
Main entry under title:

Velvet Eden.

1. Photography, Erotic. 2. Merkin, Richard—
Photograph collections. I. Merkin, Richard.
TR676.V44 1985 779'.28'0944074 85-15641

ISBN: 0-517-476800

h g f e d c b a

Acknowledgments

I would like to give a special thanks to my good friend, Mr. J.B. Rund, the Master of Willieana, who was moving out of this as I was moving into it. But he paused to help and instruct and is, to my gratitude, pausing still. I also wish to acknowledge Joe, who was there when it was all happening and who has been nice enough to tell me about it. —R.M.

For Blondie and Whitey and Steady Eddie

Several years ago, an art director friend—and the art director of this book—borrowed a photograph from me to use for the dust jacket of a book that he was working on at the time, entitled *Delta of Venus*. The book, a collection of graceful and explicit erotic stories by the late Anaïs Nin, was written in the thirties. The picture chosen for the book's jacket was slightly soft-focus, shadowy, and utterly typical of the period it was to exemplify. It depicted a classic Art Deco flapper, cloche-hatted and fully clad in a black dress. Kneeling in an armchair and lifting her hem high enough to reveal that point where her stockings met whatever it was that held her stockings up, more than likely a garter belt, she was part coquette, part hooker. The gesture was both demure and what they used to refer to as "spicy." It was *Parisienne* Peek-a-Boo to be sure, but within its camp theater, it had grace, understatement, and a kind of mystery long since gone from the realm of erotic photography. The book's jacket suggested reticence and allure, and the fact that *Delta of Venus* did as well as it did was certainly in part attributable to the graphic charms of the photo. The picture was credited to the Richard Merkin Collection which, although it had existed for a number of years, had never before been titled or referred to in print. The photo and credit prompted a number of inquiries as to just what this Richard Merkin Collection was and who, for that matter, was Richard Merkin and was that *really* his name? Since publication of *Delta of Venus*, a number of other photographs have been used in print and credited to the same source. Because *Velvet Eden* is in part the offspring of the sudden notoriety of the Richard Merkin Collection, I suggest that it might be proper, at this point, to address myself to the queries raised about it and its owner and settle them definitively.

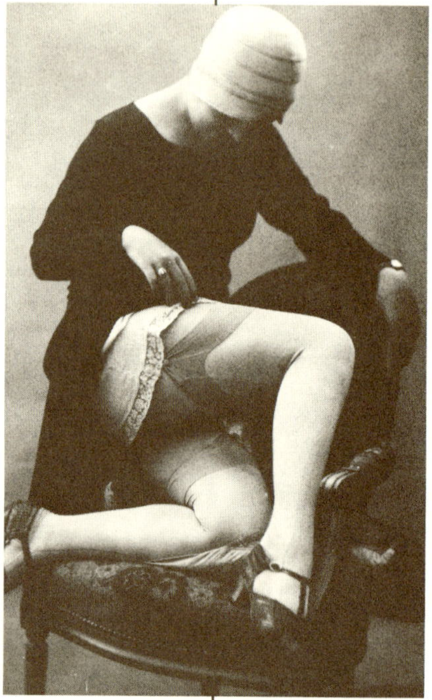

WHAT IS THE RICHARD MERKIN COLLECTION?

The Richard Merkin Collection is an archive, an accumulation of erotic and pornographic photography, ranging from the late nineteenth century to the early sixties when the nature, and the aroma, of the genre began to alter radically and, in my opinion, much for the worse. The collection also includes negatives; some early texts; films generally from the same period; pamphlets and books, providing they have been illustrated with photographs (or "Taken from Life" as "the industry" used to refer to it); and what is probably the most complete compilation of "8-Pagers" or "Tijuana Bibles" in this country. With a few notable exceptions, and a few which are not so notable, the Richard Merkin Collection excludes original works of fine art which is another concern altogether and one that interests me far less. The Richard Merkin Collection is composed primarily of pictures meant for sale to the man in the street. The criterion for inclusion generally requires the picture to have been taboo at the time of its production. This is a rather vague and shifting barometer but it does provide a vantage point from which to view the collection, and gives it a distinct flavor or character.

WHO IS RICHARD MERKIN?

That's easy. I am Richard Merkin, an always painter, a sometimes-writer, sometimes-teacher of painting and drawing, a boxing and baseball enthusiast, Bon Vivant, Boulevardier, Raconteur, and a number of other Fin-de-Siècle characterizations terribly easy to be (or at least to *say* you are) because no one really knows what they mean and no one really cares. I live in New York City (any place else is Bridgeport, right?) and I steadfastly refuse to own a television set. If it weren't for Goose Gossage I would even deny the existence of television. Lastly, I fully subscribe to the late George Frazier's definition of what constitutes the True Gentleman: to dress impeccably, to be able to recite Cole Porter flawlessly, and always to be (hopelessly) in love with a beautiful woman.

IS THAT REALLY HIS NAME?

Yes, definitely.

So now we can proceed, as the Actress said to the Bishop, to the business of collecting.

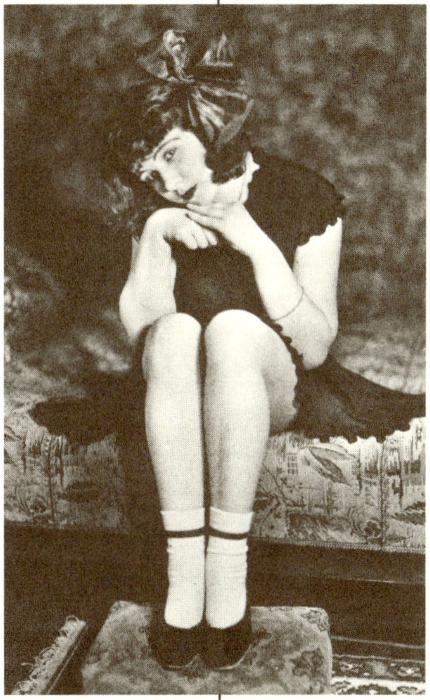

It seems to me now that a collector always collects, has always collected, and will continue to collect (no matter what he says to the contrary). I collect therefore I am, or, maybe, I am, therefore I collect. No matter. A true collector has a disposition toward preservation, toward documentation, toward the maintenance of order and civilization. Collecting also celebrates what one deems significant and it is, therefore, the assertion of personal values, what one Believes In. Indeed, the possibility of investment, of realizing eventual monetary gain through intuition and selection is some part of a collector's raison d'être, but I maintain that for genuine collectors this is a secondary consideration and after the fact. Monetary gain is sheer gravy but it is nothing to the nth power when it is compared to the heady delights of discovery and, yes, of ownership.

As a child, greeting life in Flatbush in the years just after World War II, I collected the things kids collected then (and, not so curiously, still do, albeit far more self-consciously in this age of inflation and ComiCons): comic books, bubble gum cards, and particularly baseball bubble gum cards and photos of athletes and movie stars which, incidentally, provided me with my first contact with the emporium of Irving Klaw. *Movie Star News*, then as now on East Fourteenth Street, was an epiphanic experience for an eleven-year-old in search of 8 x 10 glossies of Sunset Carson and Bob Feller. I also collected, in an equally epiphanic state, those items that could never be put in scrapbooks, but were safely hidden under mattresses, or deep in the labyrinths of the bottom drawer of a lad's dresser, way, way, way behind the *Sub-Mariners* and the Rawlings five-finger mitt, the autographed Mort Cooper model (to be sure). Like all genuine, neophyte collectors I went to great lengths to complete runs of comics and series of picture cards, but unlike other kids who collected, I managed to retain much of this childhood and adolescent archive through college and what James T. Farrell might refer to as my "early manhood." This would suggest that the entire matter of collecting meant more to me than the garden variety avocation that it was, and I suspect is, for most kids.

One of the great underlying joys of collecting, as any collector can attest, is accurate prophecy, or the ability to detect an interest, or a genre before it becomes a cult or is taken up by the public en masse. And, when the price is right. While studying painting in graduate school in the early years of the sixties, I became fascinated with the vintage American comic book and related ephemera and I pursued comiciana with Spartan fervor for nearly a decade. To me the comics were vital and pertinent and yet subterranean and, as yet, private; and the incense of serendipity that pervaded collecting them intoxicated me, a clearly diagnosed case of Collector's malaise. In time I constructed a selective and cohesive collection, largely in printed matter. I still maintain a large part of the archive, but like many collectors, I eventually became bored by it all, particularly when the prices became vastly inflated and the subject mundane because of the overkill publicity that accompanies any Pop Phenomenon. When the thrill is gone, the thrill is gone.

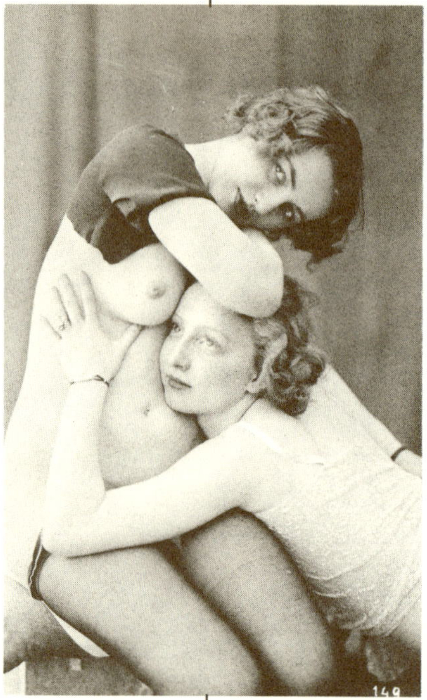

Yet no real collector can go for very long without collecting, as I told you before, and, since I have always been captivated by photographs, I seriously began to collect—in the early seventies—the kinds of photographs that constitute *Velvet Eden*. In point of fact, I had been introduced to material of this nature quite early on, thanks to the pungent potentialities available to a boy in Baghdad-on-the-Hudson. I can recall seeing pictures, in school yards and boys' rooms, at so early an age that I literally had no clear idea of what was transpiring in them, though there never seemed to be a question but that whatever was going on was first biological and, second, amusing in the extreme.

My reasons for embarking upon this particular collecting venture were stimulated by several factors. For one, by the middle of the sixties, as social circumstances became increasingly more permissive, and visual expression increasingly more liberated and explicit, it seemed to me that erotic photography as a form was losing its traditional effect and impact. The pictures seemed far less exciting, utterly devoid of their awkward charm or former theater, and not even remotely witty. In short, less human. The erotic and, more specifically, pornographic image is dependent upon the social climate and actually thrives on suppression. Made commonplace and readily available in the most mundane way, it is rendered impotent. The more erotic photography became socially acceptable, the less it had the desired effect. Without the taboo, the erotic photo, out of the closet, is like a sundial in the shade. It loses its ability to perform what is certainly one of its main objectives (and sole objective in the case of genuine pornography), which is to turn you on. To be sure, the modern counterpart could be raunchy (though rarely robust) or Super-Slick (see the photos of Helmut Newton) or Arty Infinitum (see the photos of David Hamilton); but it became increasingly apparent to me that as permission paraded, the classic form lost its special charm, its innocence and the spark that gave it breath. So it became important and exciting to collect and to preserve as much as I possibly could of that strain of unaffected and often clandestine expression that went irretrievably astray with the passing of the totally anonymous photographer.

A second consideration that prompted me to collect the pictures was that I perceived the existing material itself to be an Endangered Species. Produced, more often than not, under the most primitive and rudimentary circumstances, the photographs were subjected not only to the ravages of time and haphazard storage, but also to the social mores that guided the generations that fell heir to those secret collections. Photographs such as these rarely could be regarded as having any monetary value. They held no sentimental or nostalgic value. In most cases, the pictures were little more than a source of shame and embarrassment to the surprised heirs who discovered the accumulations among the earthly remains of the secret Bon Voyeur who had gone to his reward. Immediate destruction was generally the result, without the slightest hesitation save a disapproving head wag and a few deploring tsk-tsks regarding the scandalous preoccupations and eccentricities of the dear late archivist, Uncle Harry.

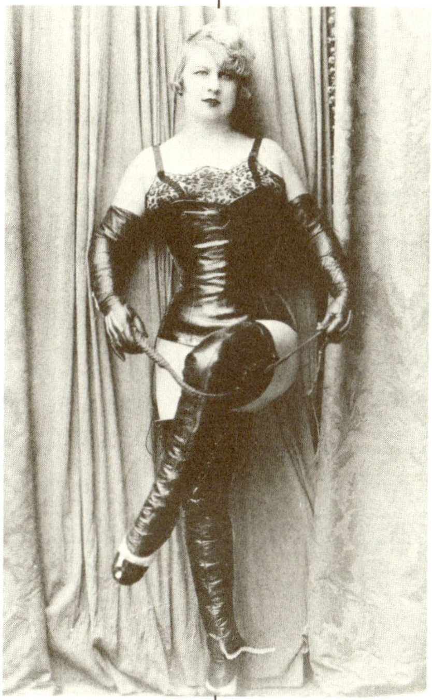

Vintage erotica thus became increasingly scarce and difficult to unearth. Again, the lure of the chase!

A few years ago, I purchased a fascinating and singular *objet trouvé:* a breadbox, black and battered, that had been walled up, literally, à la E. A. Poe, in a house in New Jersey for at least thirty years. It contained a thousand or more erotic and pornographic photos, uniform in size, numbered and filed, which constituted the stock of an itinerant, under-the-counter operator (bless him or her) whose business flourished in the period just prior to Pearl Harbor. In general, the quality of the pictures was poor and all were, of course, copy photos, many generations from the originals which were often pre-1900. Nevertheless, it was a curious trove, bizarre and informative to students of such arcane matters. The owner of the house knew absolutely nothing about this sort of thing and little more about *anything.* He did admit, however, that although he felt that the pictures were important, he was not absolutely certain as to whether or not any of them were the work of Matthew Brady! I must hasten to add that he said this with a straight face. When I regained a conscious state and my blood pressure picked up its workaday pace, I tried to convince him that not only were they not attributable to Matthew Brady nor even to any remote acquaintance of Andy Warhol, but that all were by unknown photographers and were, in fact, copy photos and light-years from the original images. I finally bought the breadbox but not before taking out yet another mortgage on my château in Touraine.

I have acquired my collection from ancient magick [sic] emporiums in New York City; back-date magazine impresarios in Baltimore; bookanistes along the banks of the Seine; auctioneers in Faulkner country; street urchins in Cuidad Juarez, Tijuana, and similar border hellholes; from flotsam and jetsam dealers along Royal Street in New Orleans; pool hall operators in Cleveland (or at least I think it was Cleveland); and some absolutely hair-raising material from a Little Old Lady in Connecticut who said to me, "Is this the kind of thing you're looking for?" It was all I could do to nod, "Yes, Ma'am," but I'm not certain why I felt embarrassed because it didn't seem to faze her in the least and I've always had the sneaking and romantic suspicion that she had been one of the participating actresses in the photographs, but I didn't ask and she didn't tell.

Another time I purchased a trunk full of memories from an auctioneer in the deep South. It had belonged to some Ancient Mariner, long since gone to Davy Jones' locker. It contained, in addition to what I had bargained for, the evidence of a lifetime on water: parts of naval uniforms, calling cards from whorehouses in remote points of the Orient, a little maroon address book with the phone numbers of chippies and good-time girls who plied their trade before Roosevelt was inaugurated, and a black silk scarf with a hole or two that I wear to this day. A touching trove indeed, and I spent a few uncomfortable hours with this dybbuk, dreaming of that "classiest abyss in Calcutta" that, alas, would never be my nocturnal domain, not for one single, solitary, opium-ridden evening. Sometimes you get more than you bargained for. ❦

There is a fundamental difference between out and out pornography and erotic photography of the sort that makes up most of *Velvet Eden*. Pornography is single-minded and seeks to do one thing and one thing only: to move you sexually, to turn you on, to incite you, to tempt you, as Lenny Bruce so well expressed it. Erotica, and here I am concerned with *Velvet Eden*, may seek to put you in touch with the sexual impulse, but along the way it pauses to reflect on other things and offers more imaginative and suggestive associations. The Snake Lady, the schoolgirls, the detail of the decor, the costumes, and the melodrama that energize these pictures offer echoes of sensuality, humor, and social conventions from days gone by. The photographs that appear in *Velvet Eden* dwell upon dreams that pornography has neither the time nor the interest to convey. Erotica can even comment on pornography, caricature it, satirize it. In the end, erotica can and often does approximate art. Pornography, on the other hand, is only pornography, which has little to do with anything else, especially art. ❦❦❦ ❦❦❦

The taking of pictures of women to be looked at by men is as old as the camera. *Velvet Eden* is a rich, appreciative collection of these images. Some are art, some are record, some are both. It is a sampling, a selection, a symphony of moments stolen from secret rooms of what the novelist Nelson Algren has called our "split level bedlam." *Velvet Eden* evokes a fantasy-form that was nurtured by its own suppression. These photographs, compositions made in haste, evoke the atmosphere of run-down hotel rooms and Deco boudoirs. The All-Seeing Eye of the Anonymous Camera transforms down-on-their-luck Burly-Q queens, with their seamed nylons and snakes and masks and garter belts, into romantic objects of desire. Yet they remain poignantly human, elusive. In their frailty and elegant clumsiness, they reach out to us from this *Velvet Eden*, before our expulsion, before we all of us fell from grace. ❦❦

Although most of the photographs in this collection in fact derive from France, it would be next to impossible for anyone other than a seasoned scholar of the erotic monochrome chlorobromide to establish their exact time and place of origin simply by taking a good hard look at them.

This is not entirely due to the deliberate web of anonymity that until very recently always linked the subject, the photographer, and the end consumer of erotica in their conspiracy to elude detection by the moral Gestapo of the time, and the subsequent absence of telltale signatures or trademarks. True, German *Fräuleins* might be broader in the beam and their toenails cleaner than those of their French sisters, who in turn could be depended upon to manifest less sultry pouts than the sirens of Naples or Seville; and, if not exactly cornfed coeds, American volunteers for erotic display have always seemed by and large to betray the New World's relative lack of sexual sophistication by a certain winning awkwardness of form, a hint of strain in their seductive smiles. But these are fine distinctions, the esoteric province of the dedicated connoisseur. Remove her clothes, drape her across a chaise longue, tell her to take a good deep breath—and *click,* the nude, Caucasian, under-thirty female belongs not to France or Germany or Liechtenstein but to the borderless land of erotica.

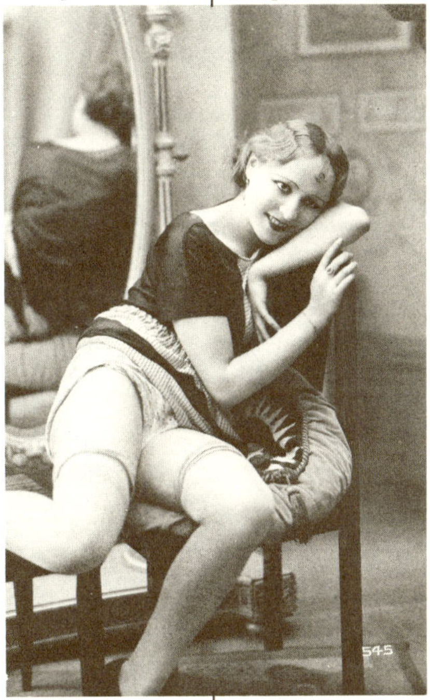

And yet if the land of erotica could be said to have a queen, that queen for most of its modern history would by universal acclamation be France.

Erotica had been fashioned over the past few years into something different by the hot, horny hands of the Larry Flynts of the world. But few living males who attained puberty much before 1960 or so can even separate the words "France" and "erotica" in their minds. For them and for their fathers and for innumerable generations preceding, the simple fact of being *French* conferred on any woman, any picture, any item of lingerie or sexual gadgetry, an ineluctable musk, a guarantee better than Tiffany's or Cartier's that these were the authentic goods, stamped by the equivalent of an erotic *Good Housekeeping* seal of approval. Indeed, so sexually supercharged had the very word "French" become by the middle of the twentieth century that it powered itself right out of its adjectival form and became an energetic verb, a term for a lovemaking activity so debauched that it could clearly have been invented only in France.

But whether the French race ever was in fact any more interested in sex than the rest of us, any more daring or adept at it, is something best left to the social scientists and cultural historians to answer. What is clear is that the idea was universally perpetuated and accepted and handed down from one decade to the next. And the way this was accomplished may have constituted history's earliest version of the media blitz.

That most of the photographs in this collection happen to be French is less a matter of conscious selection than one of statistical inevitability. The French produced more of them by far than anyone else. Rifle any shoebox or a scrapbook or steamer trunk where printed erotic images of the pre-*Playboy* era are preserved, and they will be unfailingly, preponderantly Made in France. From the *cartes de visites* of the late nineteenth century to the packets of "postcards" that were their lineal descendants in the early to middle twentieth, through the *films troublants* and *livres d'amour* and *photos vivantes* they spun off, the art and industry of erotic depiction was always as native to France as the panda is to China; a national if sub rosa heritage, immortalized in the well known—and heavily French-accented—informal generic term, "feelthy peectures."

Perhaps most Frenchmen were too busy sampling erotica in the flesh to bother much with merely staring at it in cardboard recreations. In any event, the bulk of this erotic mother lode found its way abroad. Not in giant packing cases stamped *Erotica, Keep In A Cool Place,* but bit by bit in tiny stacks and sets and sheaves surreptitiously nested into this businessman's shoe and that doughboy's duffle bag, the better to smuggle past Customs and the kids and into the upstairs bedroom bureau. The shutters snapped, the presses rolled; France produced, and avid innocents and jaded collectors alike consumed. Thus was French hegemony in the erotic arts confirmed and reconfirmed generation after generation, all around the world.

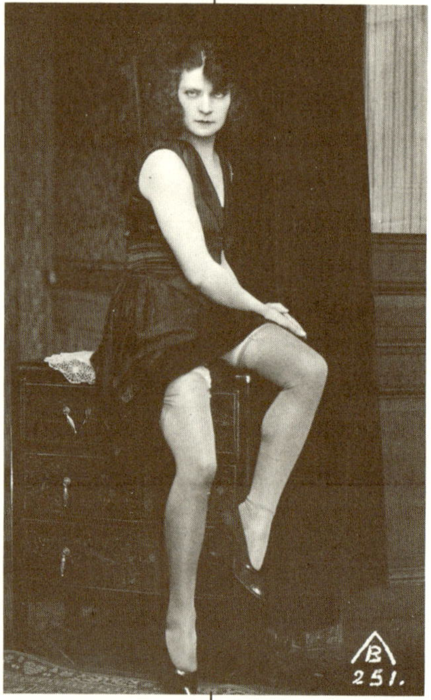

It can be argued that France enjoyed a head start in the production and perfection of the printed erotic image: After all, it was Parisian Jacques Daguerre who in 1838 had exhibited the world's first photograph to the bedazzled residents of his native city. Given the creative and other predilections of the French, and in particular the Parisians, it is effortless to imagine that certain among them soon glimpsed the camera's possibilities as extending well beyond a means of immortalizing the noonday shimmer on the River Seine or the glory of Uncle Hector's amazing nose. It is inviting to imagine that the precursors of Bob Guccione with his Rollei and his strobes were already barking instructions to one recumbent Fifi or other in garrets and ateliers all over Paris, when Queen Victoria was still but a sylph of twenty-one.

Daguerre and his bewitching laboratory curiosity provided one impulse for early French leadership in the erotic picture trade. Paris provided another. What better stockpile of raw materials, and what more hospitable climate in which to work them? Here was a metropolis that had been prompting eye-rollings, winks, and elbows in the ribs among the Continent's sexually sophisticated since it first reached the status of commune in the late fourteenth century; and layer upon layer of gloss had since been added to this underlying legend of sexual license by the colonies of poets and sculptors and artists, with mistresses and actresses and models in their train, who by the middle of the last century had helped establish in Paris an ambiance that rendered all rival cities so many sad-sack Dubuques.

The cast changed, the preoccupations shifted, styles waxed and waned, but the image of Paris as Western civilization's erotic mecca and creative epicenter only flourished as fin de siècle gave way to *La Belle Epoque.* Its techniques polished by half a century's worth of practice, its craftsmanship fast advancing in step with the development of ever more sensitive cameras and film, erotic photography was by now approaching something close to maturity and the beginnings of its modern age.

A pause occurs while World War I fractures European society, and erotic tastes and appetites reform in its aftermath along coarser, less decorous lines.

The female who before 1914 had stood statuesque for the birdie in one frozen pose or another, looking for all the world as if a lascivious notion had never entered her head and Maman herself stood just off-camera, holding her knickers, by 1920 had learned to unbend. Nanette took the cane to Babette and tried not to look entirely cherubic. The look in Georgette's eyes as she reclined on the fur suggested that she might be thinking of something other than tea.

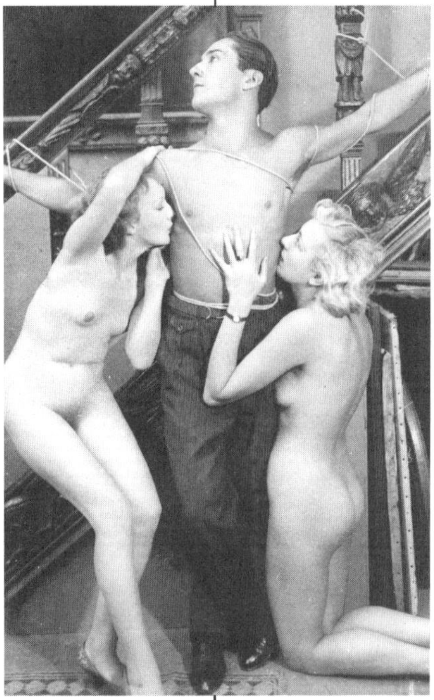

The body temperature of erotic art was finally beginning to climb. It had begun doing so when photography at last reached a sense of its own possibilities as art, and ceased courting legitimacy by trying to palm itself off as only a technological version of nineteenth-century French painting. Erotic, like all other kinds of photography, had until then imprisoned itself within the rigid aesthetic confines—even the static style—of conventional studio painting. The tingle of fleshly pleasure was hard to find in photographs modeled on garlanded wood nymphs or *Lysander Dying, Attended by the Fates,* as evoked by artists addicted to the shrouding of the female form in as much gauze and laurel as could plausibly be wound around it, then loading the immediate vicinity with every lyre and wreath and Ionic column that heavy symbolism could bear. It was a school of art that defined the desirable woman less as a physical being than a figure in some allegorical frieze; when confronted with her—her Statue of Liberty face, her body arranged in postures that suggested knockout drops more than sexual arousal—a man was forced to work hard indeed to extract his erotic thrills.

But now all this was ebbing. As the creative horizon gradually widened and deepened before them, photographers for the first time became free to explore the erotic possibilities flickering everywhere in that short distance between camera lens and willing female subject. This artistic emancipation mirrored what was happening in the surrounding culture. The lid was coming off. Spurred by the democratizing influence of the motion picture and the phonograph record, popular taste—more vulgar but also more expressive of real human feeling—was throwing off the dead weight of all that artistic moral uplift, that sickly preoccupation with antiquity and allegory ad nauseam. The body of a pretty girl could be admired as the body of a pretty girl, not as a metaphor for the Spirit of Music. A new frankness was abroad in the popular arts, pushing the dust and the cobwebs away, and in its wake, erotic photography was becoming more frankly erotic.

It is in this atmosphere, the period of the late twenties and early thirties, that most of the photographs in this collection were made. It is interesting to consider the backdrop.

The Paris of these times was a different one from that which had hosted Hemingway and Gertrude Stein and company a decade before—at once racier and more openly flouting convention as the new generation ever more completely liberated itself from the clammy grip of the old; and yet at the same time darker and more cynical. Rocked by the effects of a worldwide depression and overlaid with a kind of malaise, a post-twenties hangover of the spirit, France tottered through economic and political chaos, no longer certain of what it meant or where it was going. It was a time not of great undertakings or ambitions but a time of stagnancy and scandal—when the wife of a high politician could walk into the office of the newspaper editor who had slandered her husband, and blow his brains out; when the arch-swindler Stavisky's machinations threatened to topple the Republic.

It was a time of every man for himself, of turning inward to hedonism, and the wider world be damned. This was the Paris of Henry Miller and Jean Genêt, where half a million prostitutes were known to patrol, where the number of visitors to the Louvre every day might well be equaled by those stopping off at their favorite bordello or opium den.

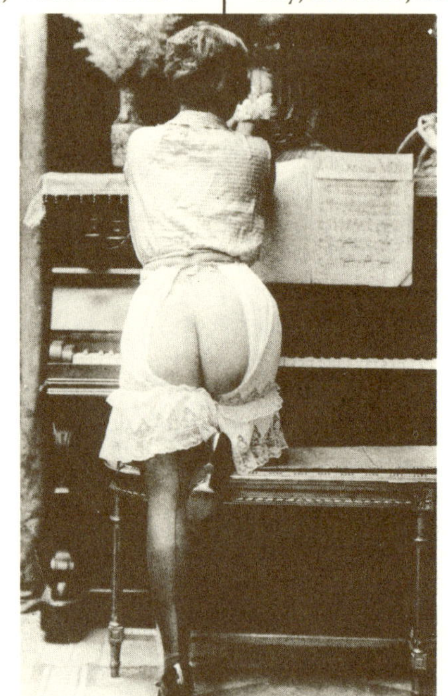

For the erotic photographer planning his next batch of studies, it made for a buyer's market in modeling talent. It wouldn't be difficult to draft willing subjects from among the whores and the artists' models, the dancers and actresses, the bar girls and the girls with no known vocation, who formed a vast and teeming underclass on the wrong side of the Seine in the Paris of the day.

One need only frequent the countless bars and clubs and *bals-musettes* in the areas of Belleville, Ménilmontant, Charonne, Porte des Lilas, or the *quartiers chauds,* the "hot spots" of prostitution in the tenderloin area surrounding Les Halles. Girls could be found who had done worse things, for less money, than to spend half a day with their clothes off in some studio or rented flat, having photos taken in exchange for a hundred-franc note.

Indeed, erotic photography would have ranked near the top of the list in terms of desirable work for women whose careers were involved with an intertwining of their bodies and sex. Above it in the status order, the possibilities were few and remote: a millionaire's mistress, perhaps, a legitimate actress or dancer or chanteuse; or the billion-to-one shot of stardom on the stage or in the cinema. Below it, the rungs led down through the ever darkening depths from prostitution to hard-core pornography and worse; meaner work, conducted in a nether world of pimps and thugs and shabby rooms; rife with brutality, disease, and the police.

The girls in these photographs must have thought themselves lucky, then, to have landed such relatively dignified and respectable work. And the photographers must have chosen them, free as they were to pick and choose from more candidates than even this busy industry could use, as the *crème de la crème*—the most provocative and exceptional creatures available, so many Eves in the velvet Eden of erotica.

They may hardly seem so now. Fashions change, in erotic appeal no less than in clothing or automobiles. The ideal of feminine allure, constantly evolving even in so brief a span as from one decade to the next, has taken many a turn and undergone many a transformation in the long years since the shutters snapped on these scenes.

If the *femmes* in these photographs often seem rather less than *fatale*—less believable as the knowing scarlet women they frequently were than as giggling amateurs, innocent shopgirls doing it for a lark—it is well to remind oneself that they did not always register so. A sly, Nabokovian juggling of time is at work. Time lends distance, and in erotica, distance is fatal: It dissipates the heat.

Nor is this phenomenon something confined to our time. The most sexually agonized adolescent fifty years from now, encountering a 1979 copy of *Hustler,* will no doubt be less impelled to tumesce instantly and bolt for the nearest bathroom than to wonder vaguely how such stuff, impossibly bland and stale, could have ever stimulated his forebears.

What remains to be considered in these photographs is erotic enchantment, softened and clouded by time. It is made almost gentle. To the eyes of our present age, the faces and bodies, the poses, even the lighting, seem chosen and arranged by someone attempting less to quicken pulses than to slow them down. Over and over, a spirit of near detachment seems to isolate the subject from her purported mission of inciting sexual arousal—titillation, at the very least. Where are the moist and hungry mouths, where is the sweaty abandon, where is the hovering on orgasm's very brink that charges even the routine erotica of today?

All far in the future. For the average man in 1929 and 1936 and as late as the middle forties, what he got from these photographs was enough. The respectable everyday world in which he lived and fantasized was a far more inhibited, buttoned-up place than we know today, from which sex had wherever possible been airbrushed or censored or otherwise rendered invisible. The sexually curious were left so famished for gratification that the merest peek at a bare breast, an undraped female buttock, was sufficient for propulsion into Nirvana. Even to think of asking for more marked a man as well advanced into the latter stages of sexual depravity, driving him deep underground into the secret, sleazy world of hard-core porn.

Faces so sweet, postures so dainty, the pastime of sexual frolic made to seem almost limpid, almost demure: what is preserved in this collection of photographs is not erotic excitement so much as a record of what represented the peak of erotic excitement to those of an earlier age. The day when such pictures as these could make the mouth run dry and the heart beat faster are long gone, along with the youth and beauty of the *jeunes filles* who graced them. Gone too is that particular Paris. But across the years a certain delicate atmosphere of mystery, a charm, has managed to survive.

It might not be entirely out of order to close with one quick "Vive la France!"

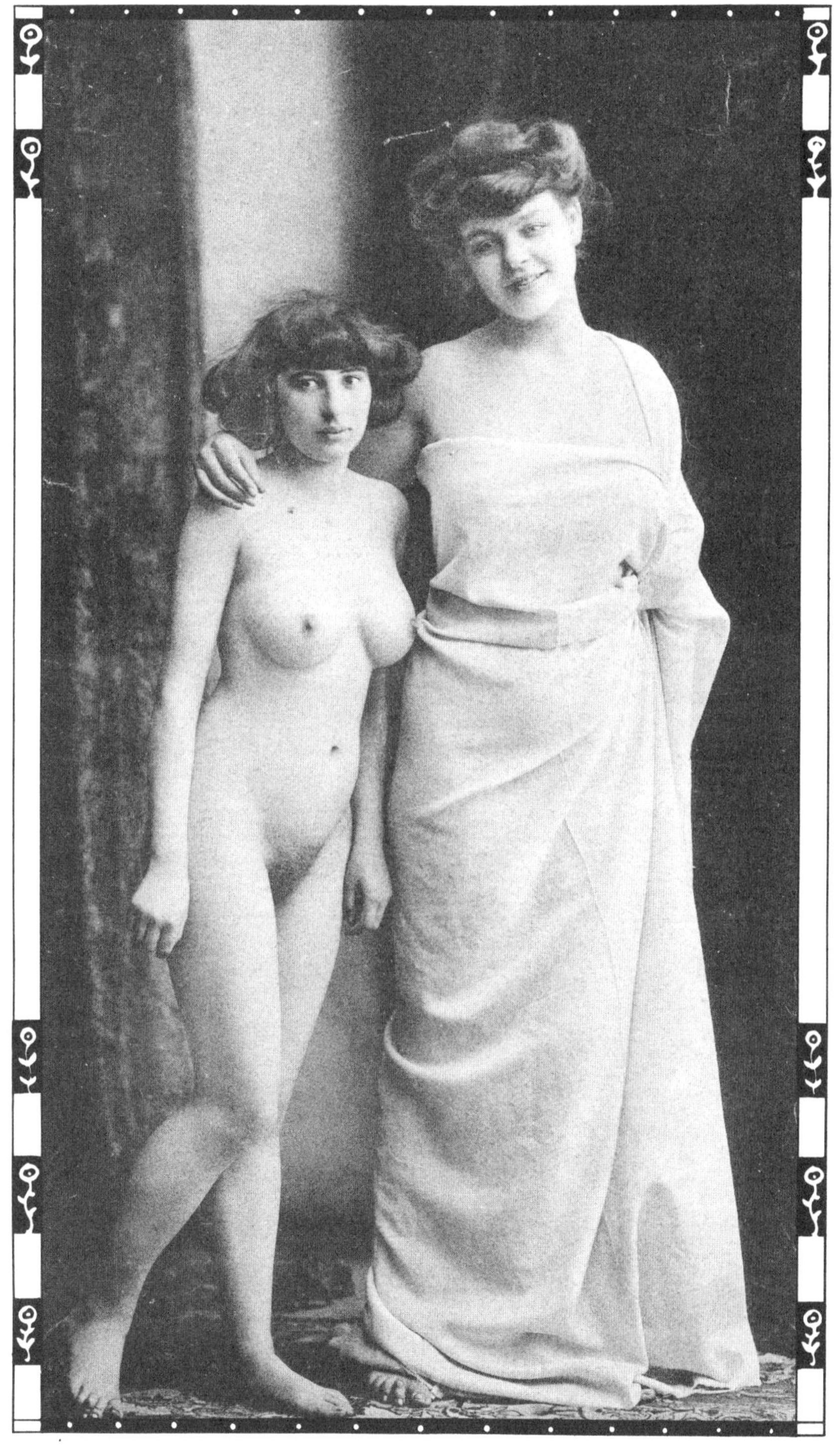

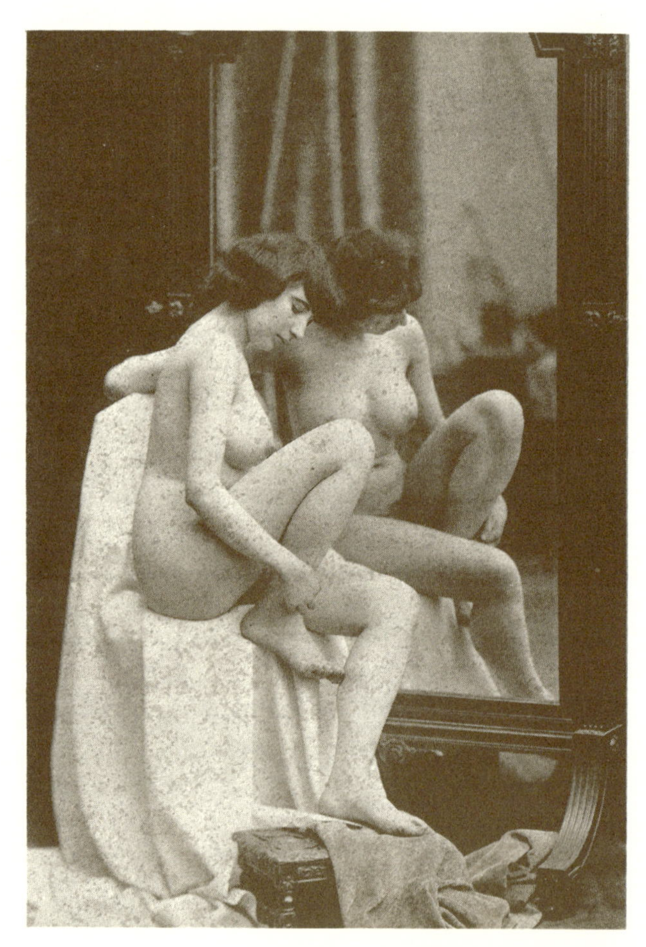

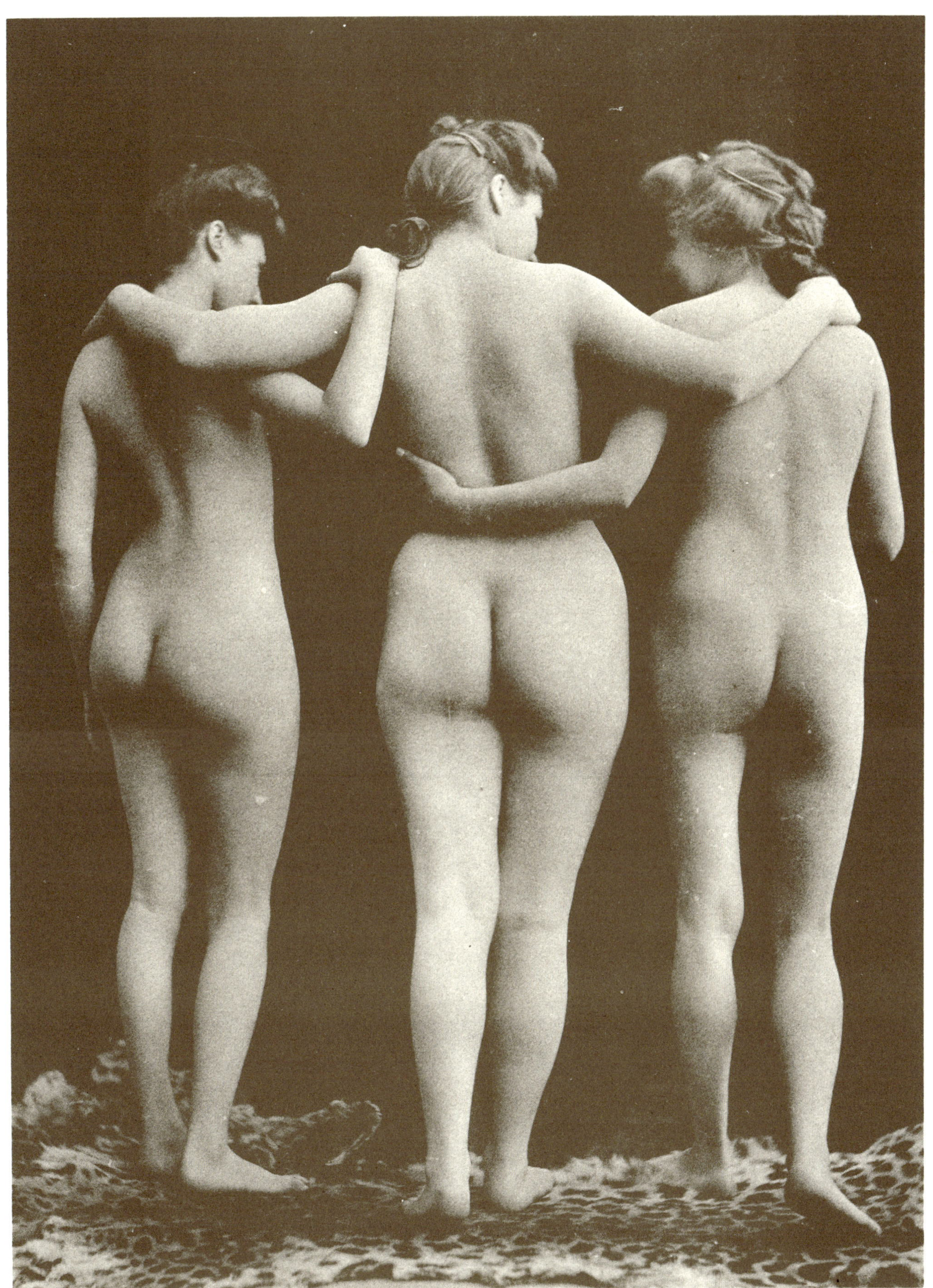

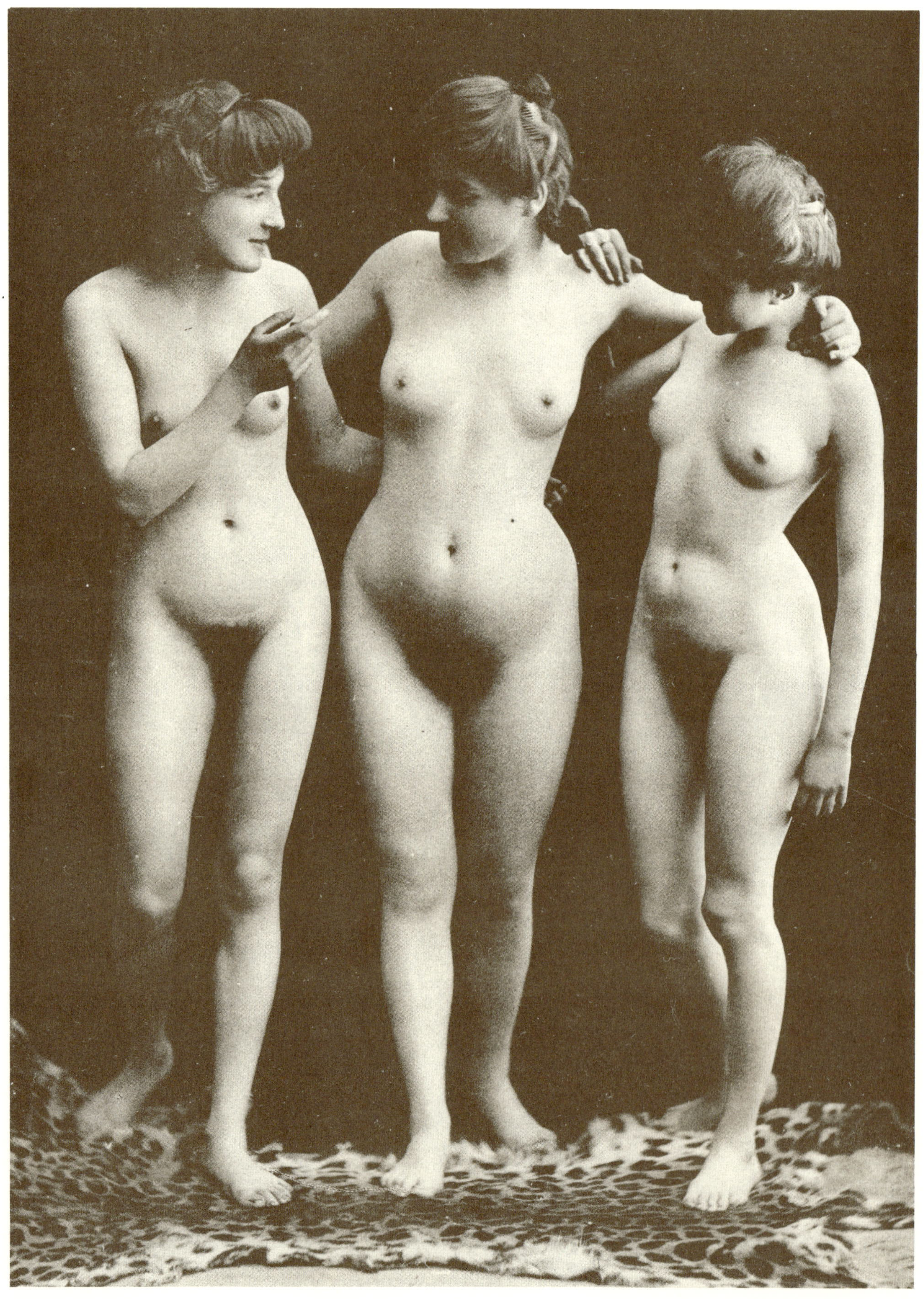

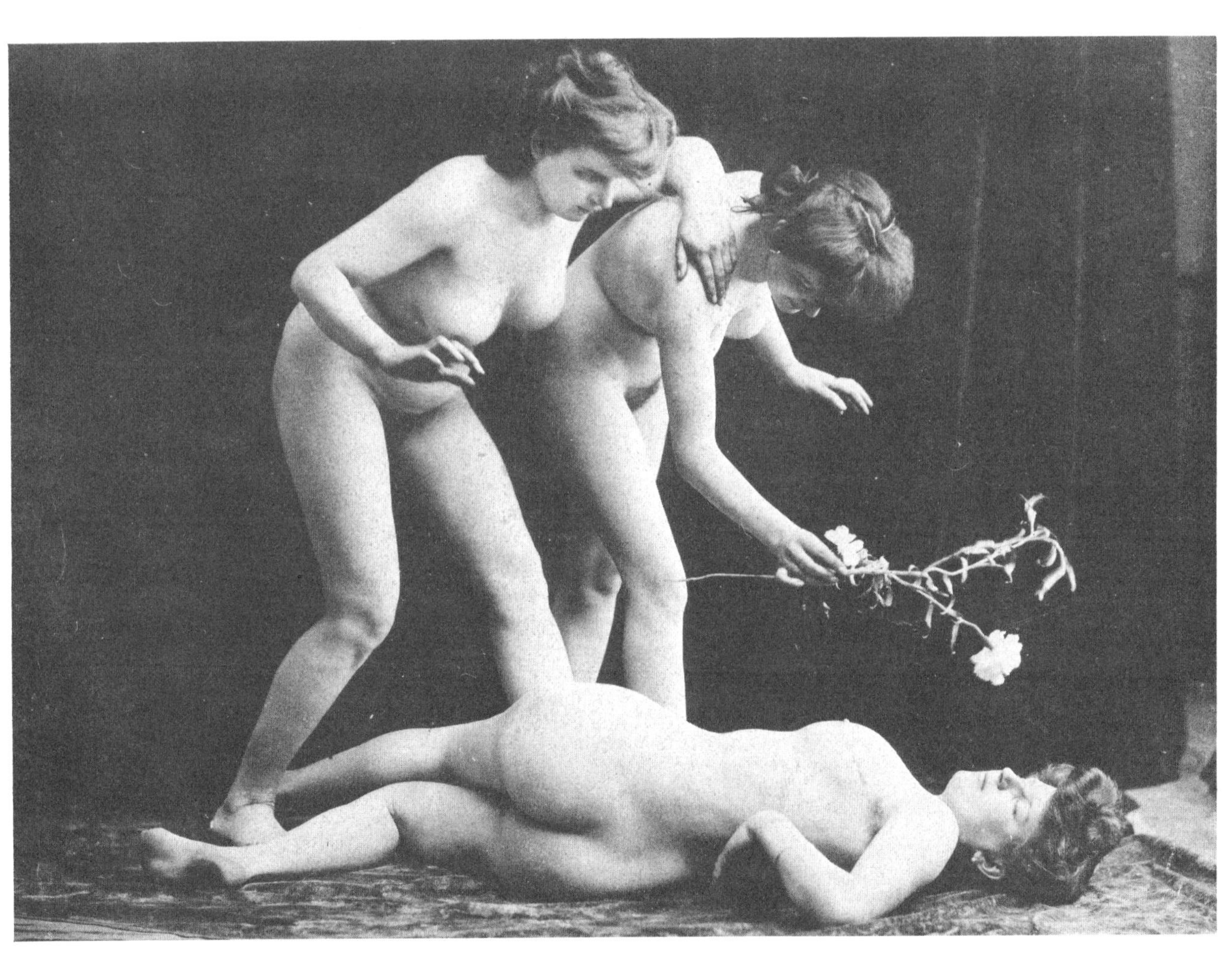

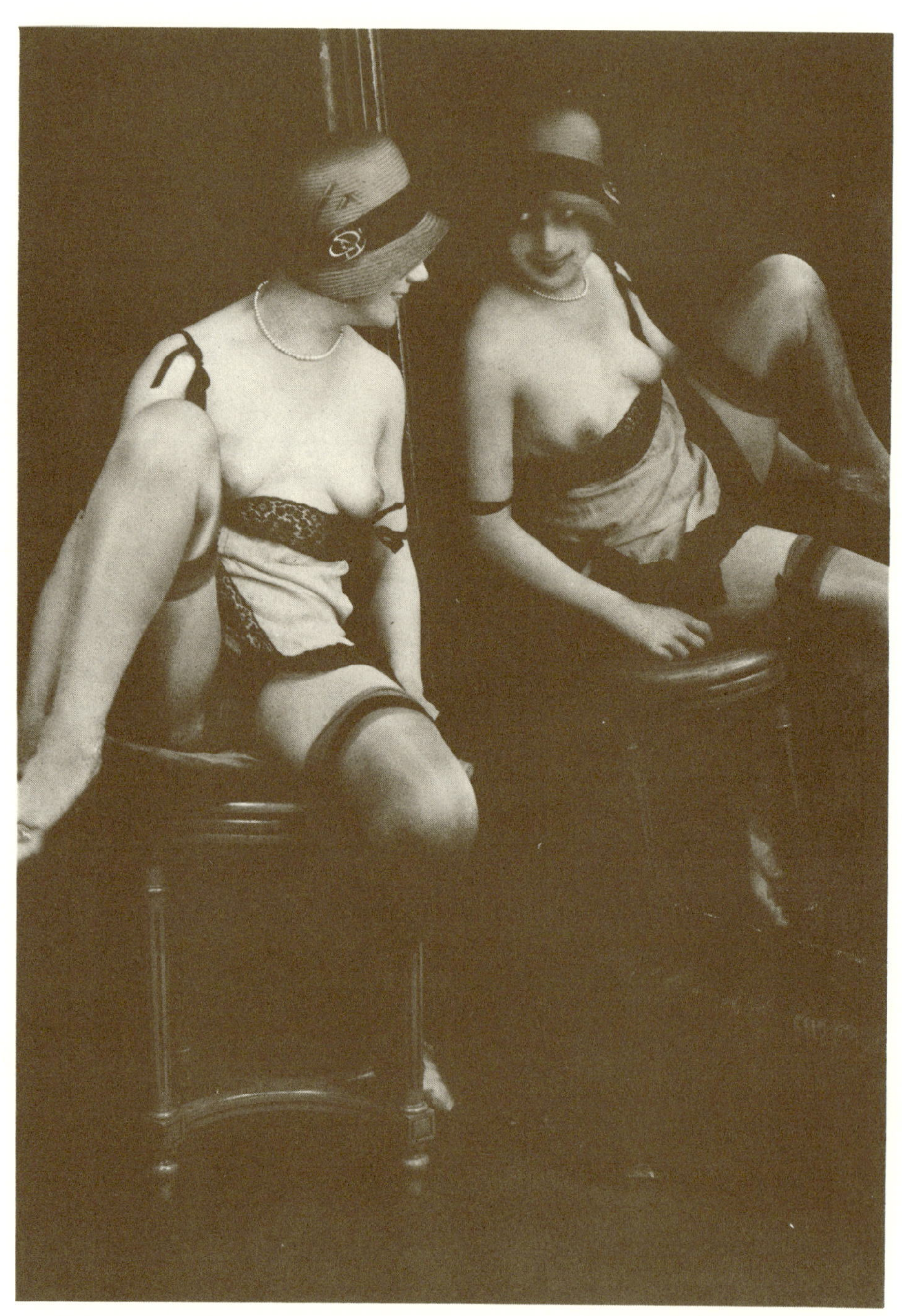

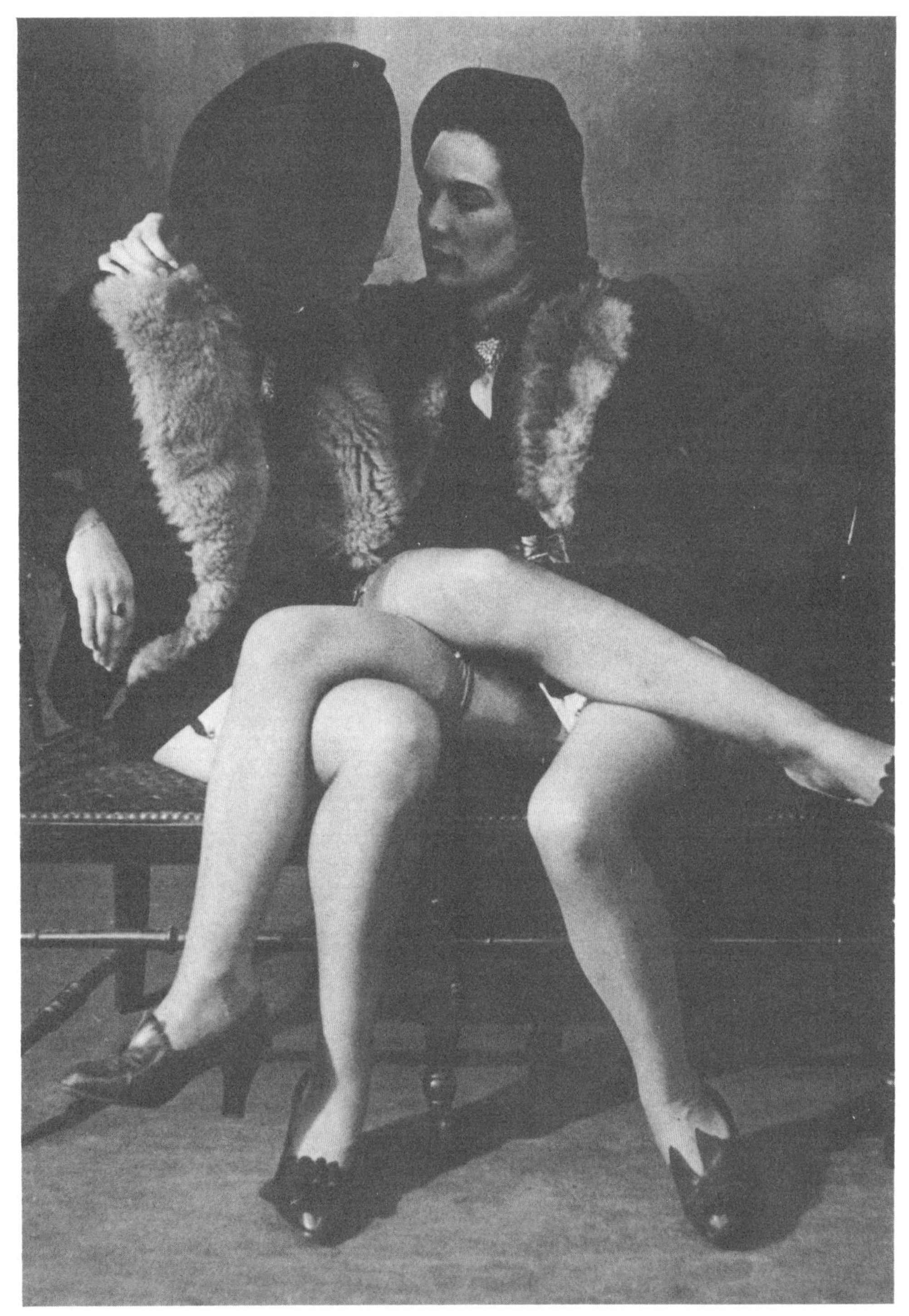

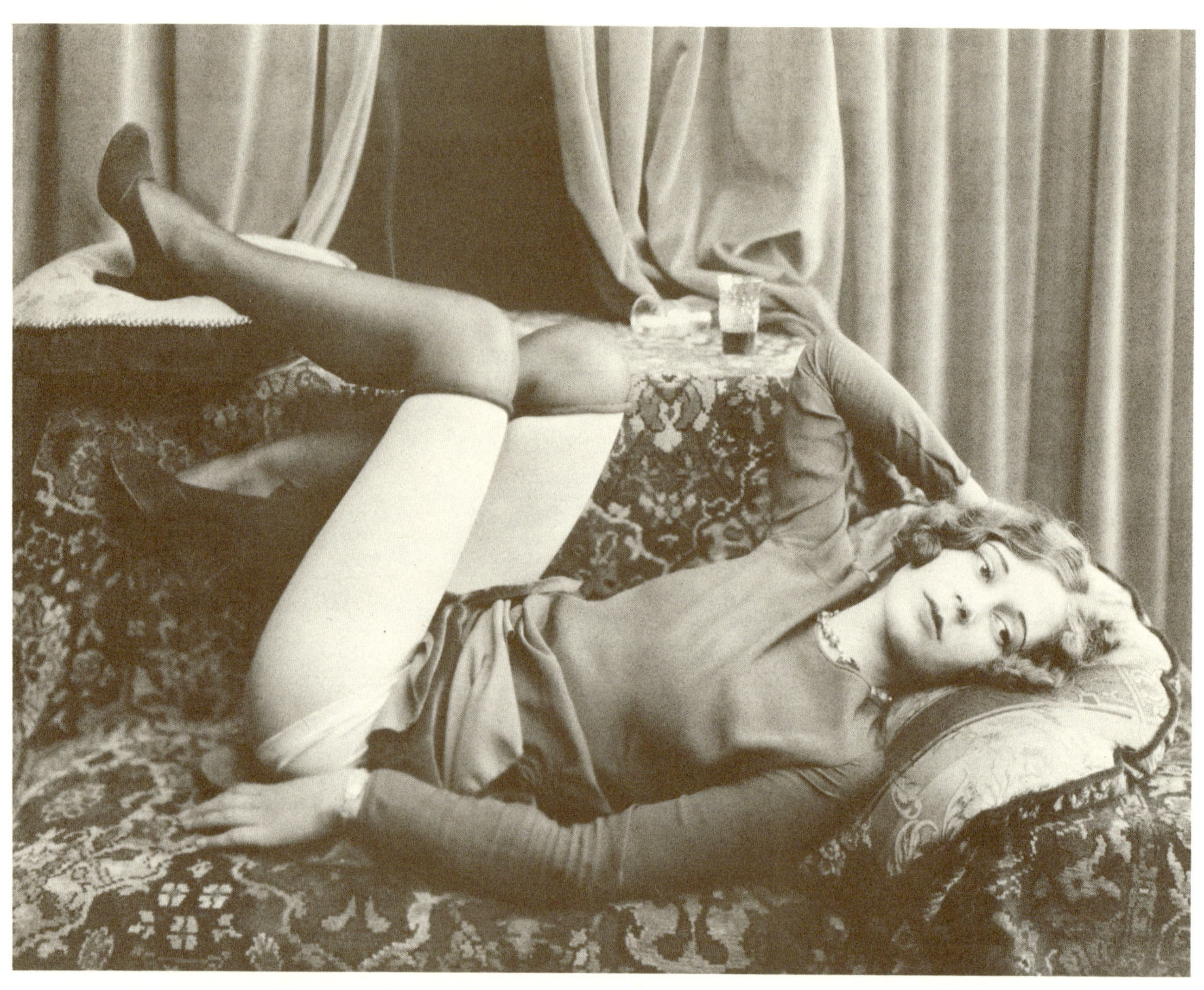

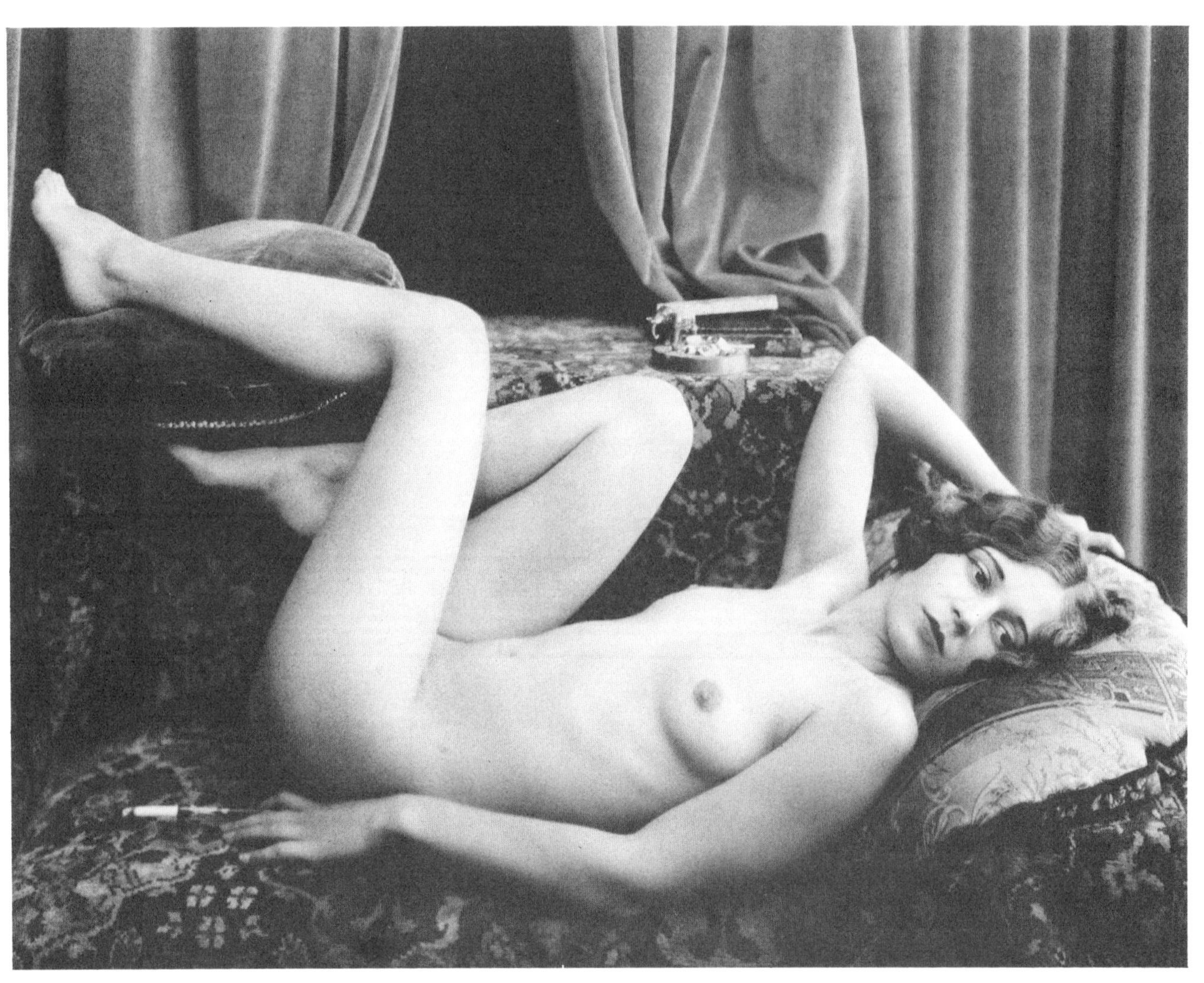

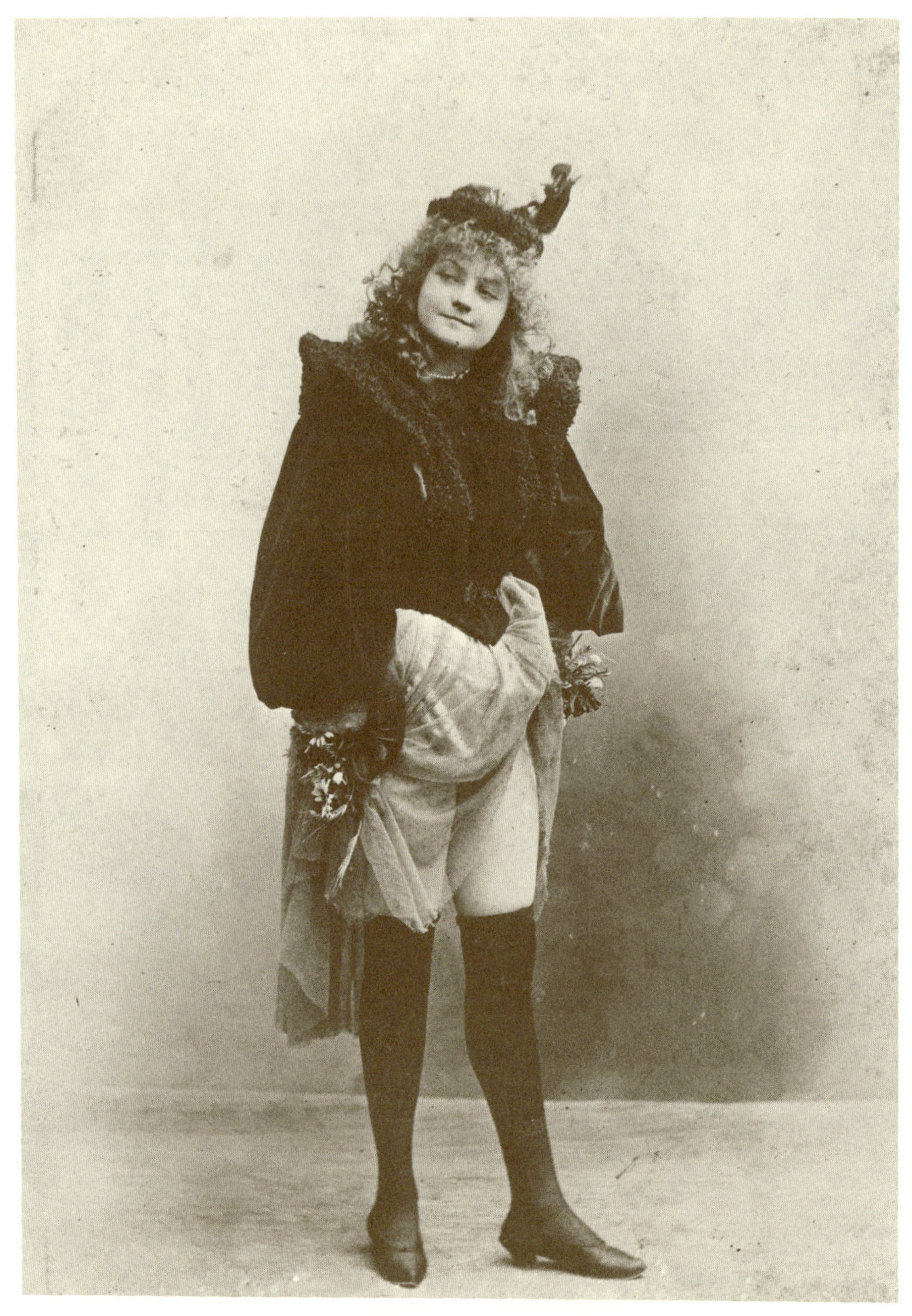

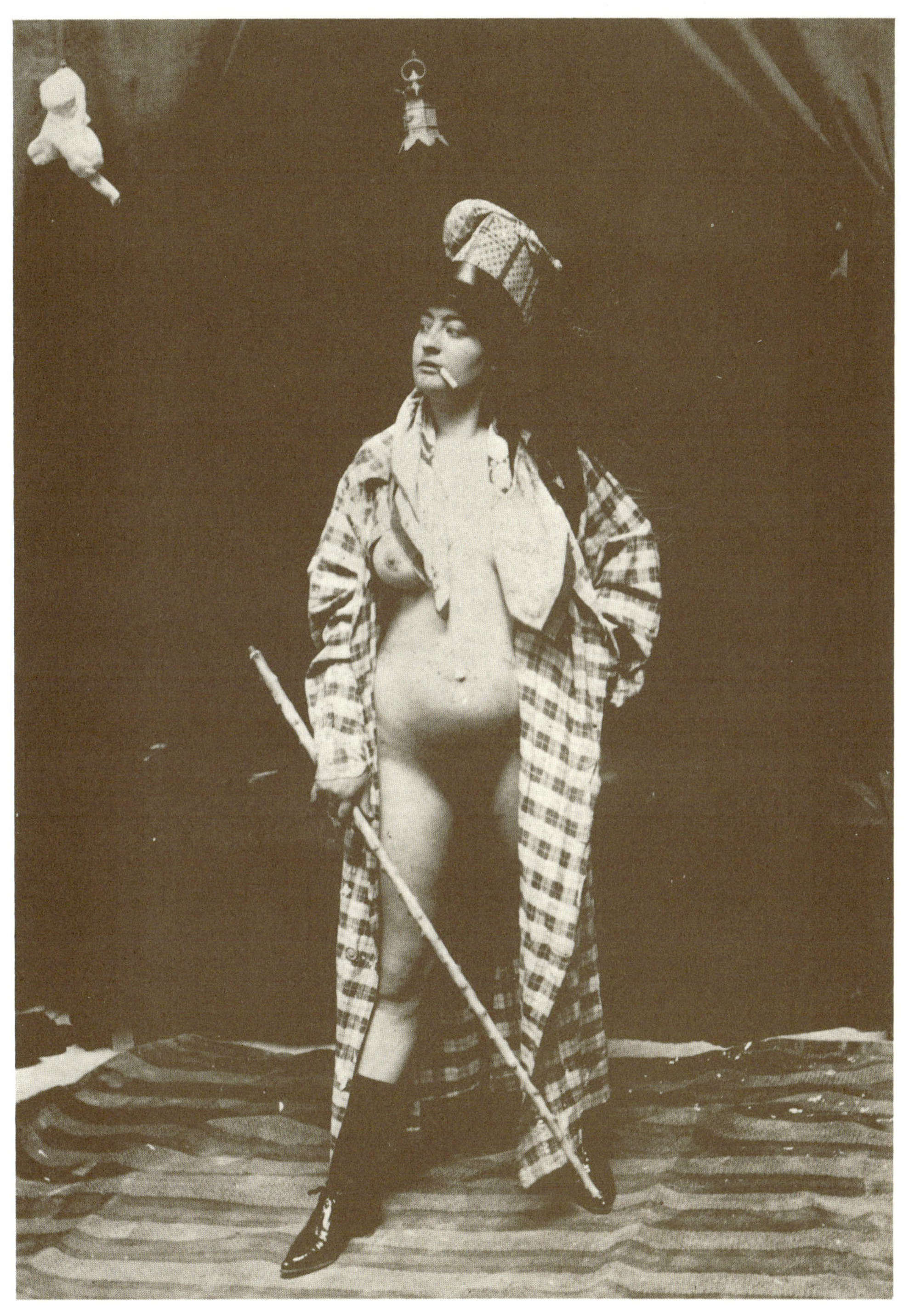

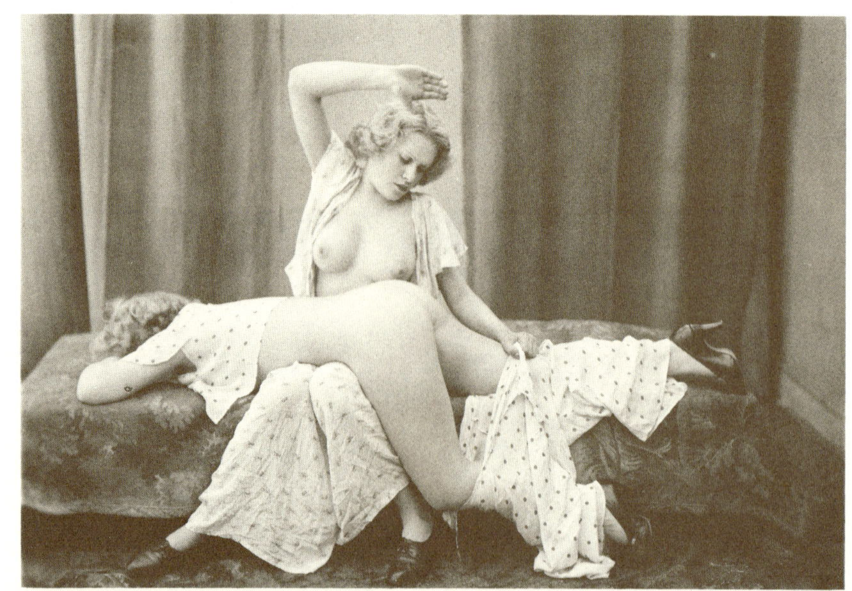

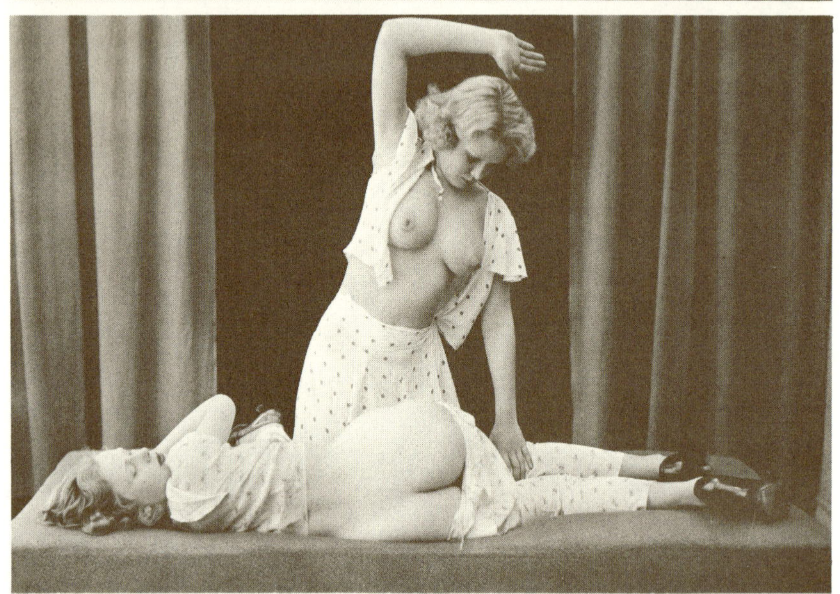

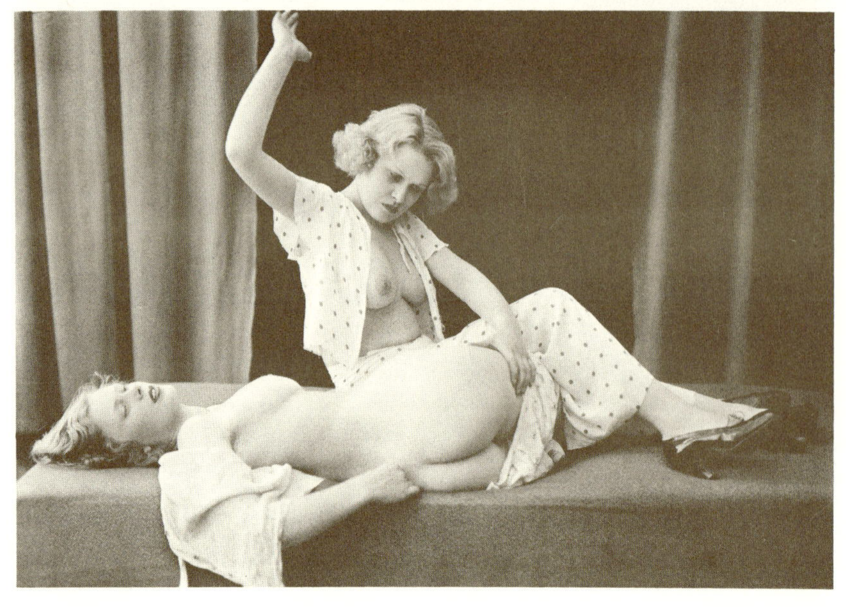

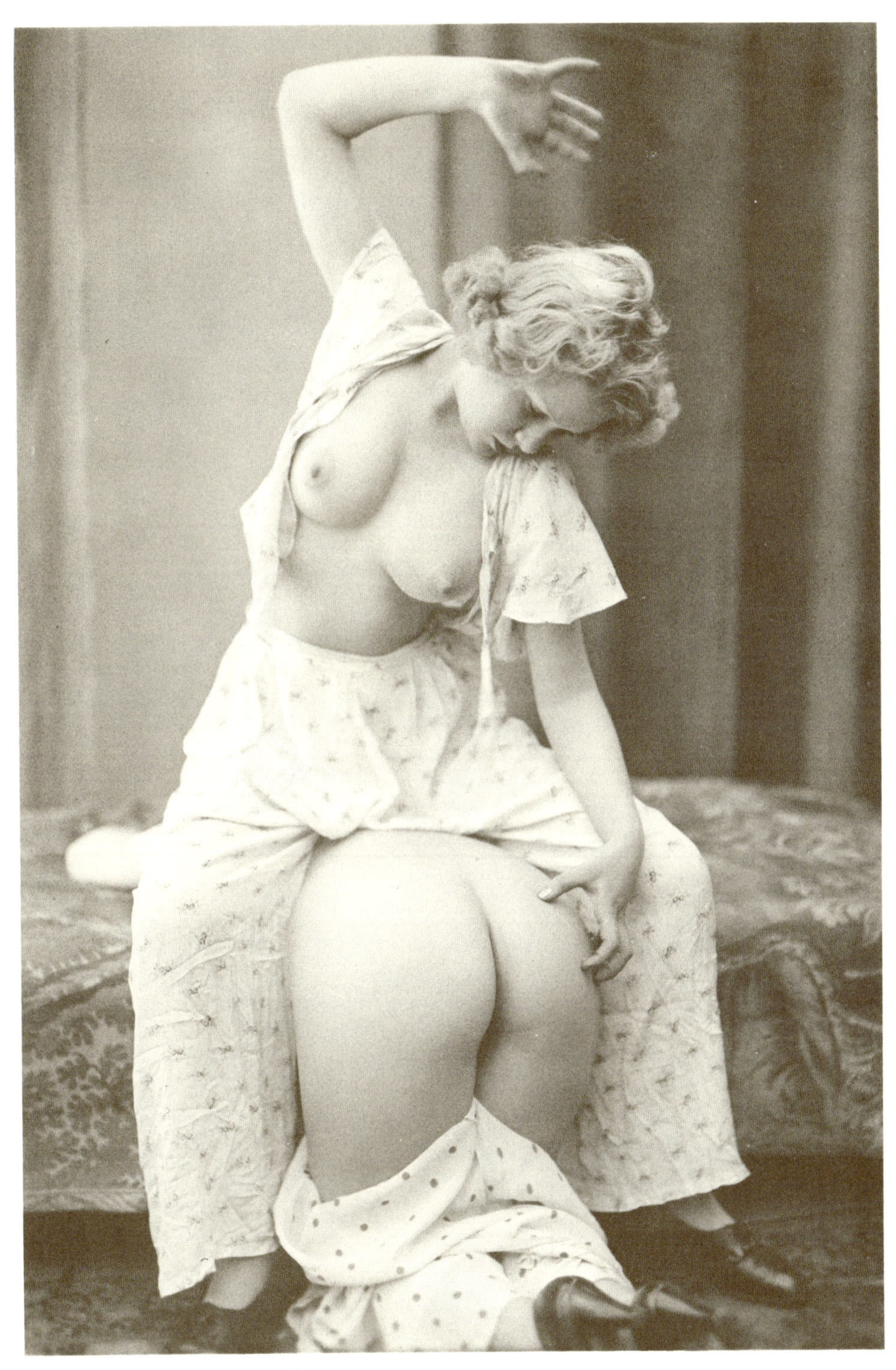

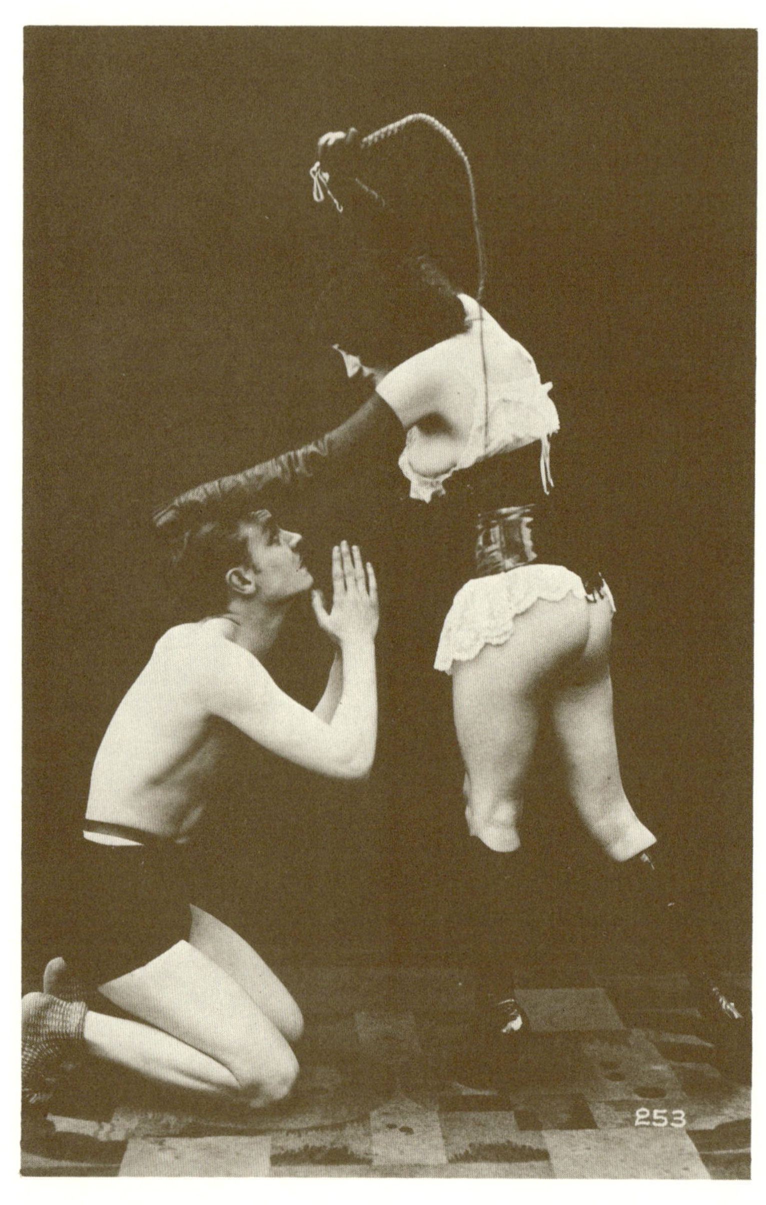
253

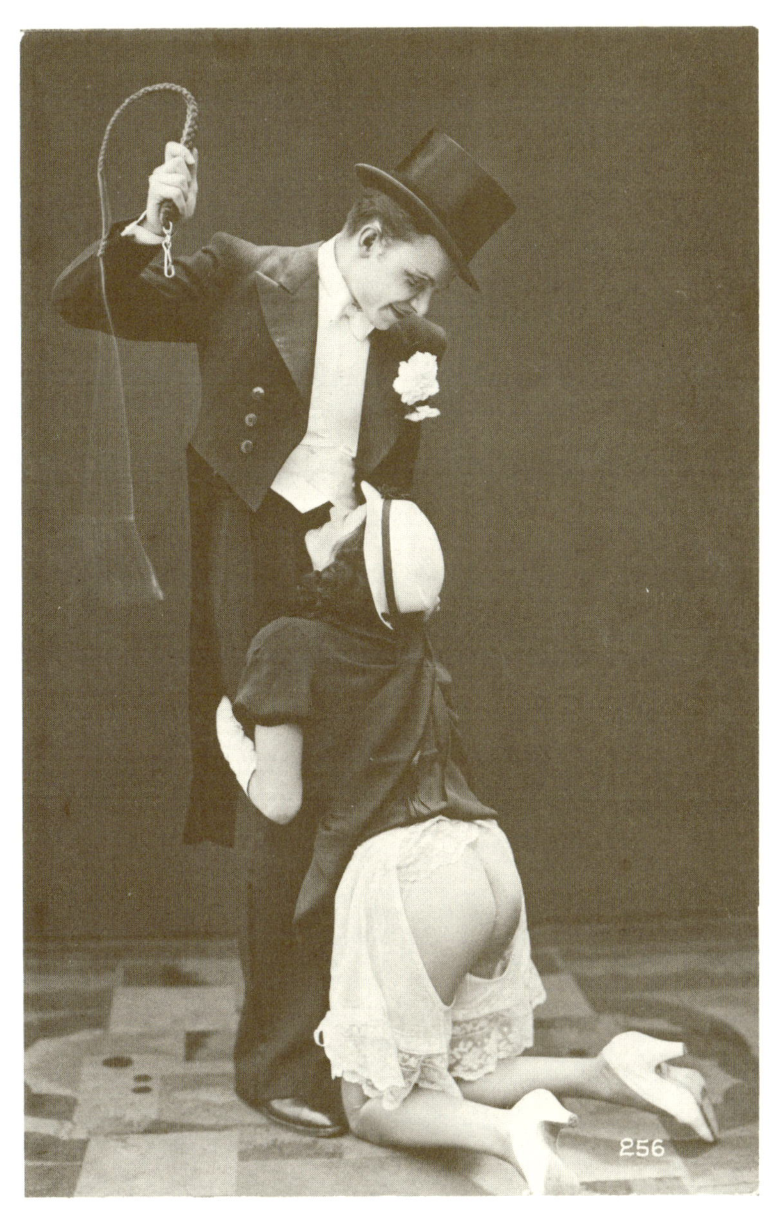
256

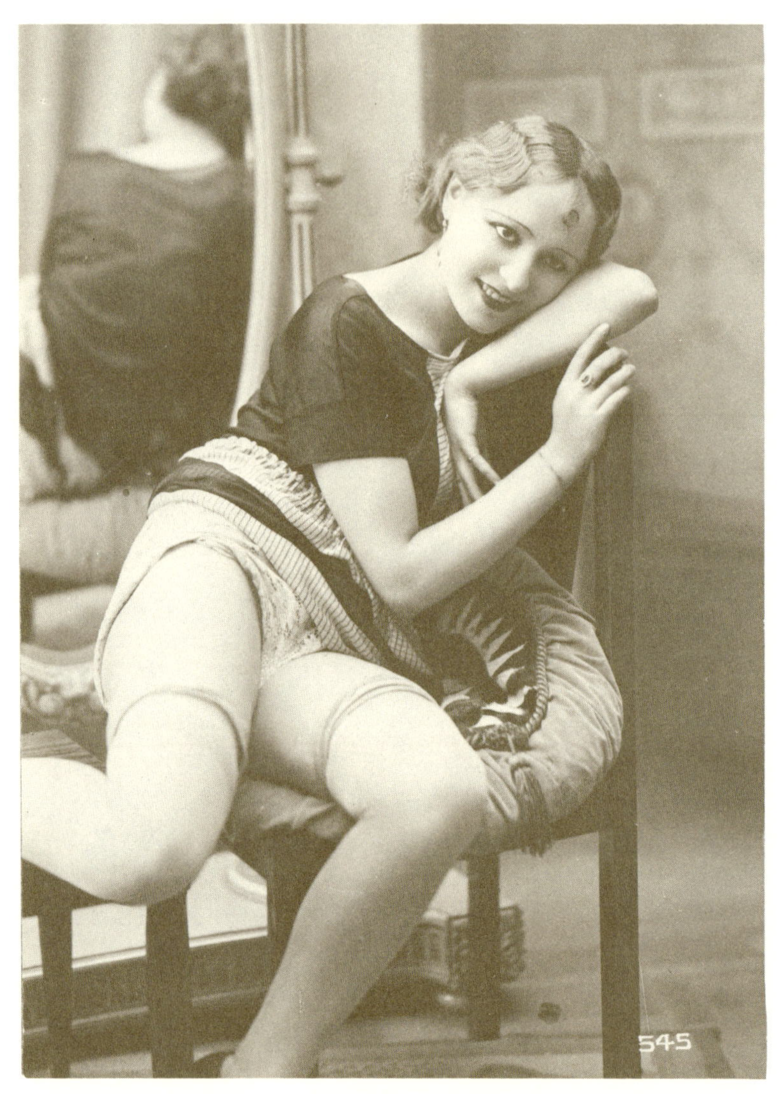
545

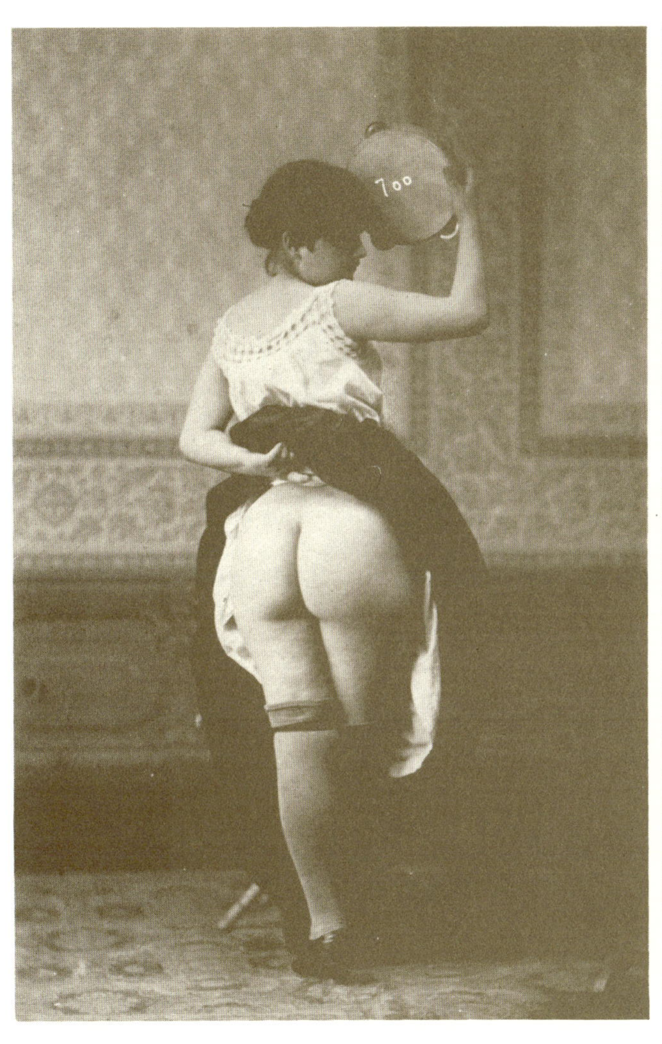
700

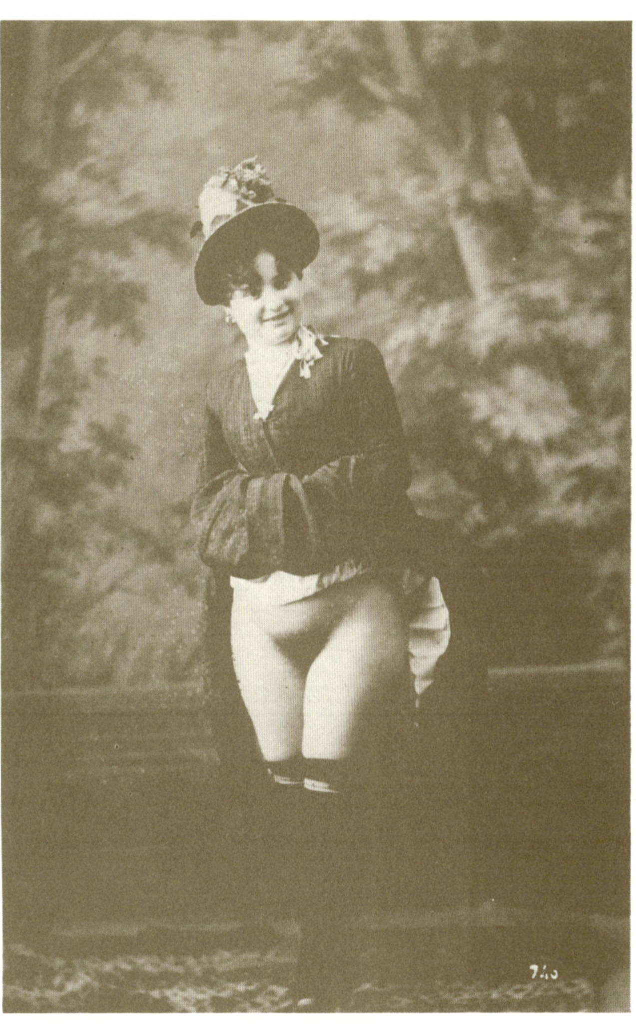

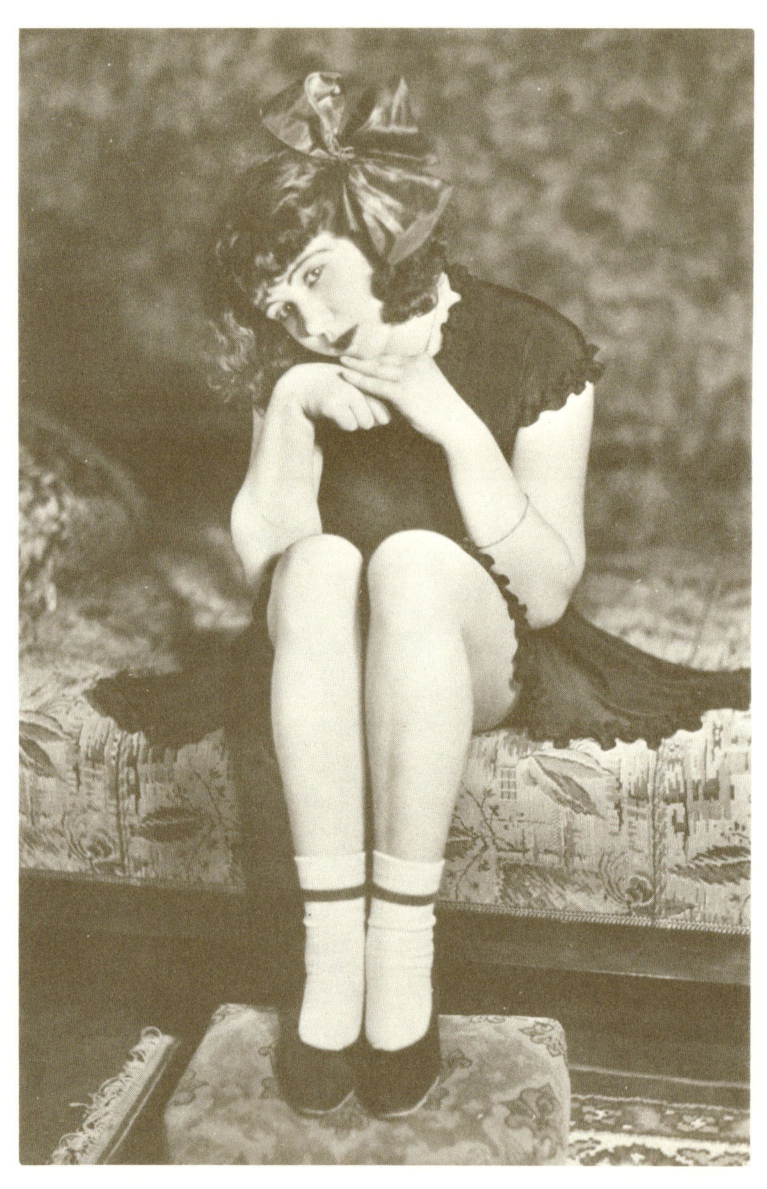

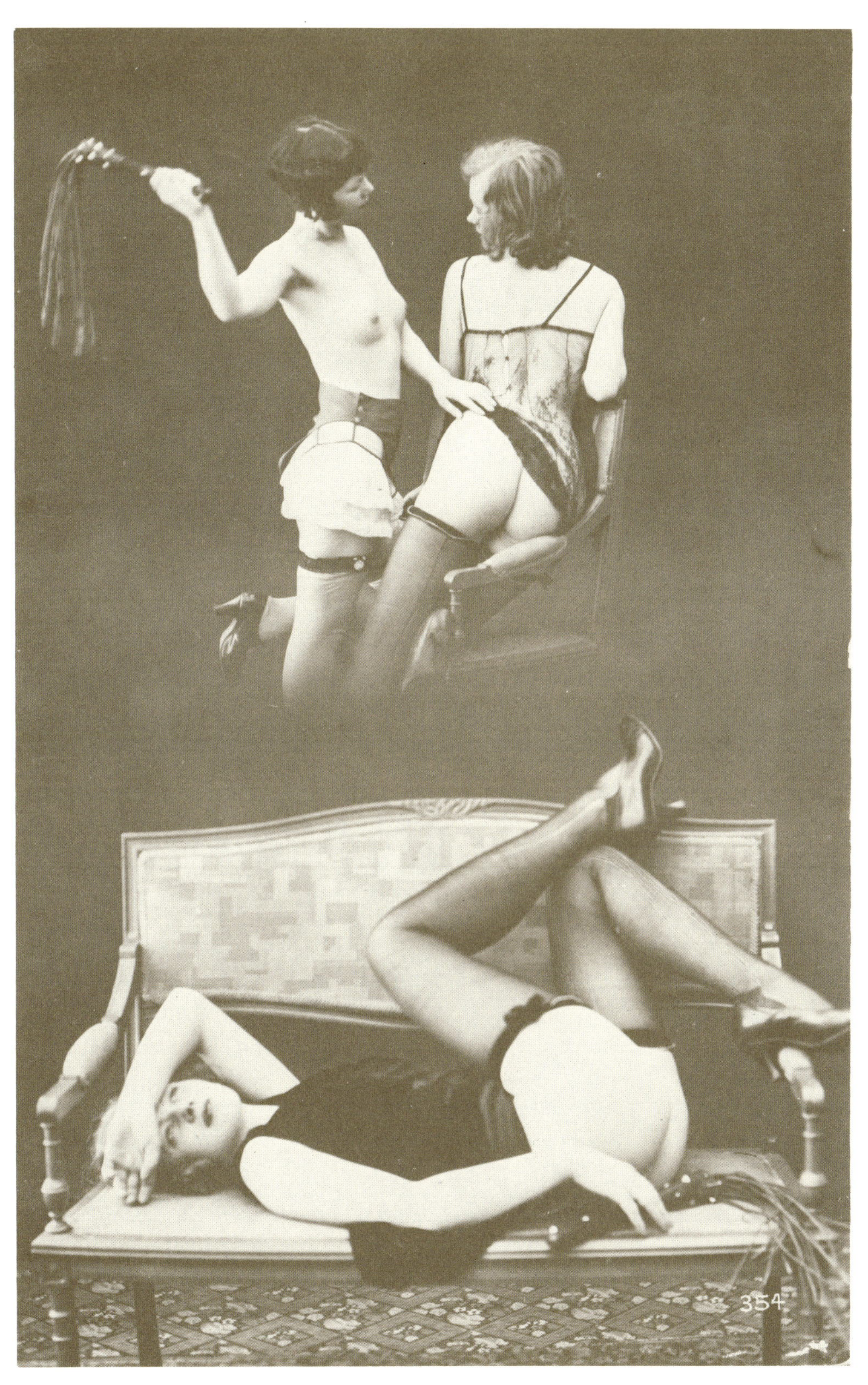
354

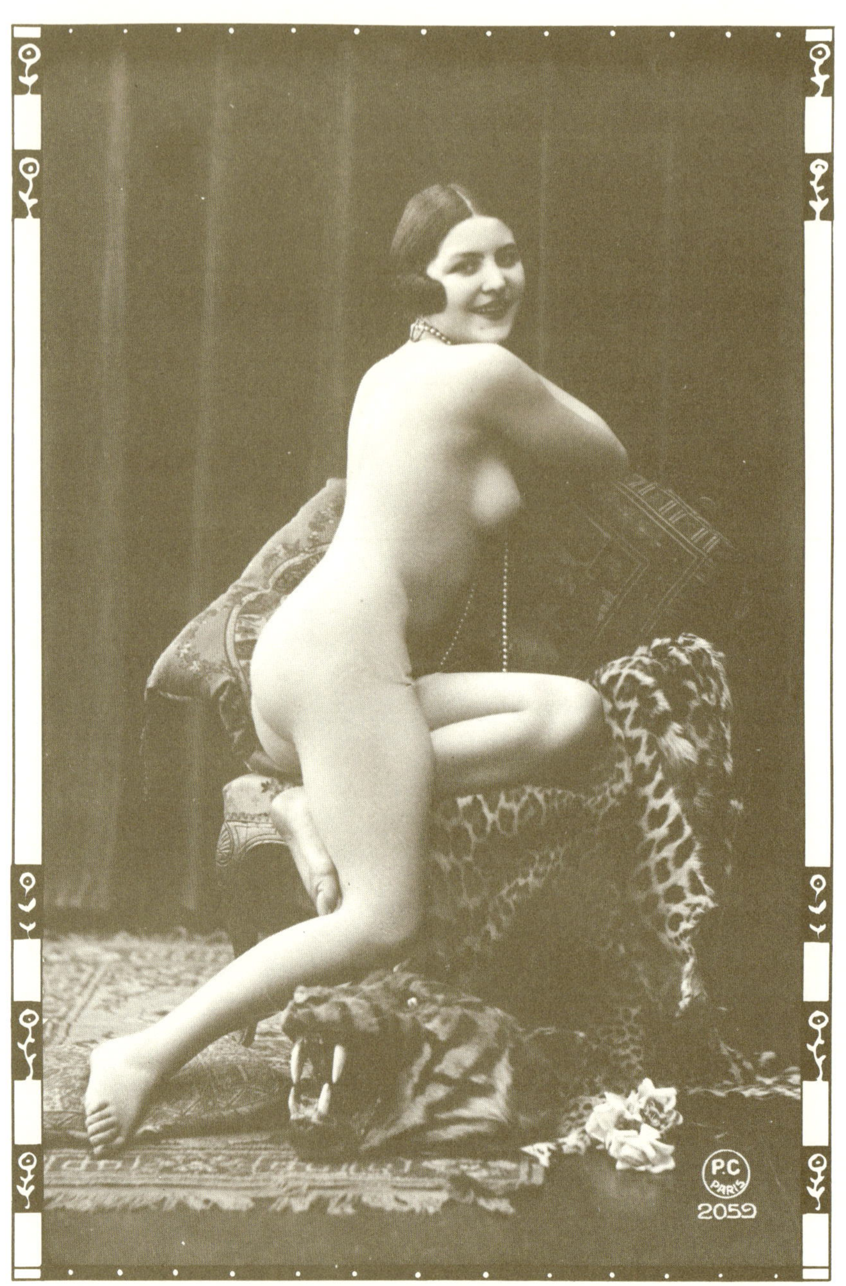
P.C
PARIS
2059

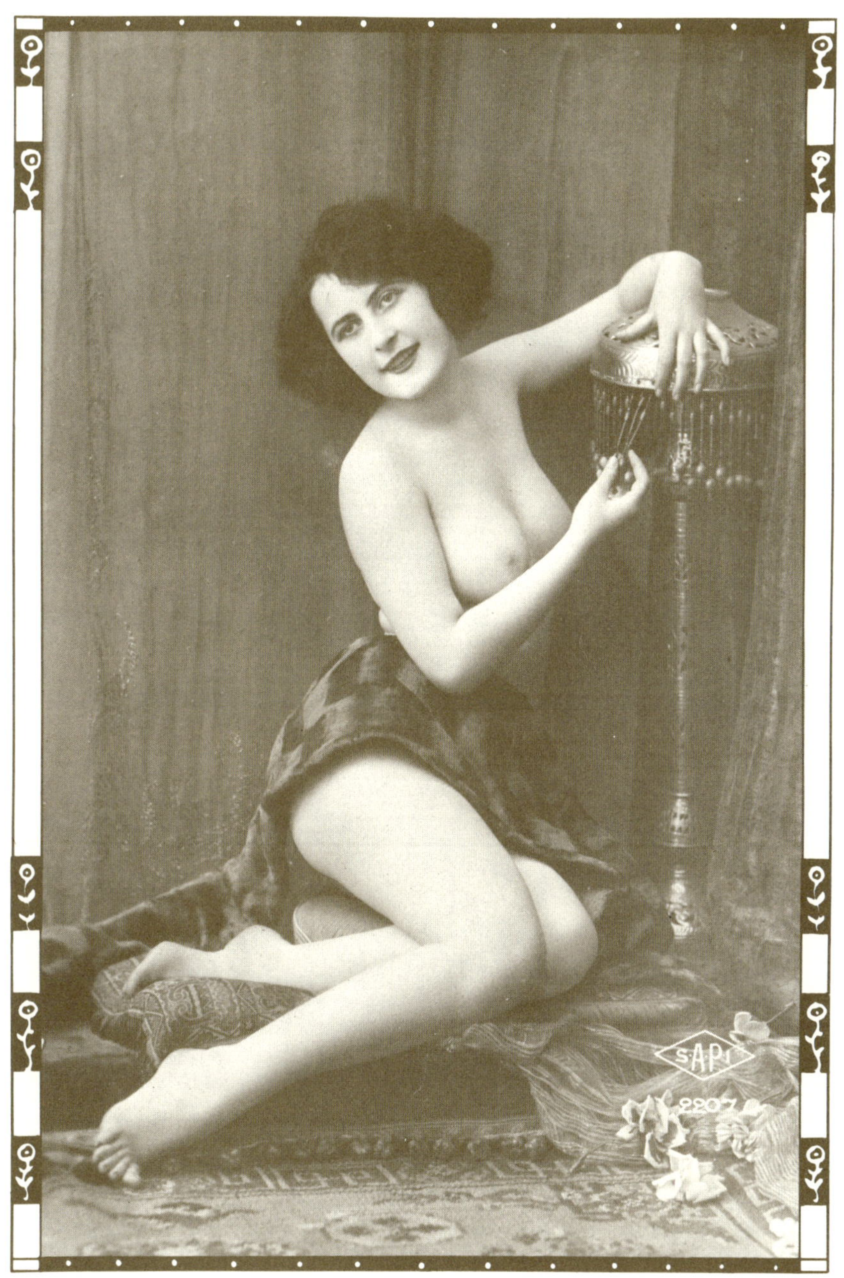
SAPI
2207

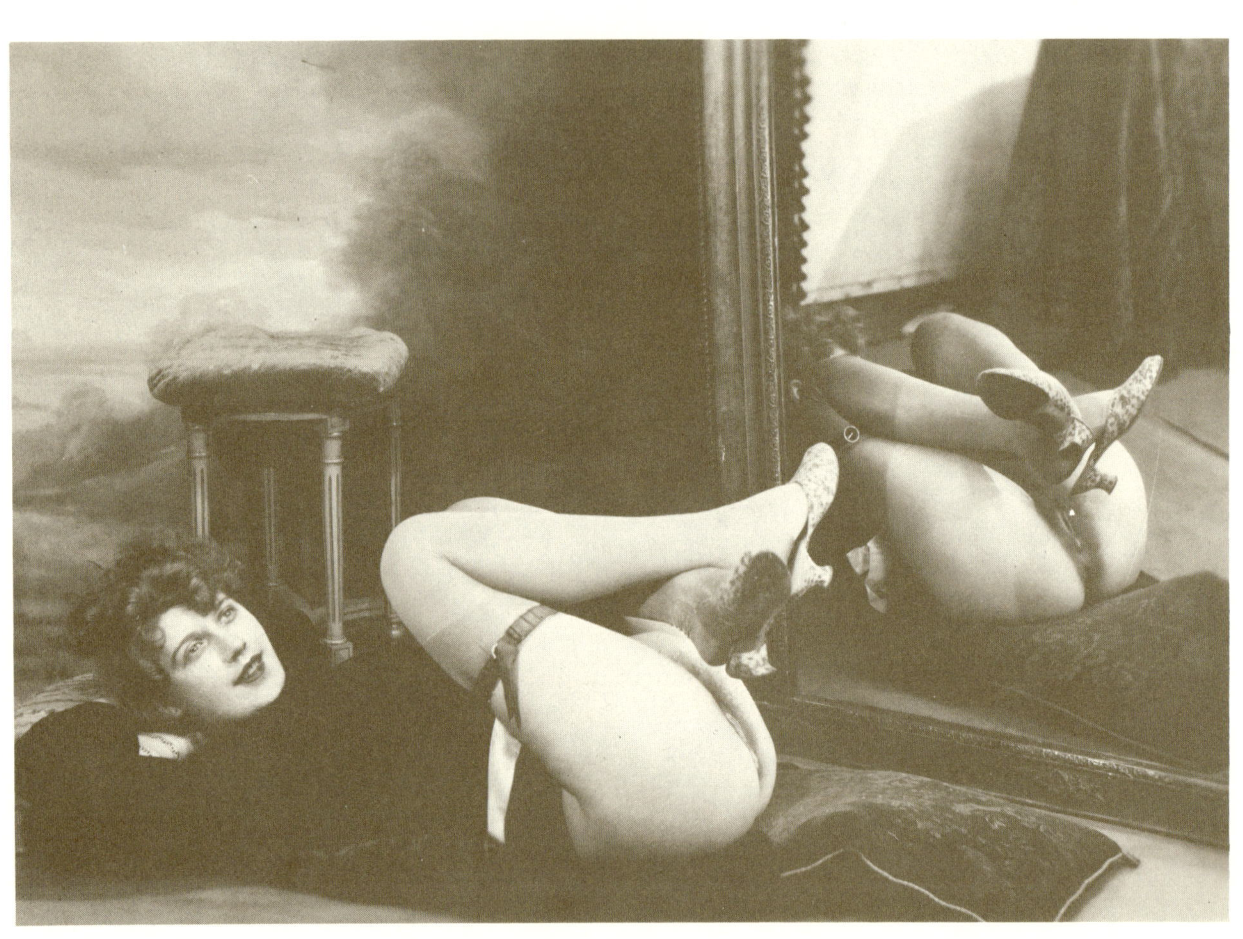

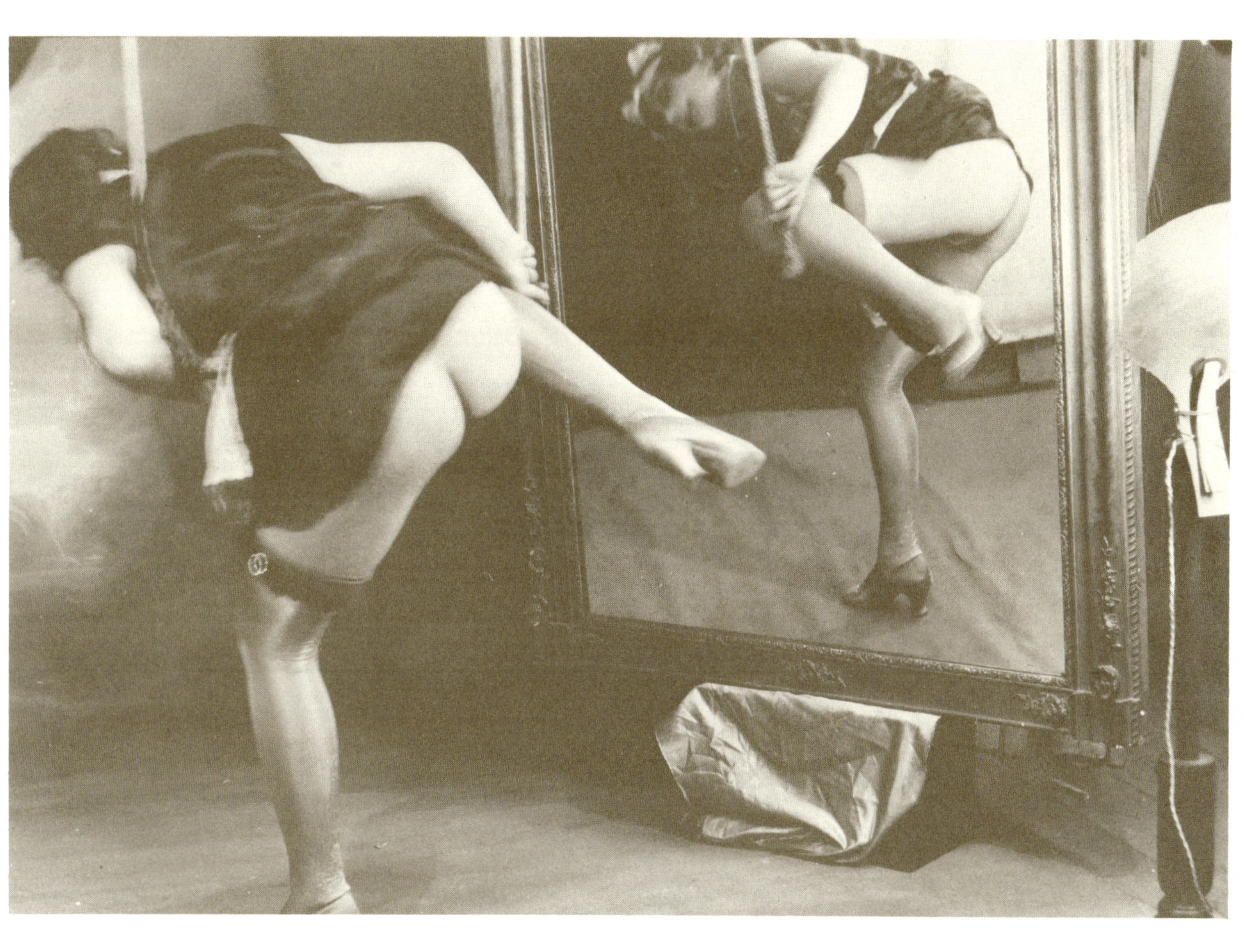

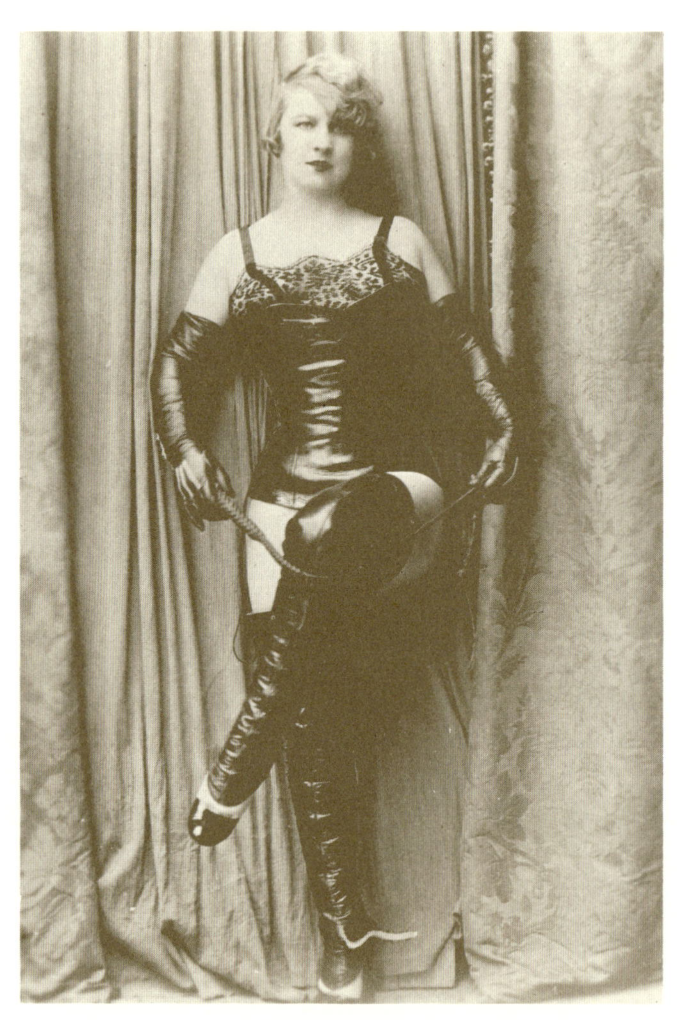

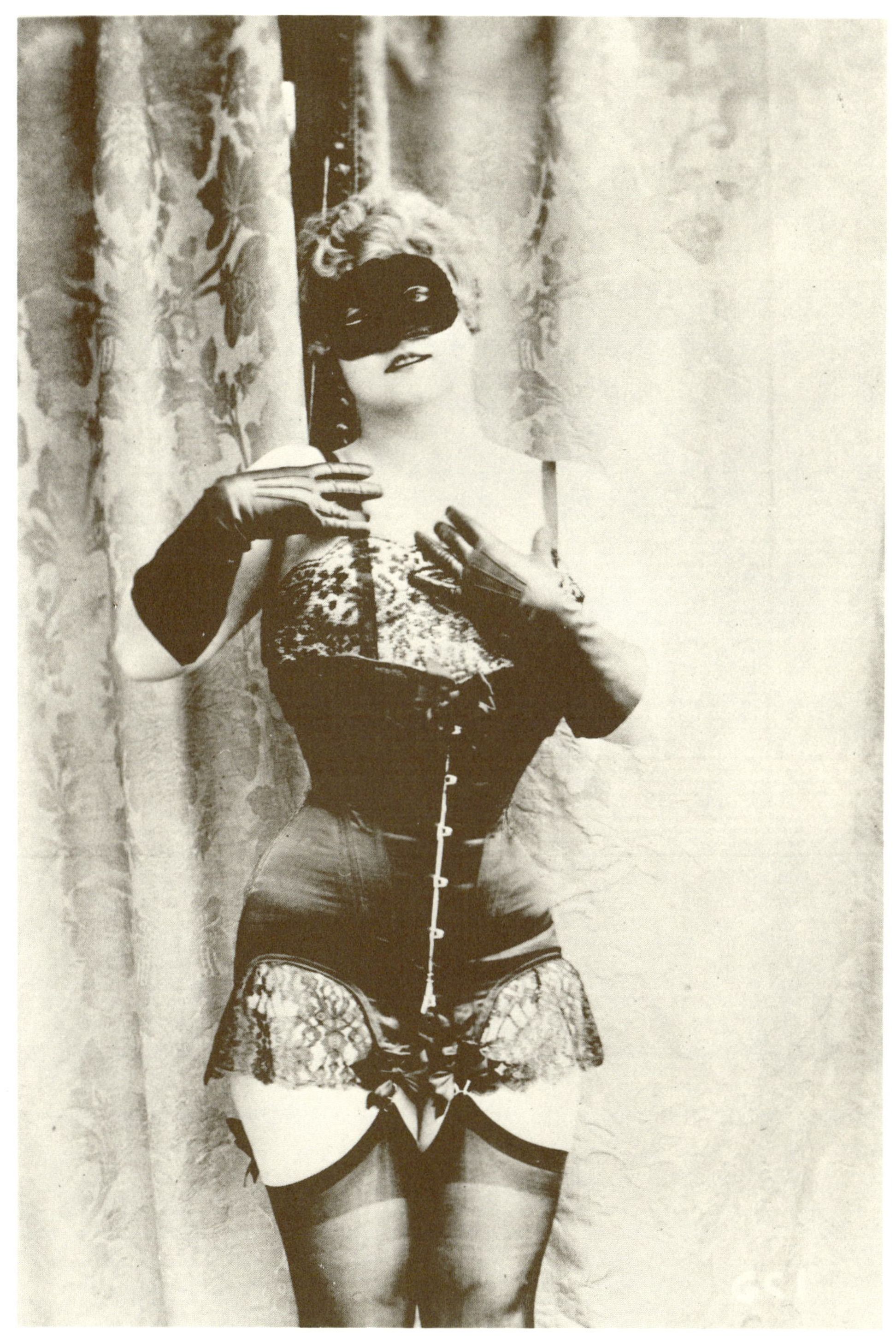

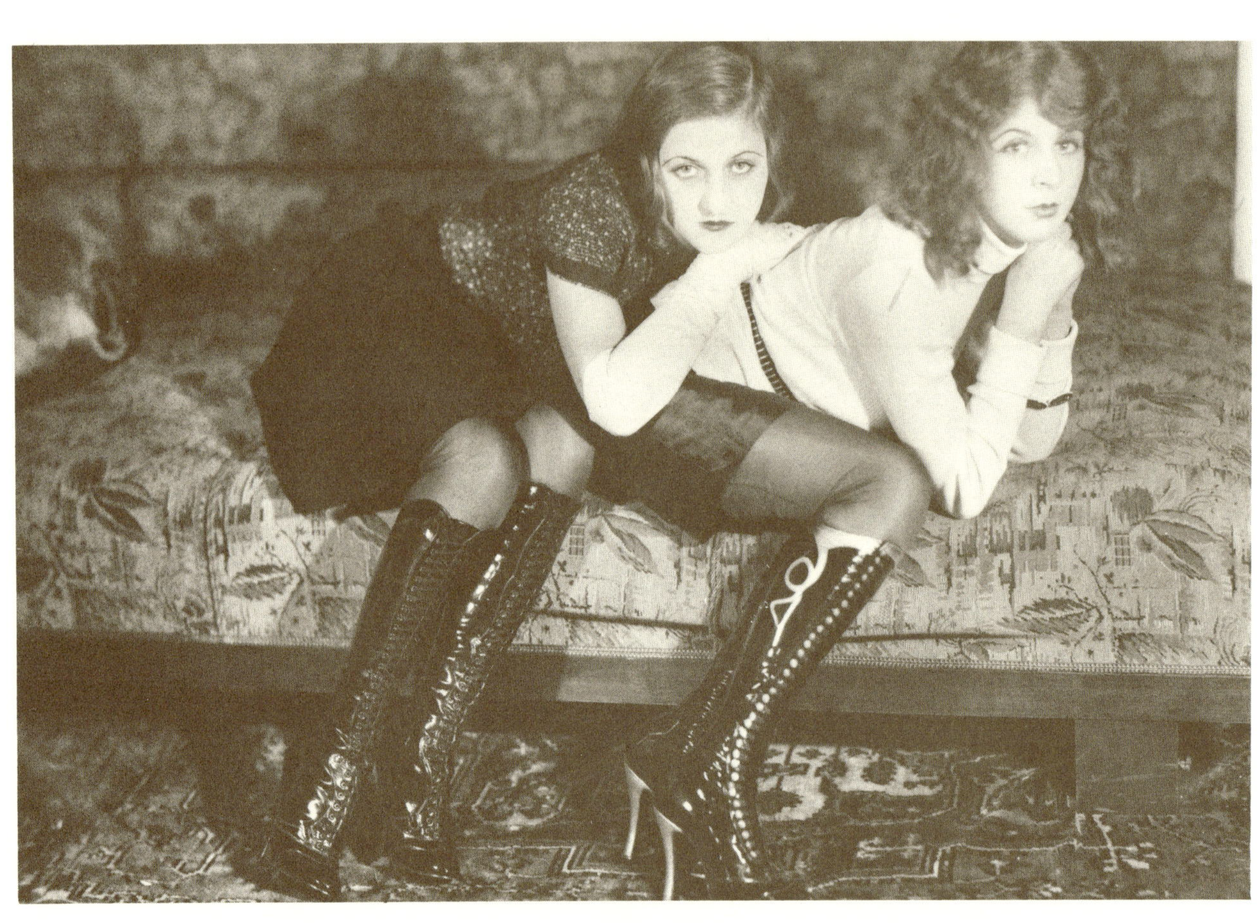

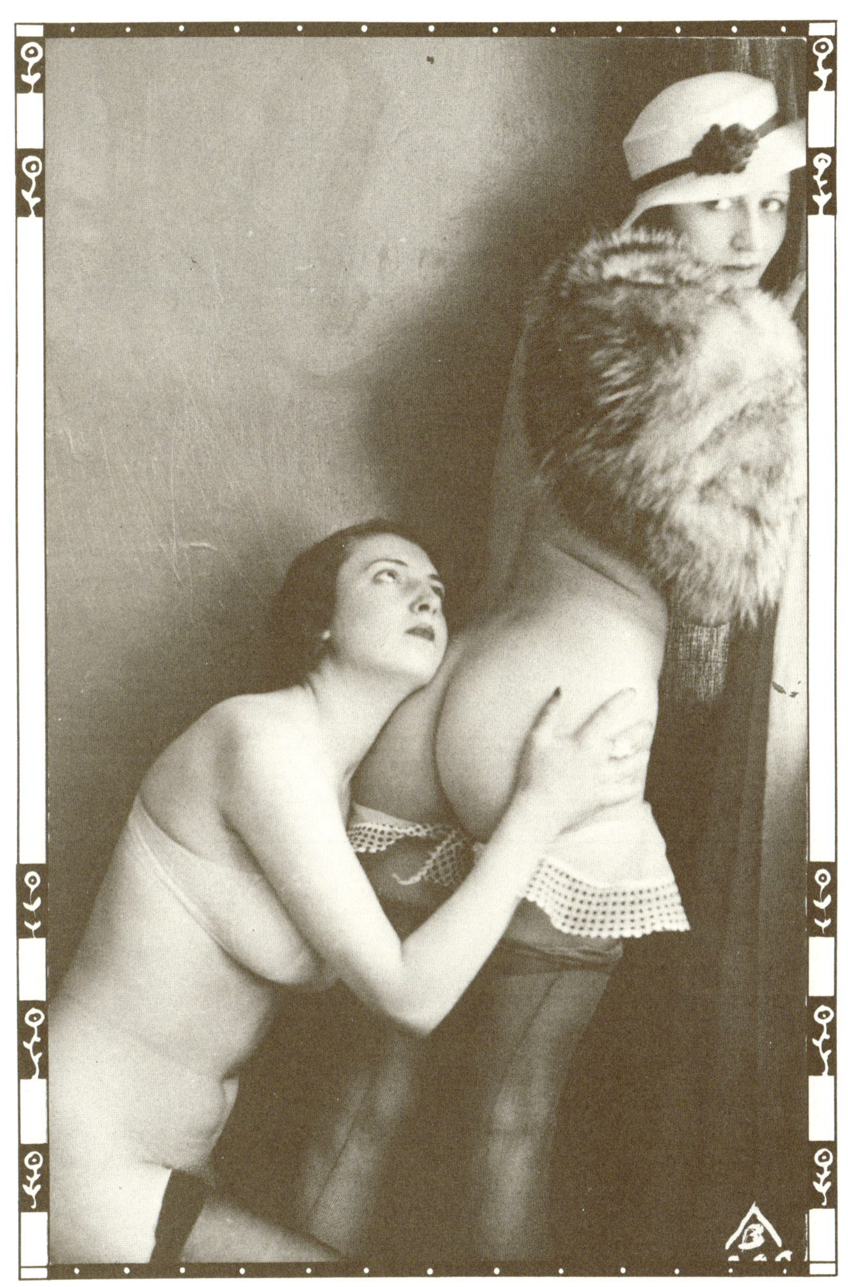

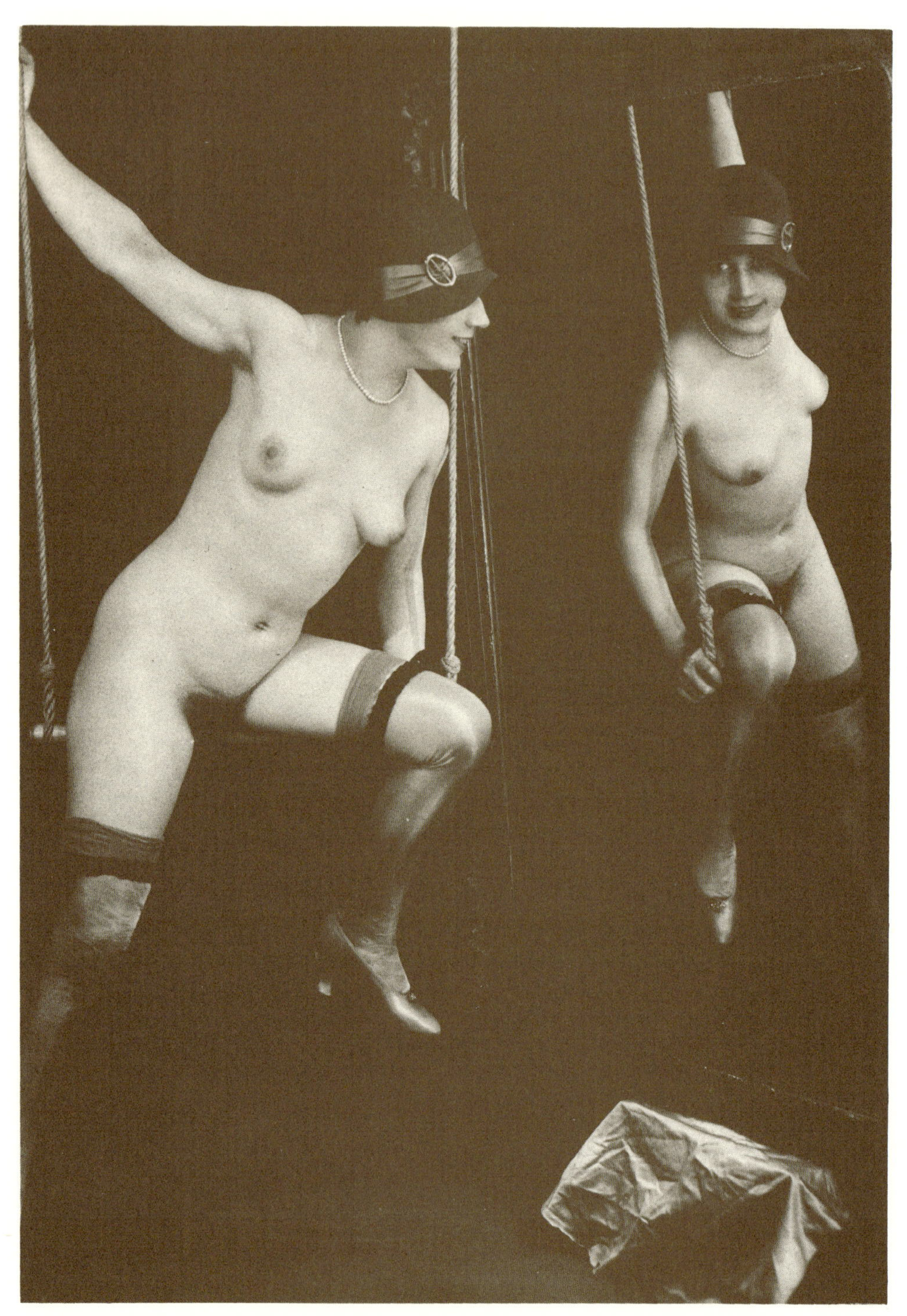

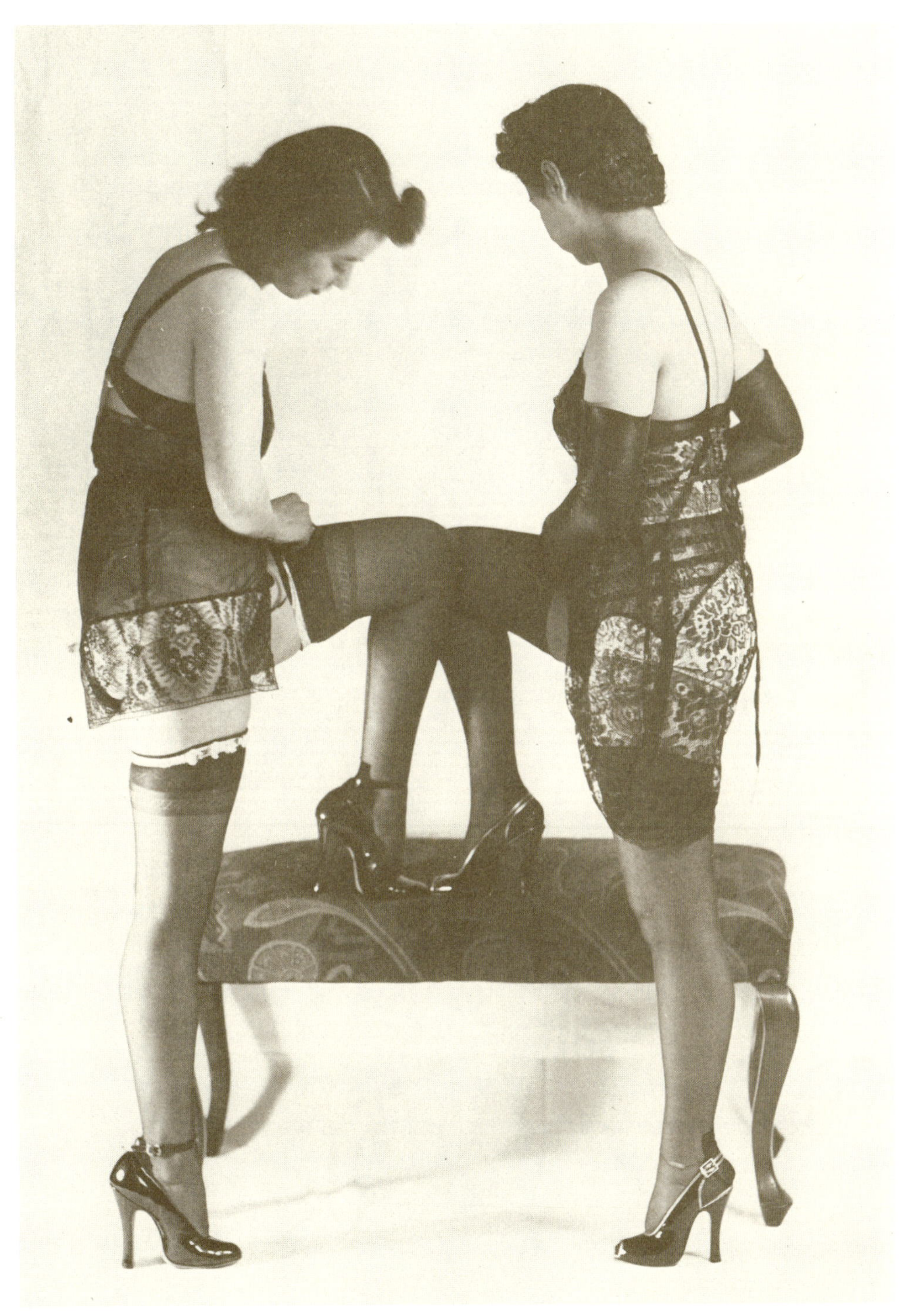

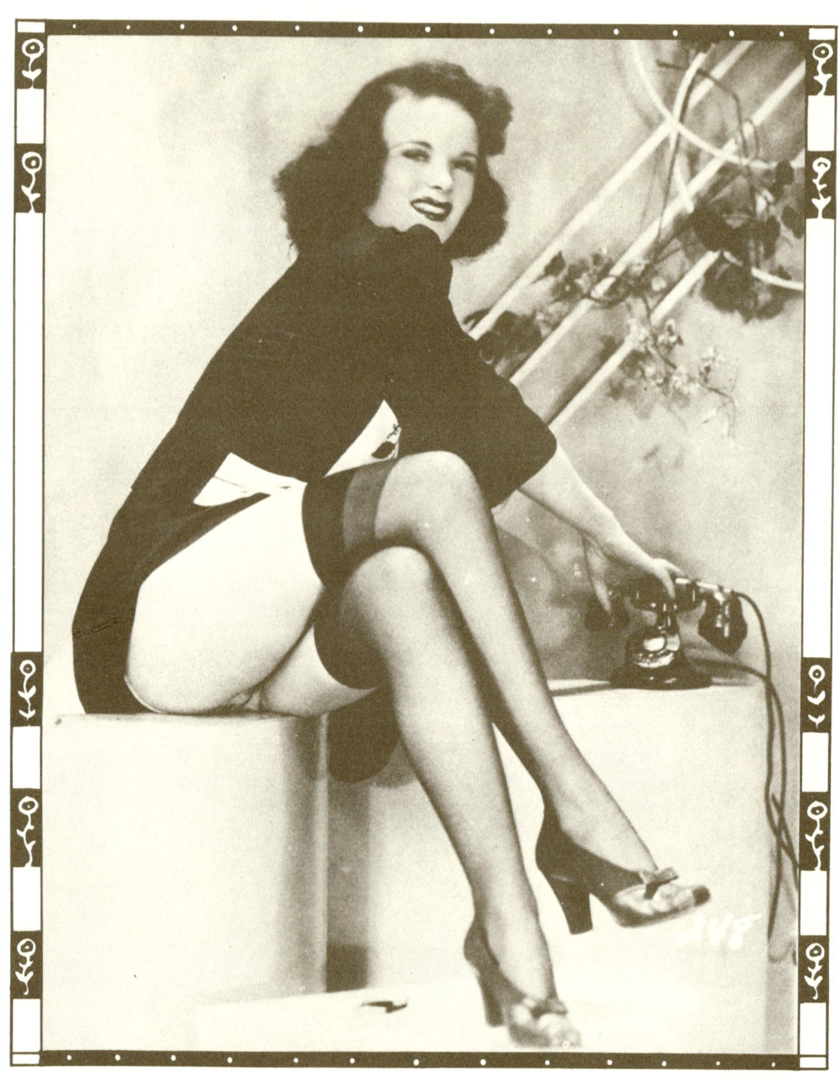

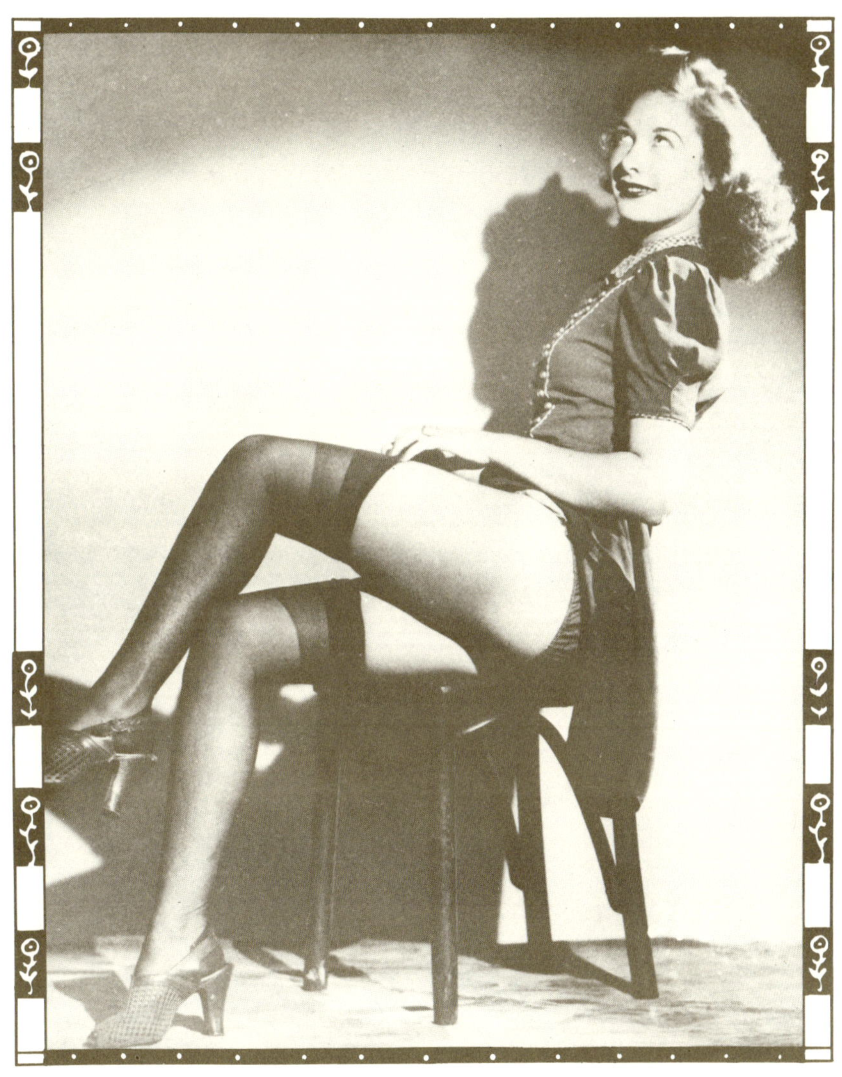

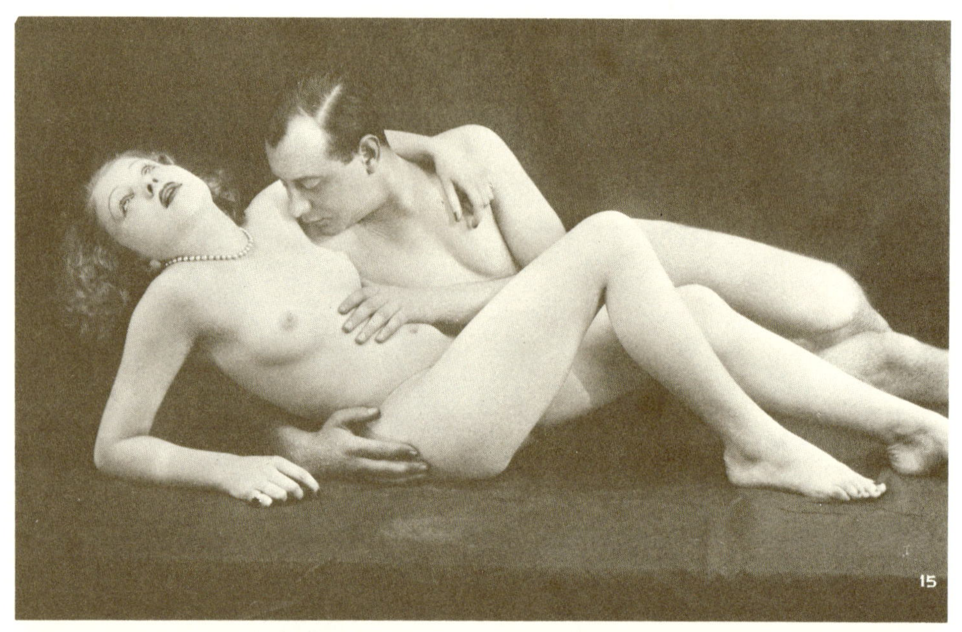

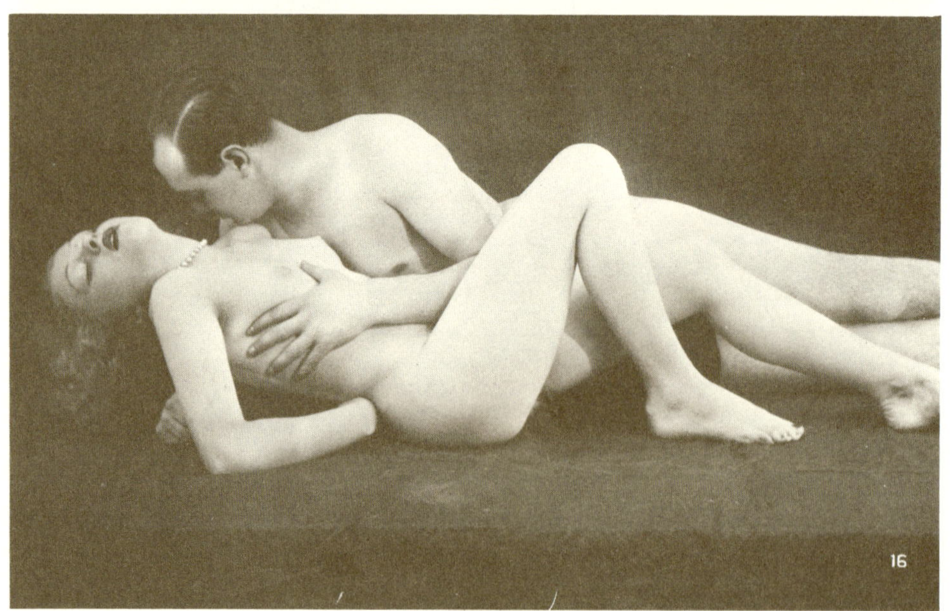

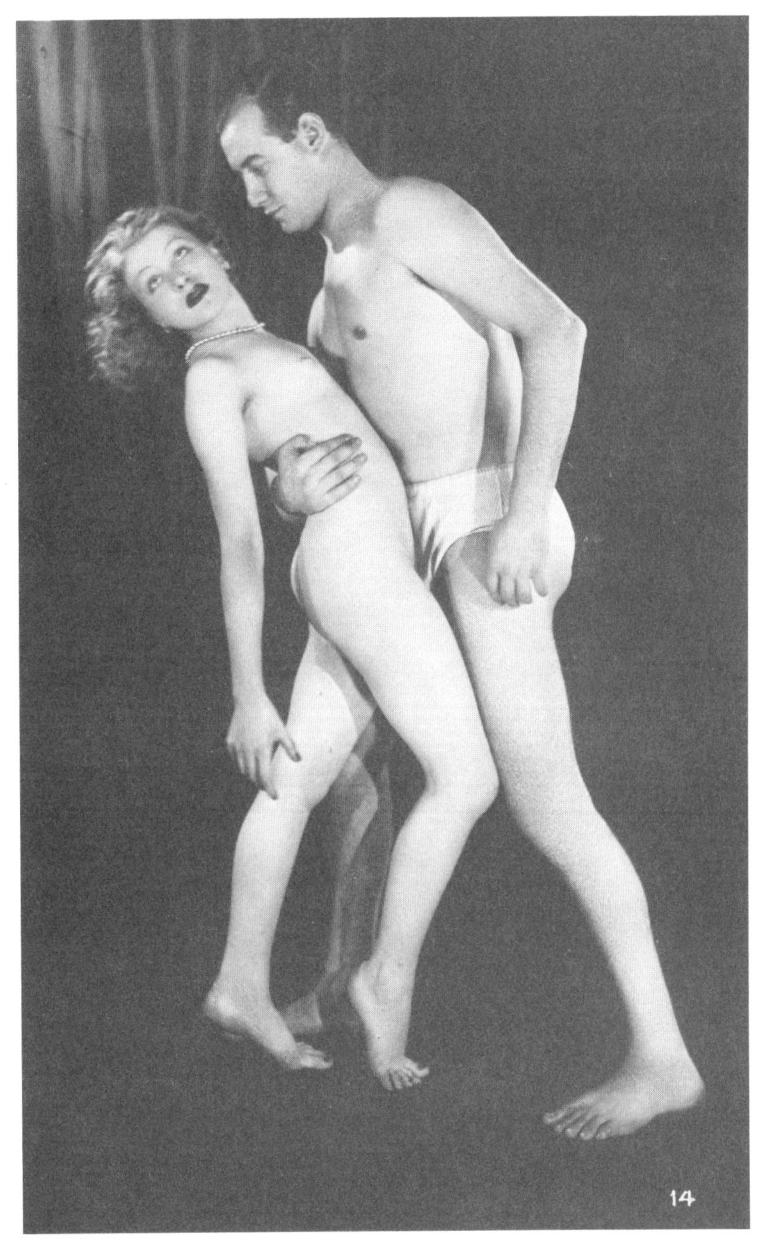
14

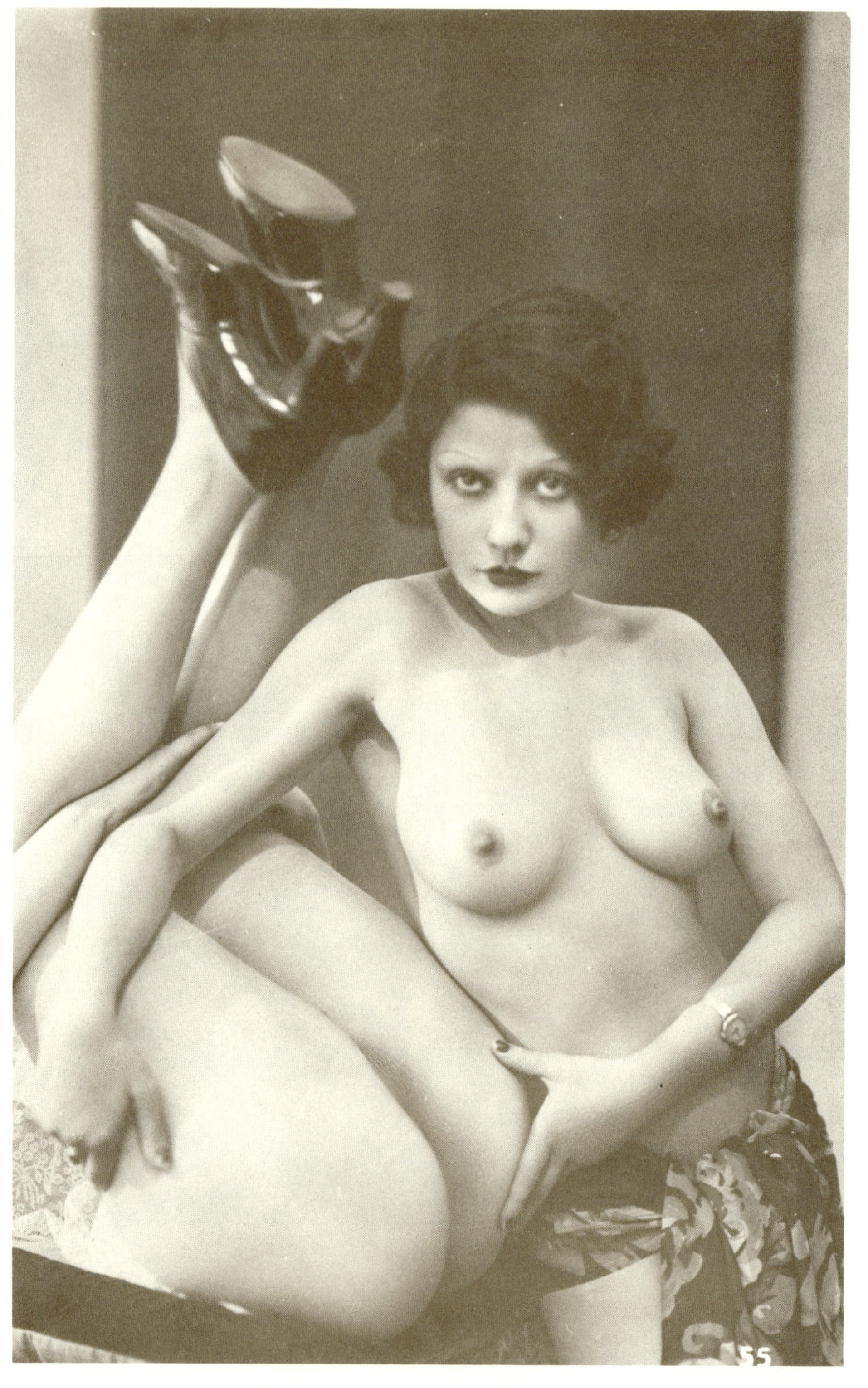
55

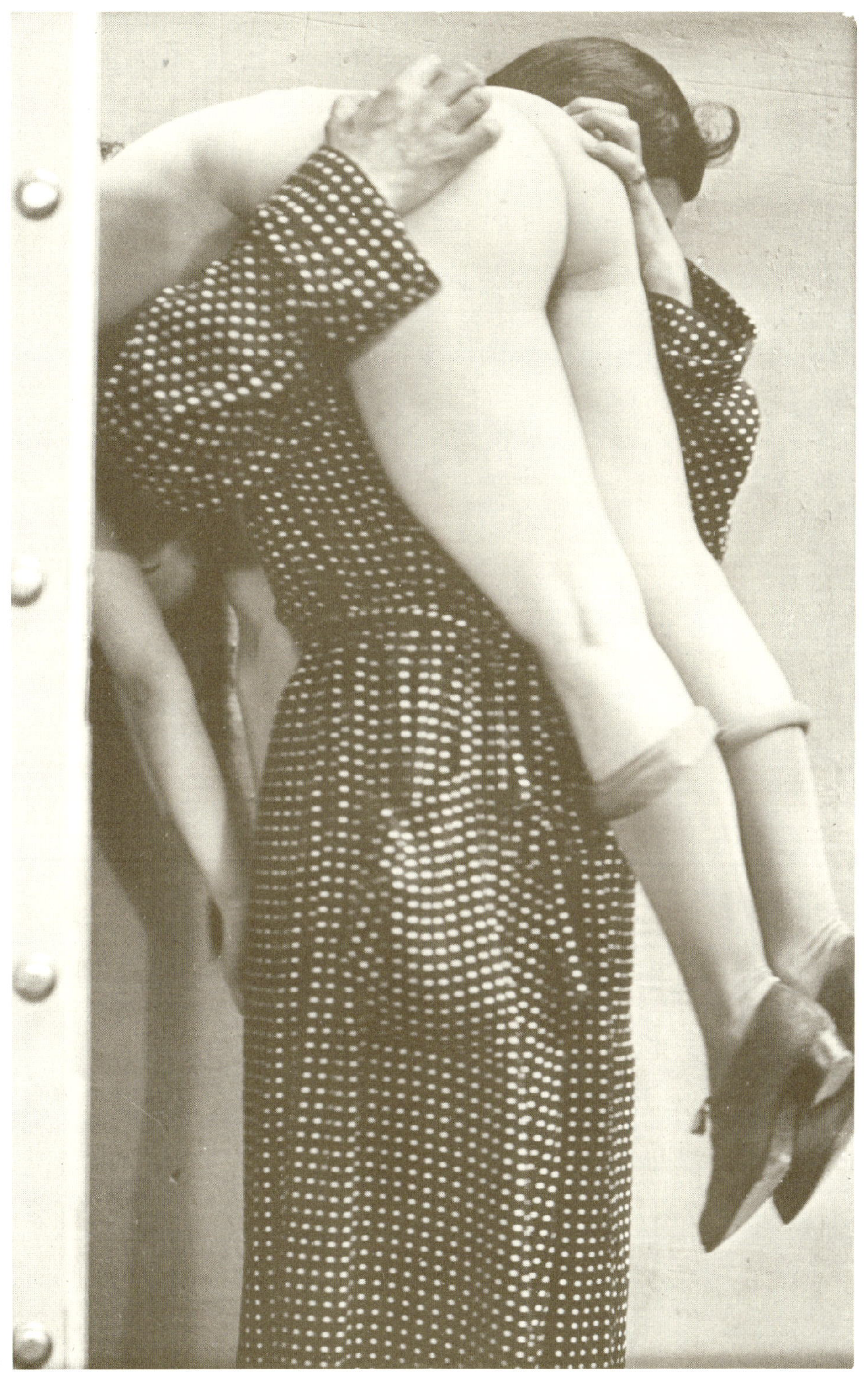

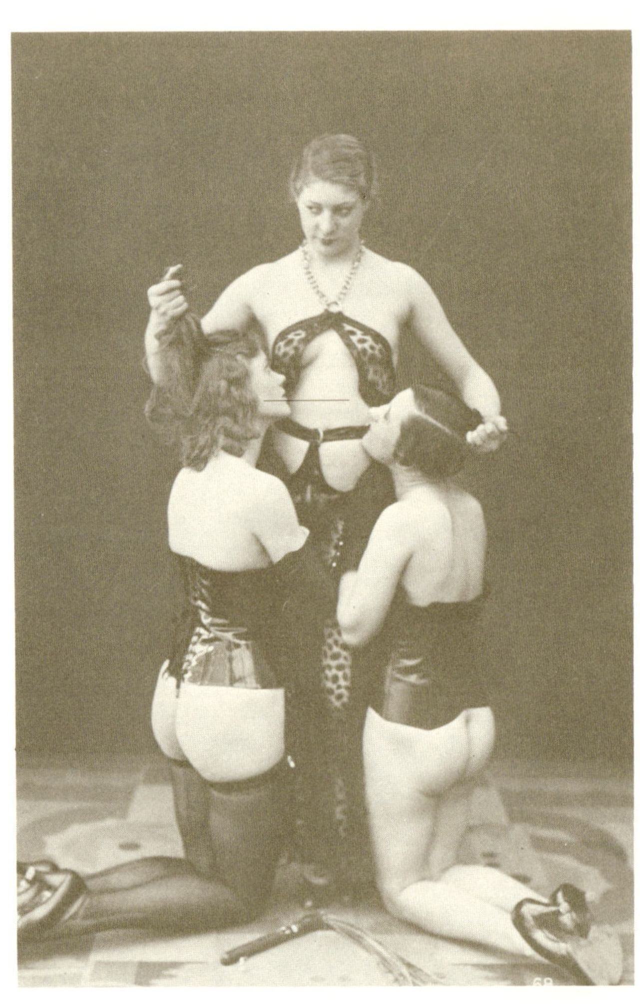

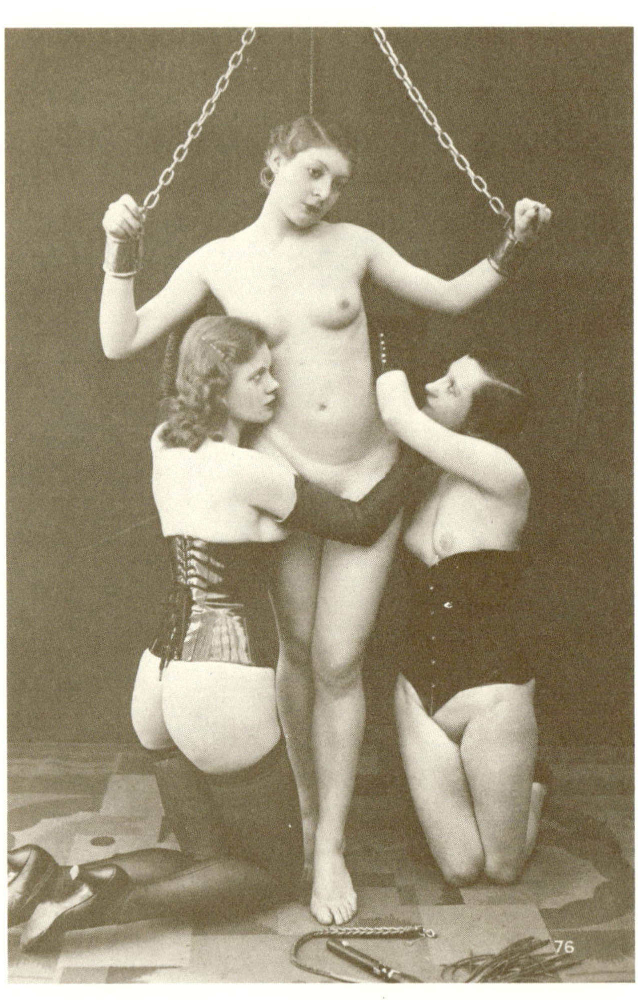
76

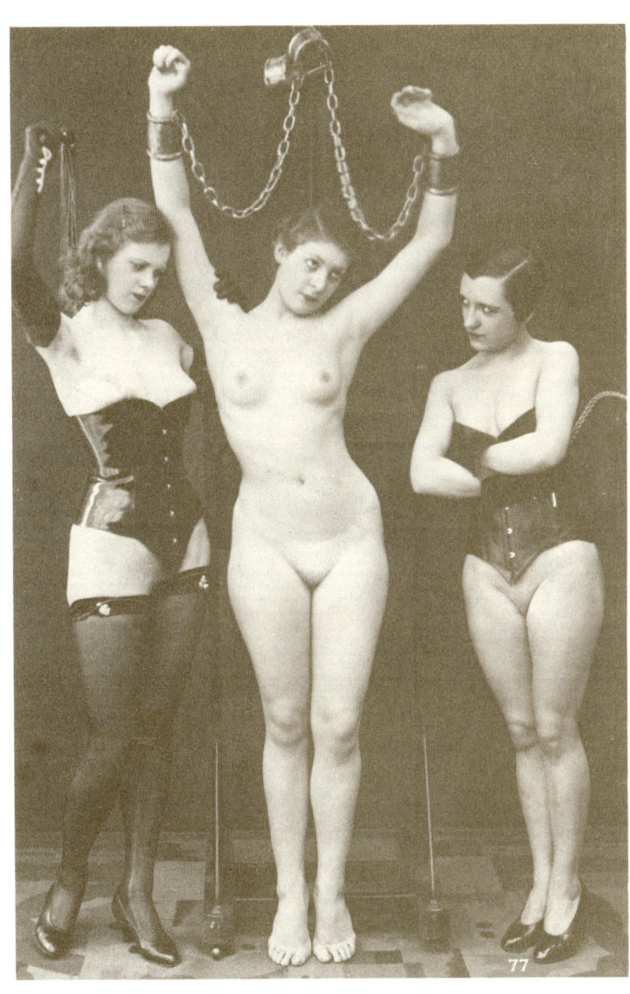
77

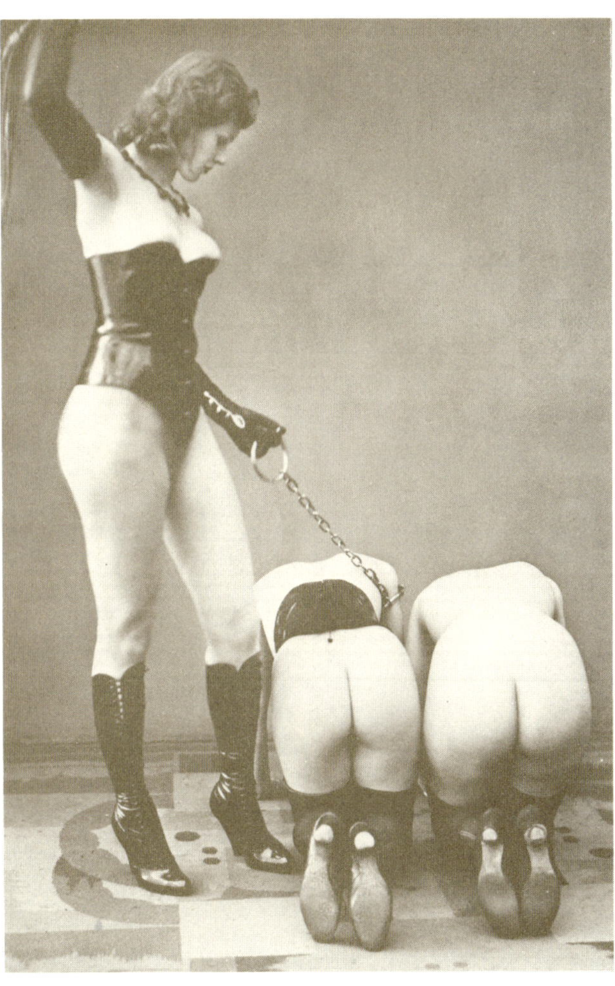

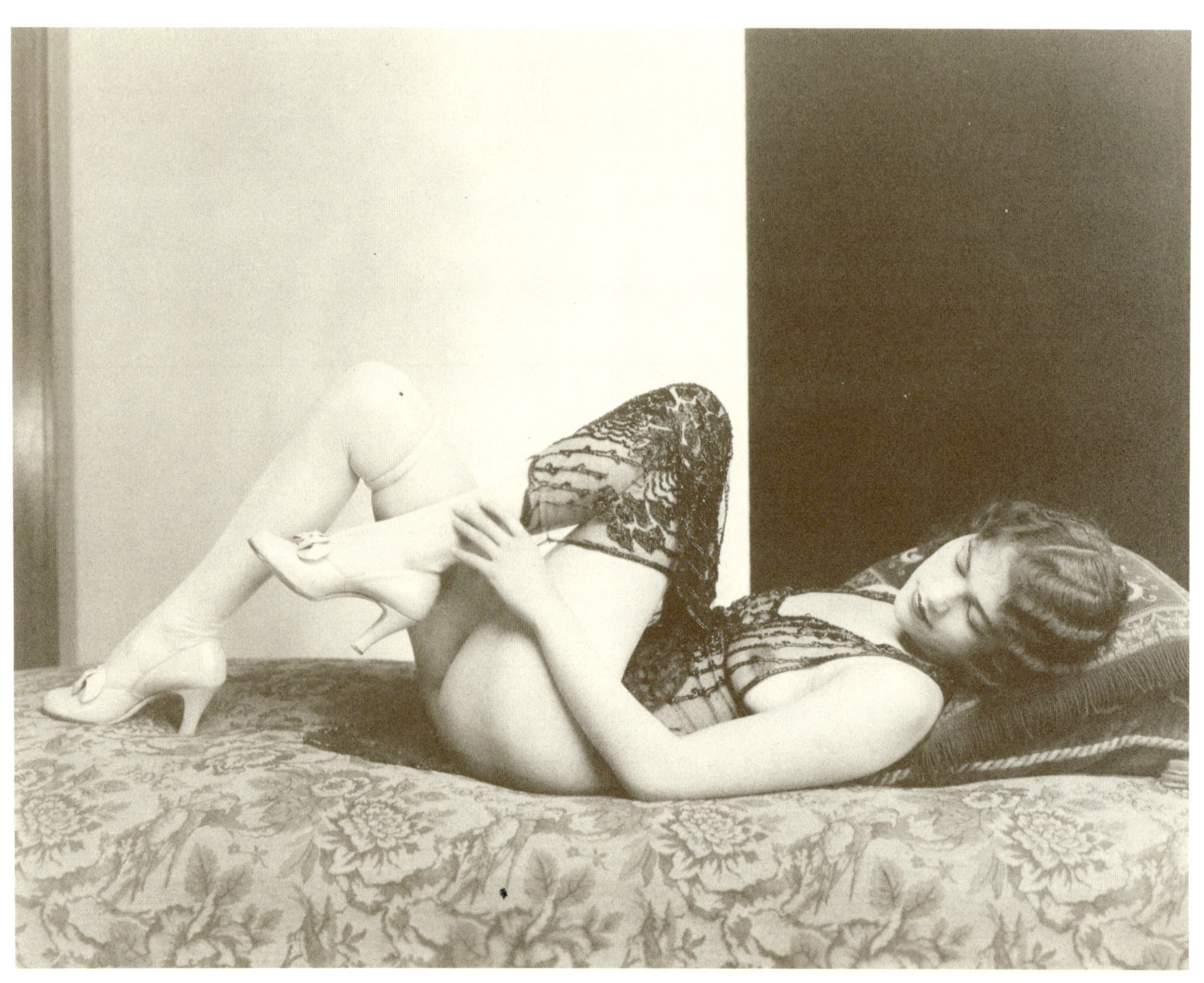

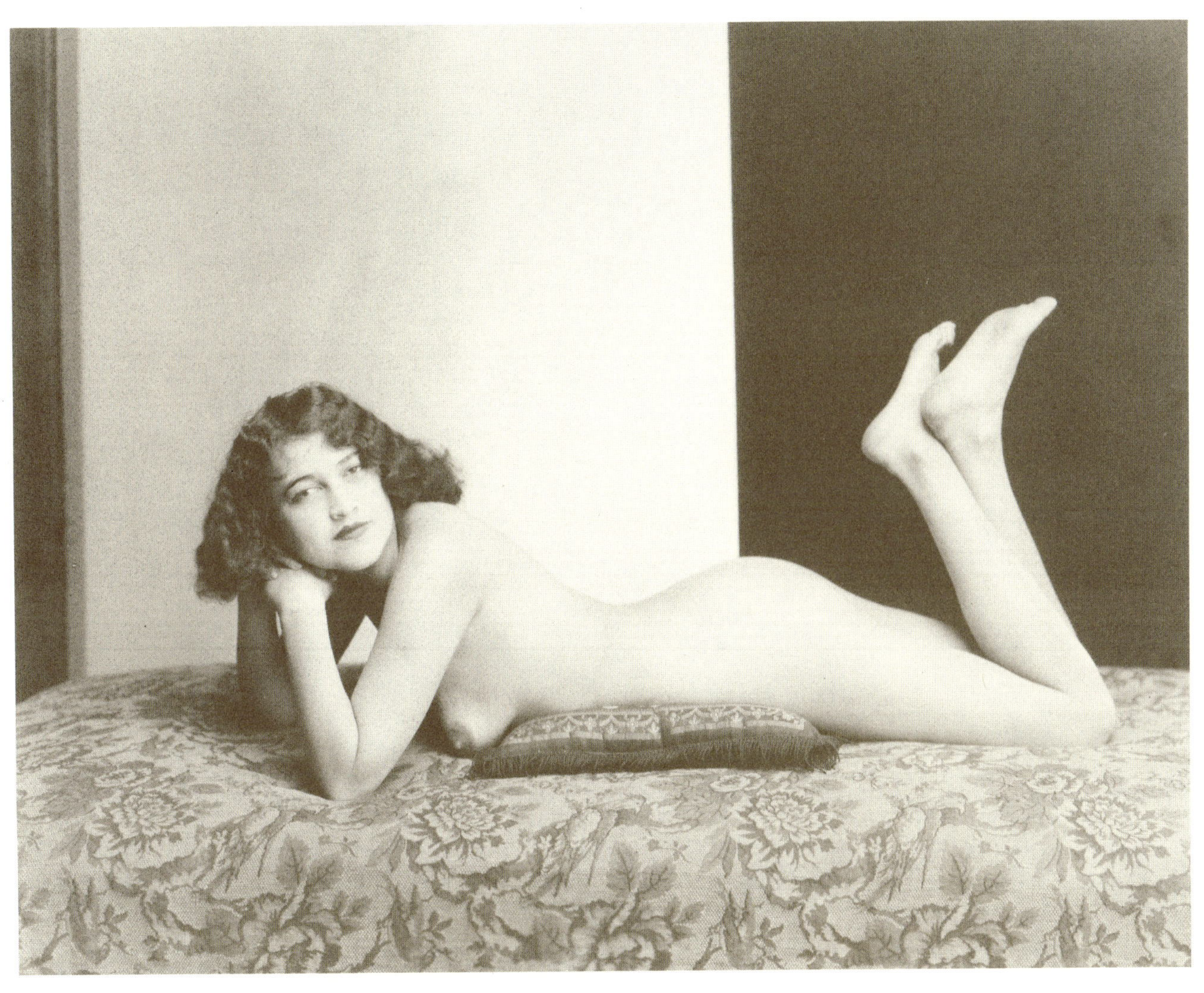

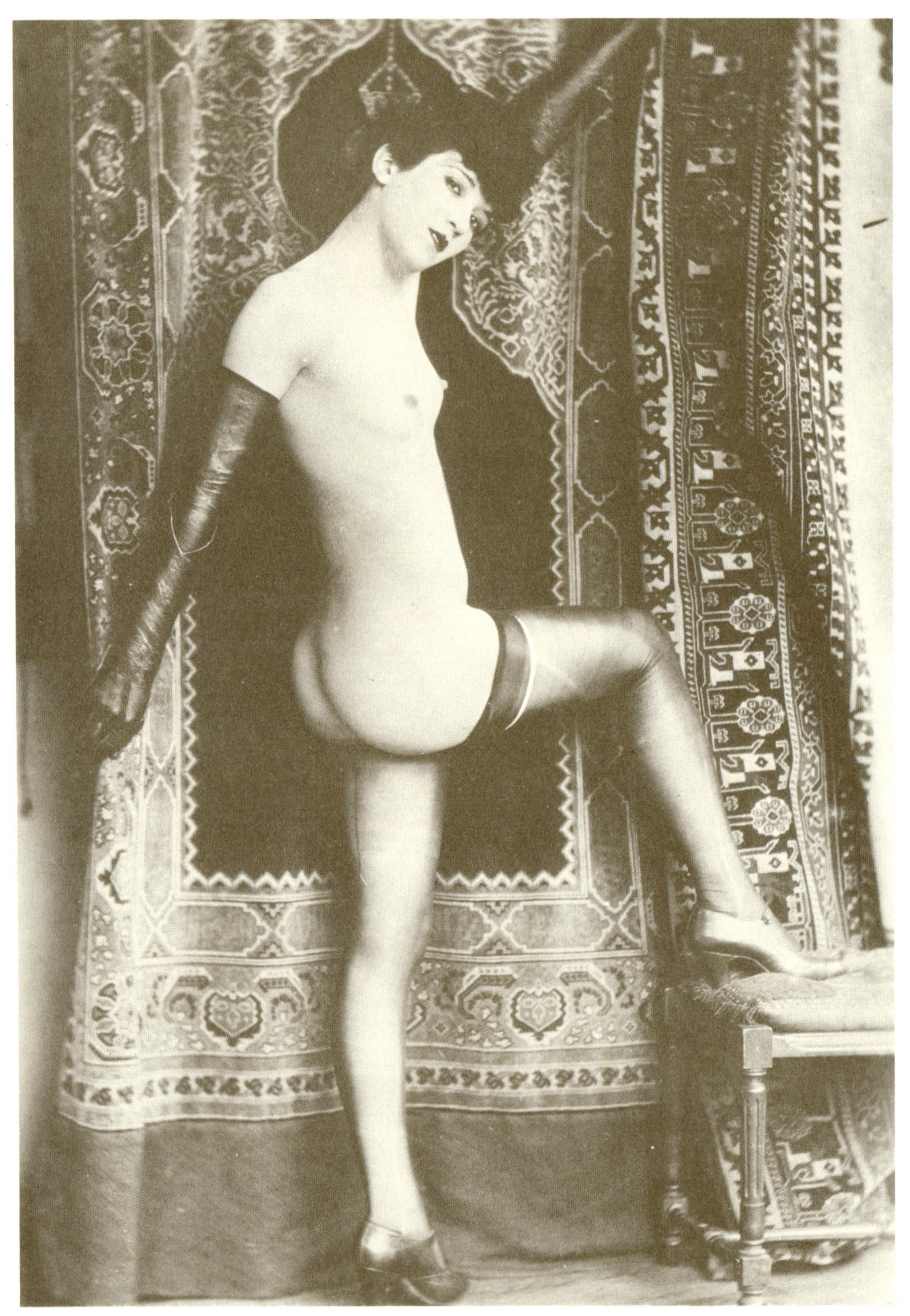

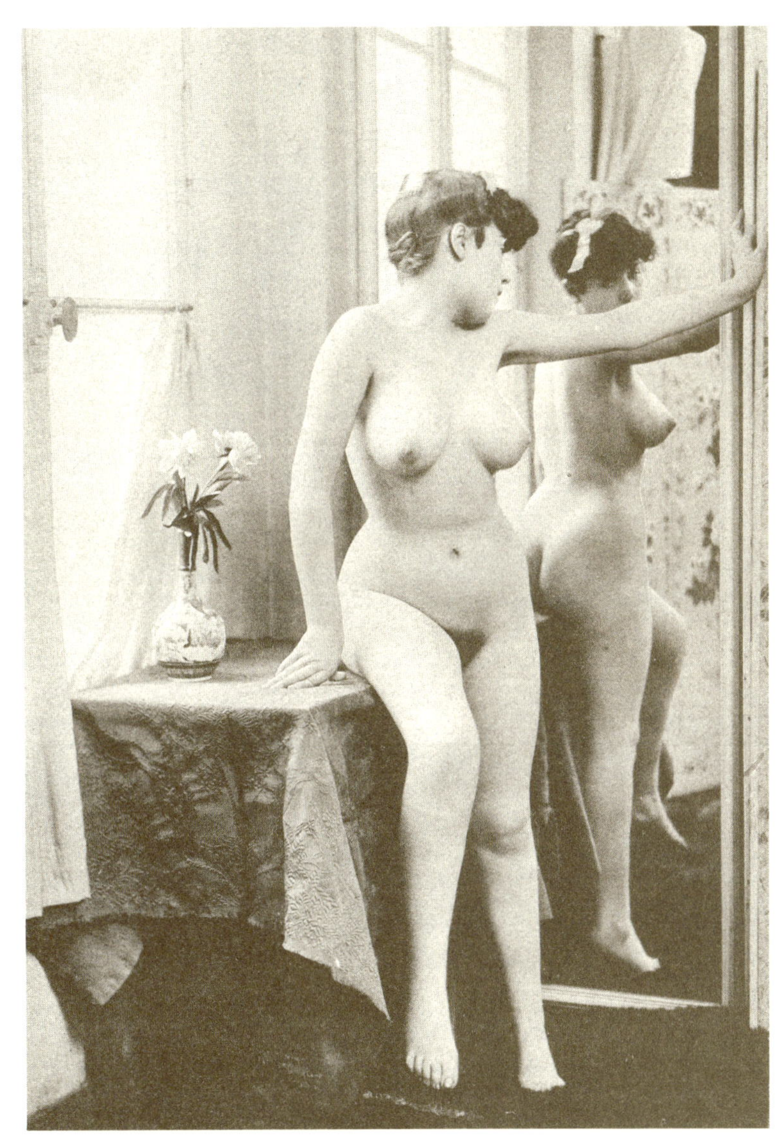

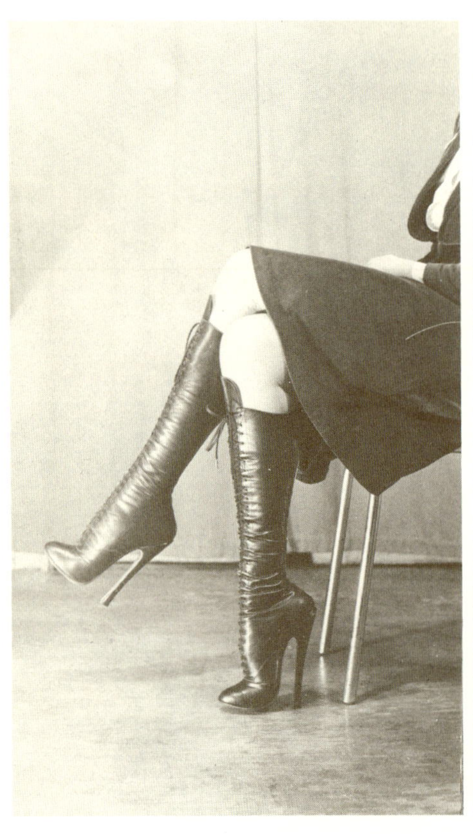
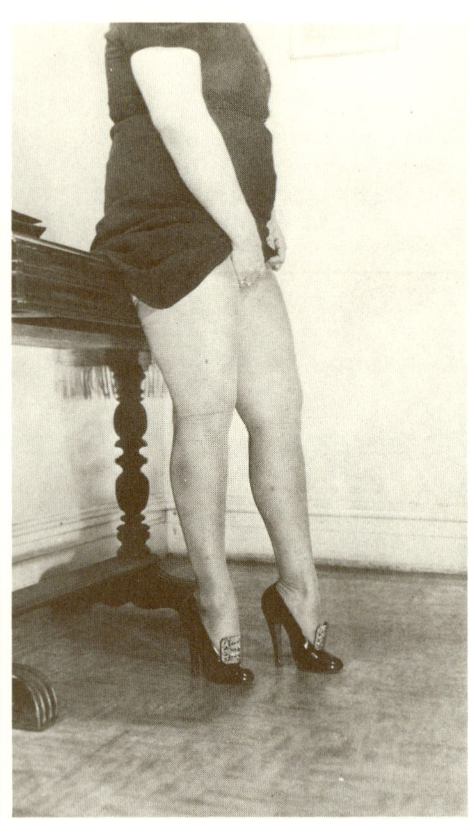

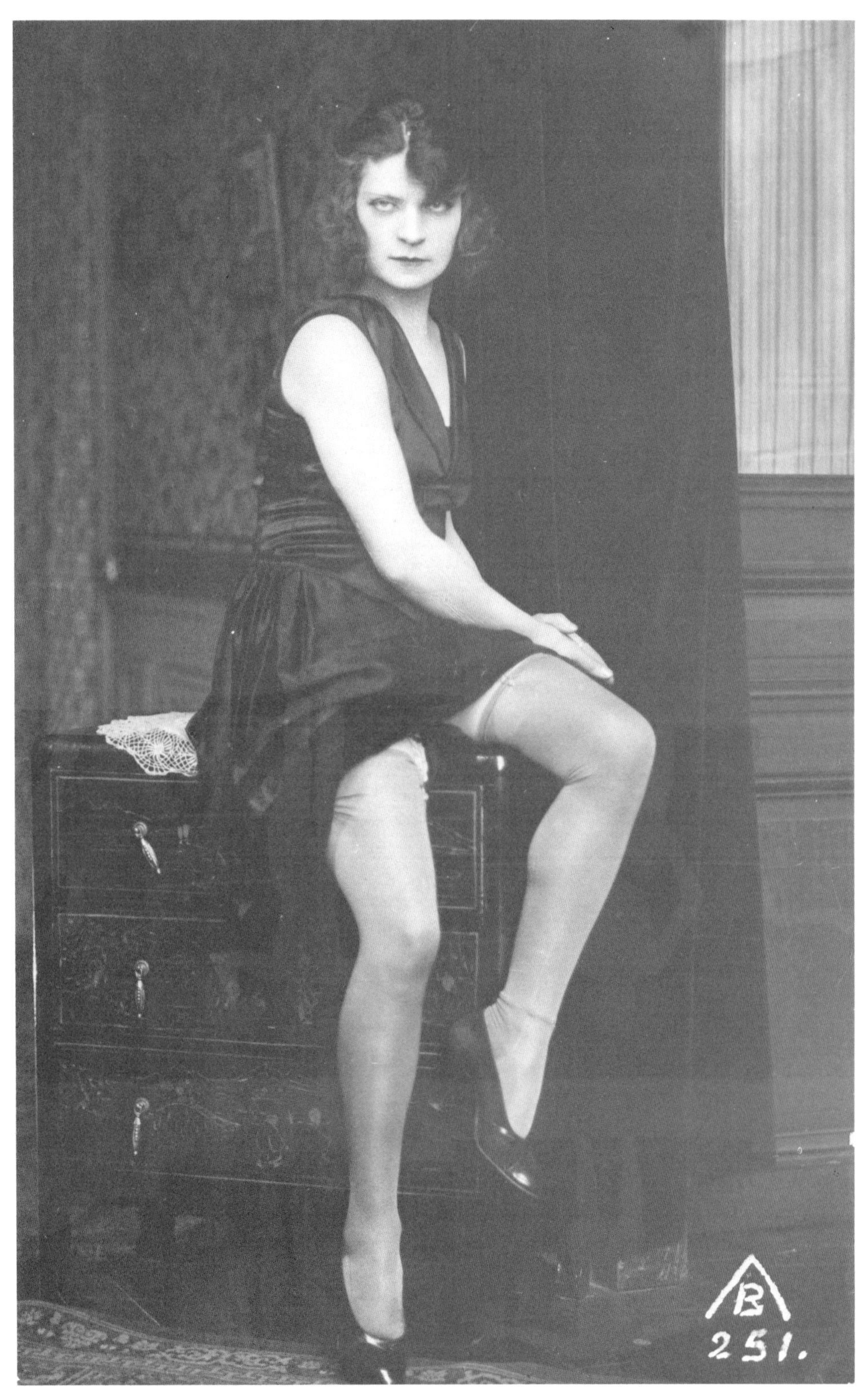
B
251.

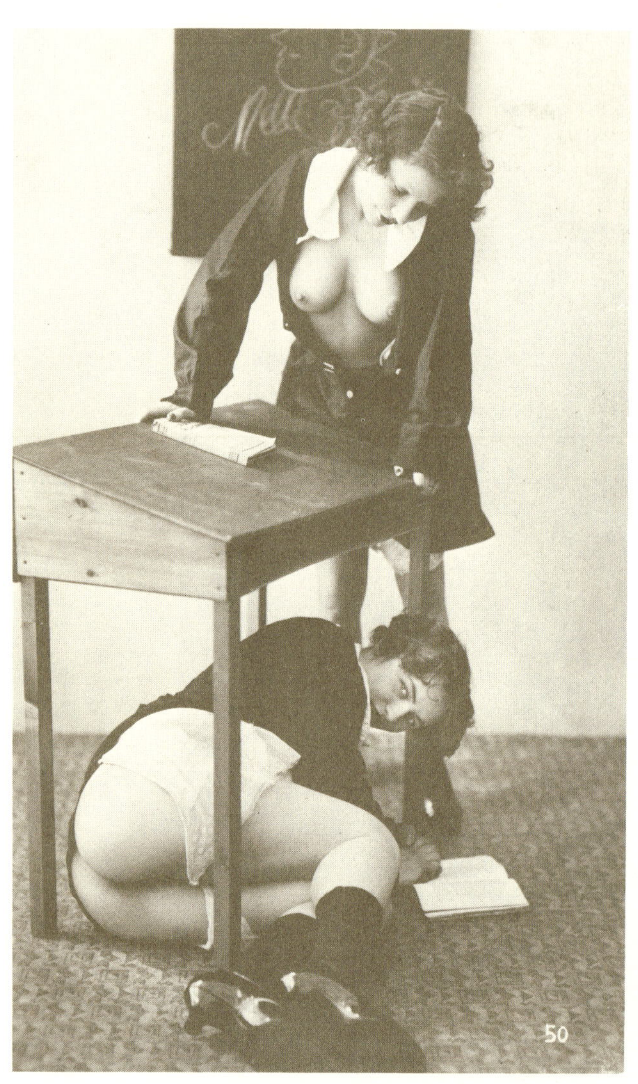
50

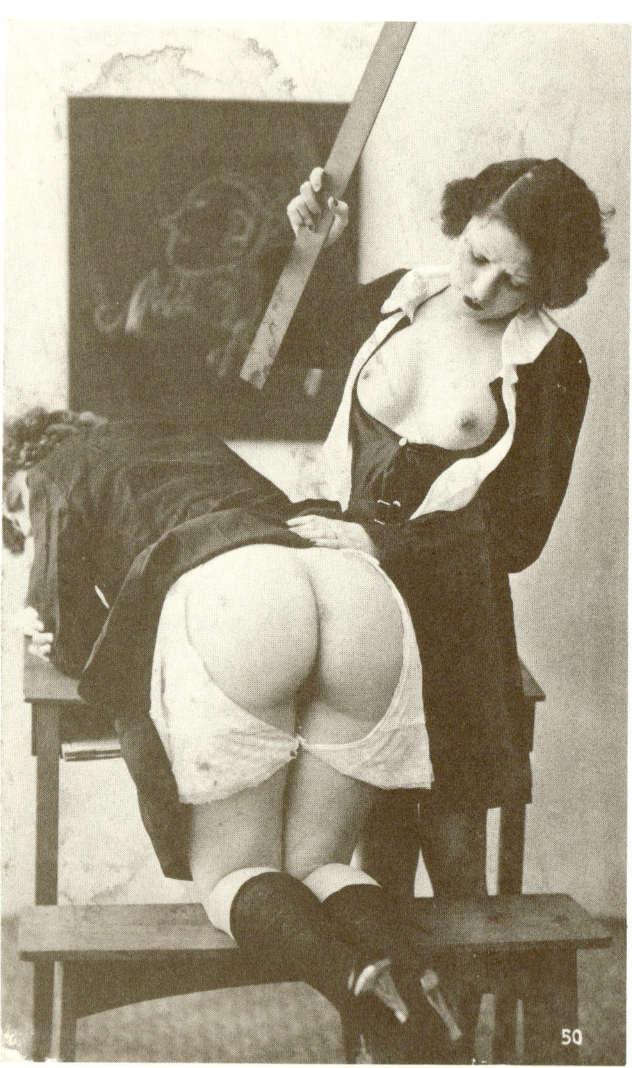
50

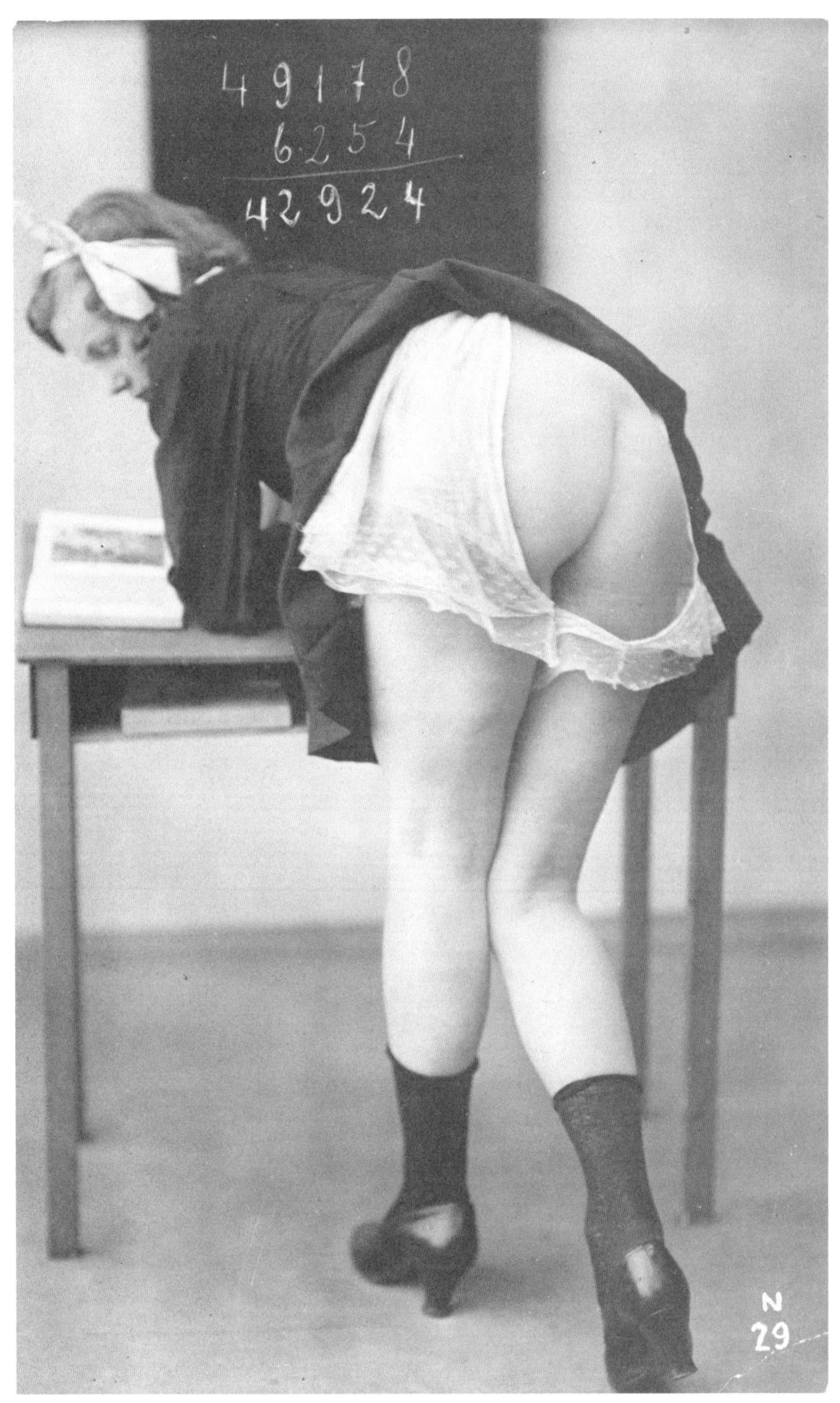
4 9 1 7 8
6 2 5 4
4 2 9 2 4
N
29

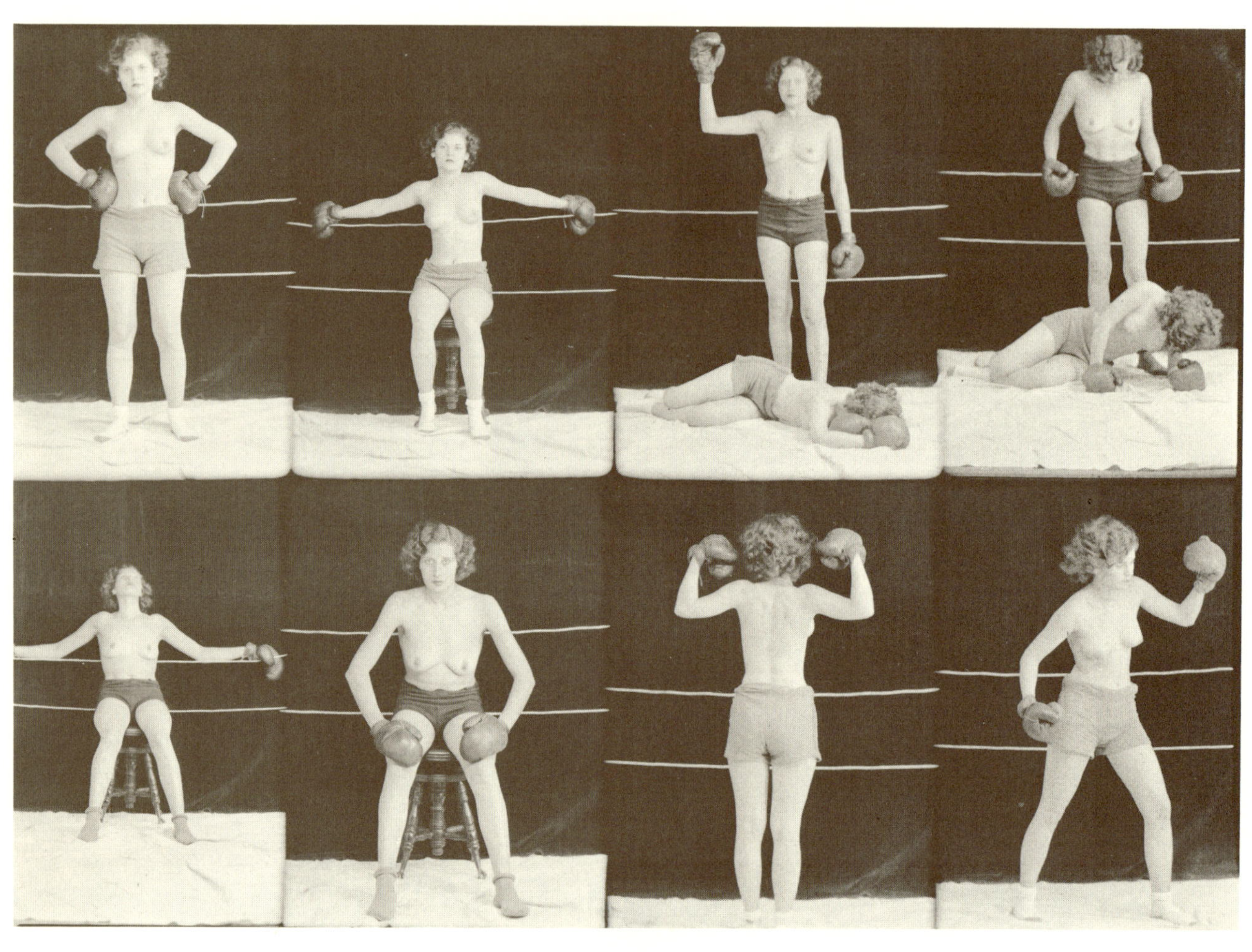

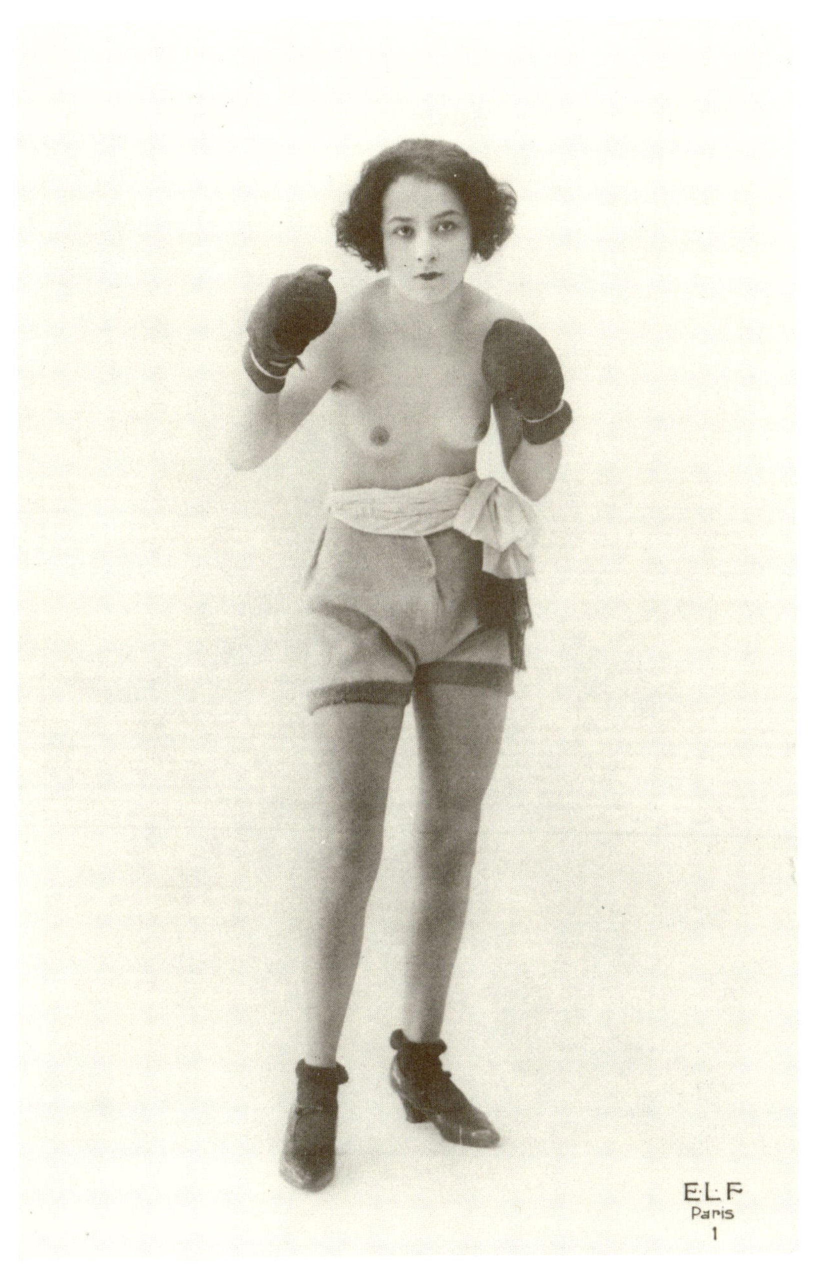
E·L·F
Paris
1

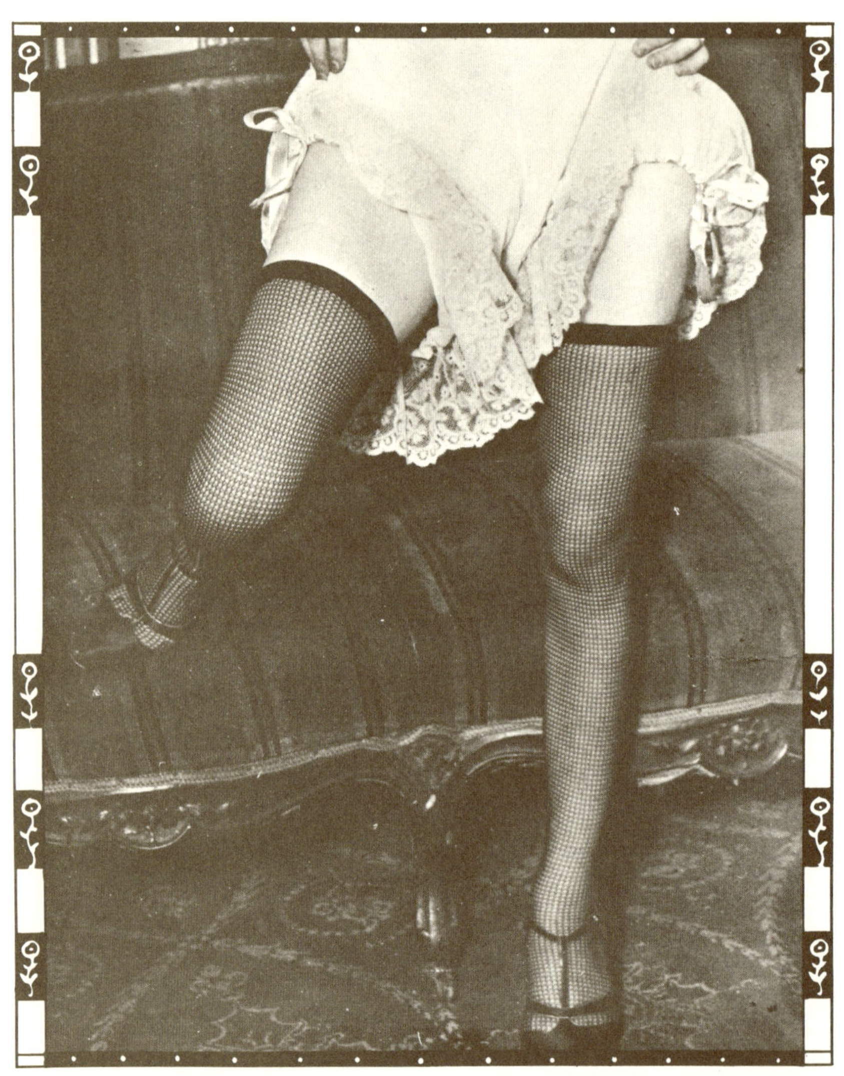

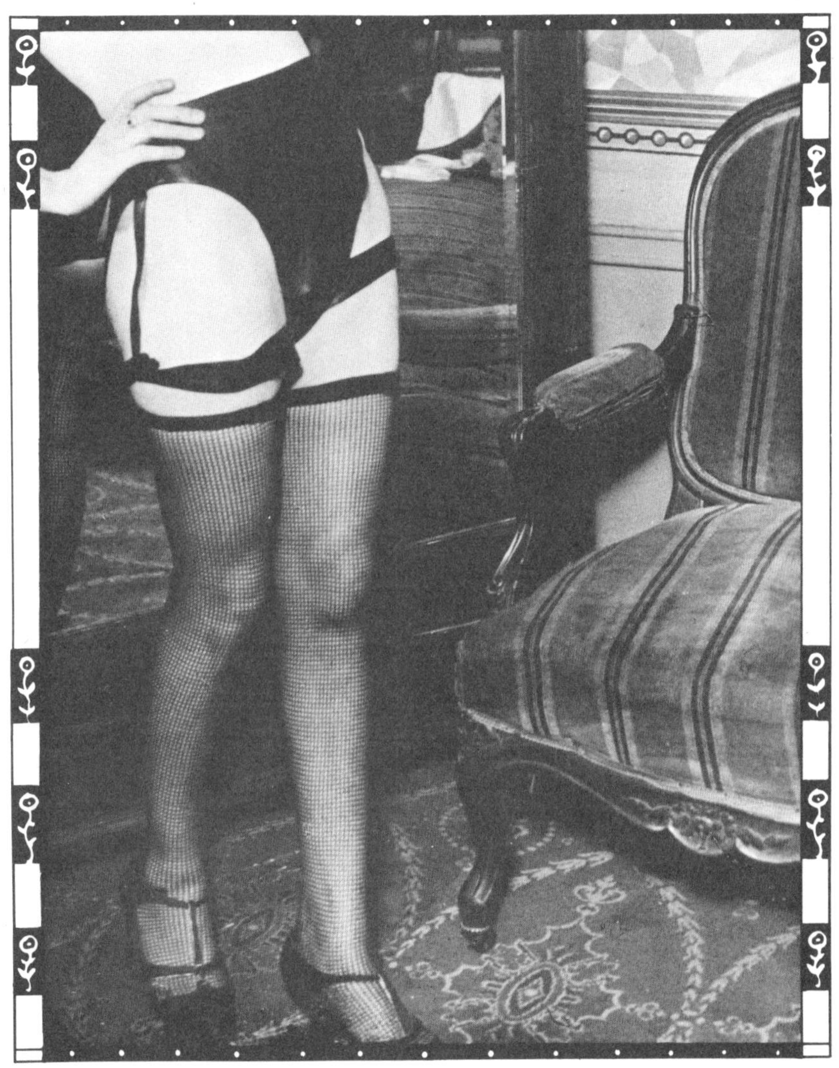

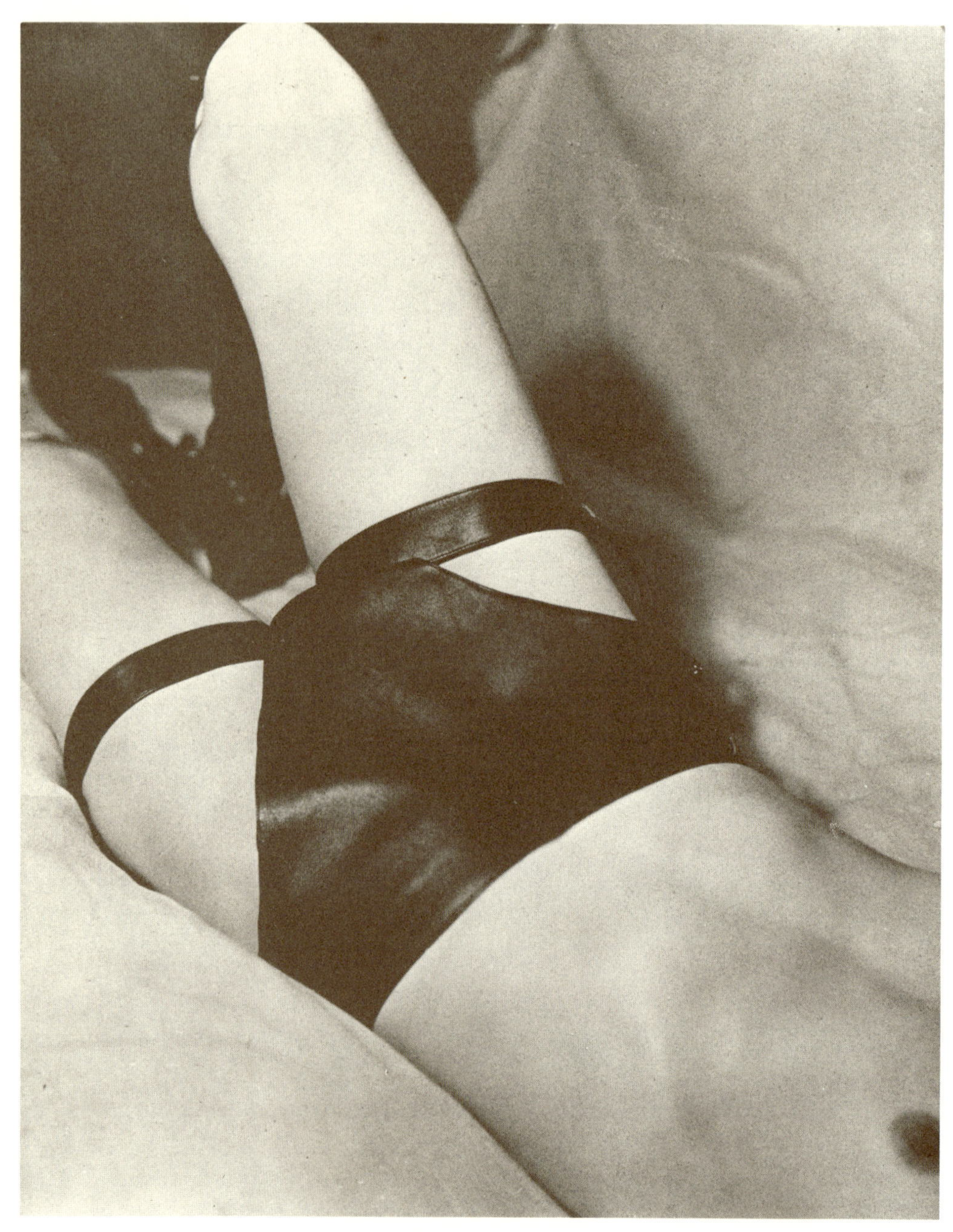

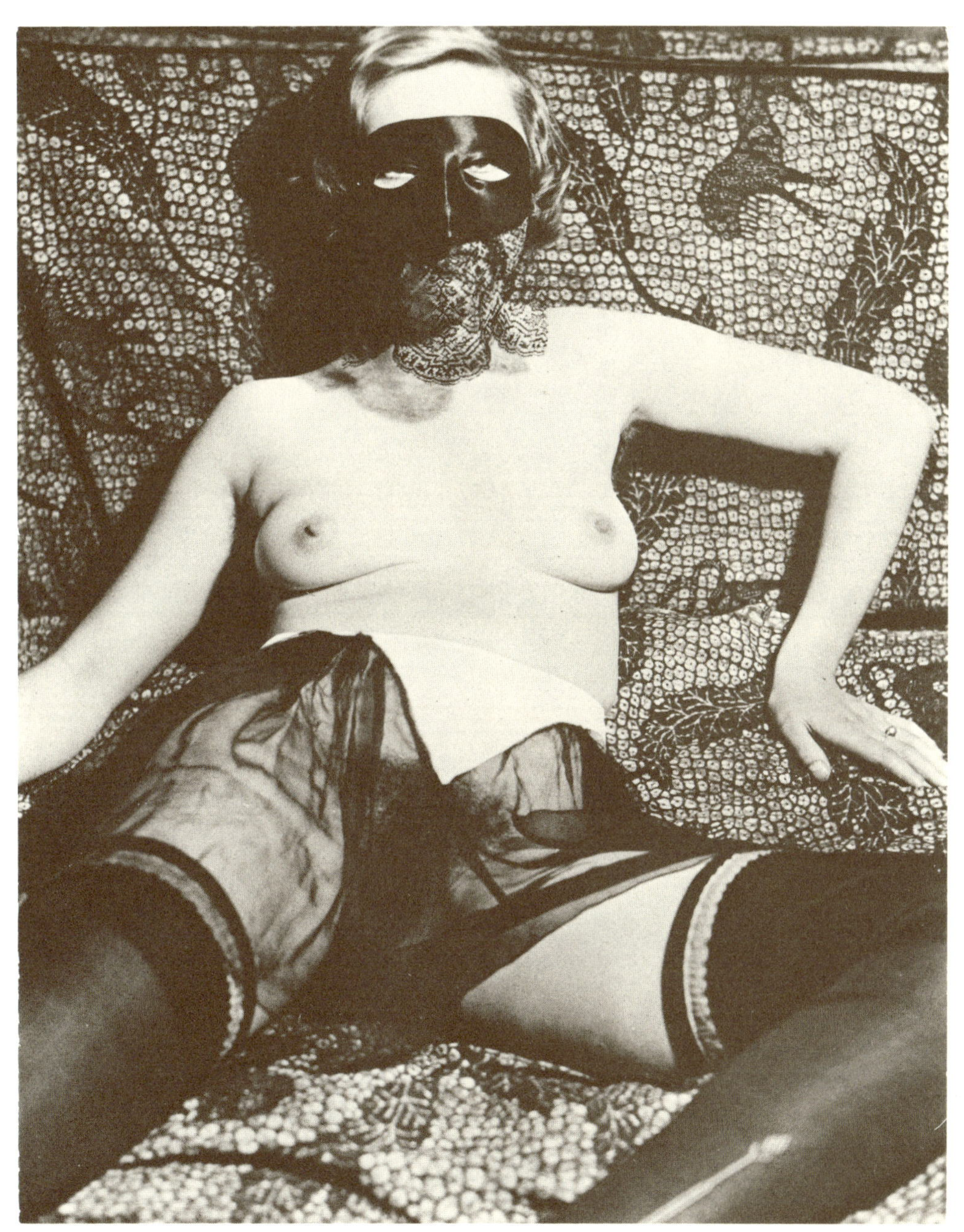

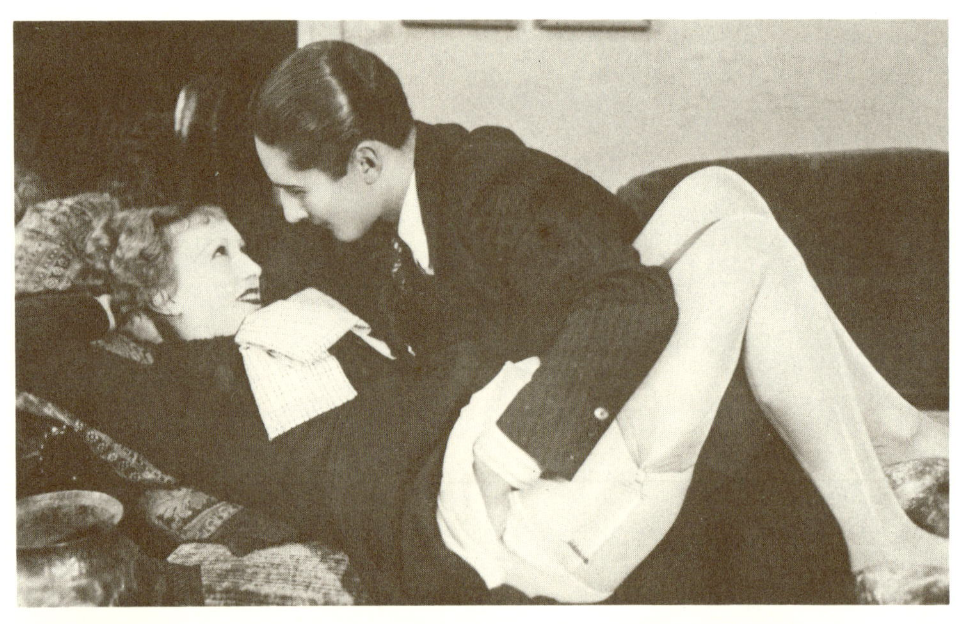

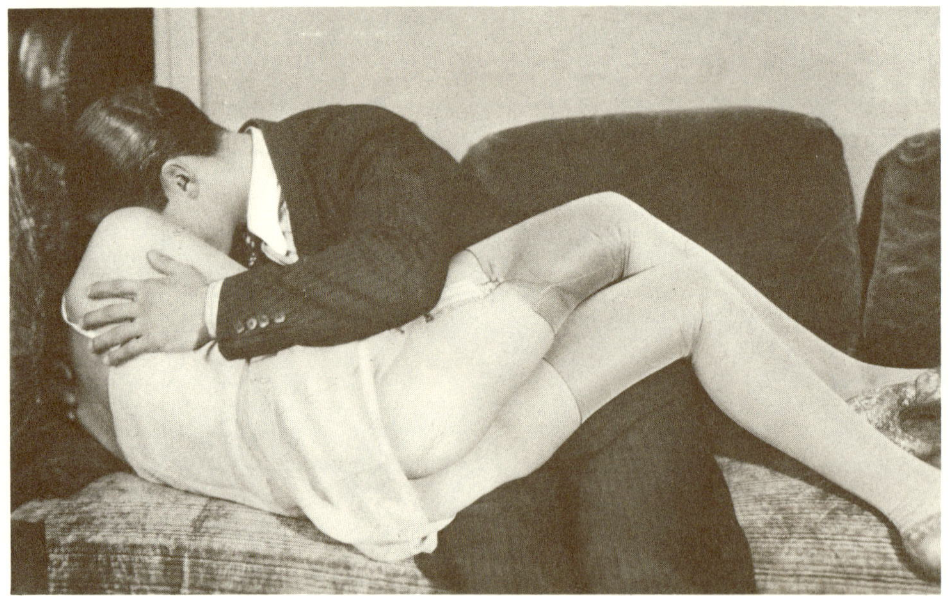

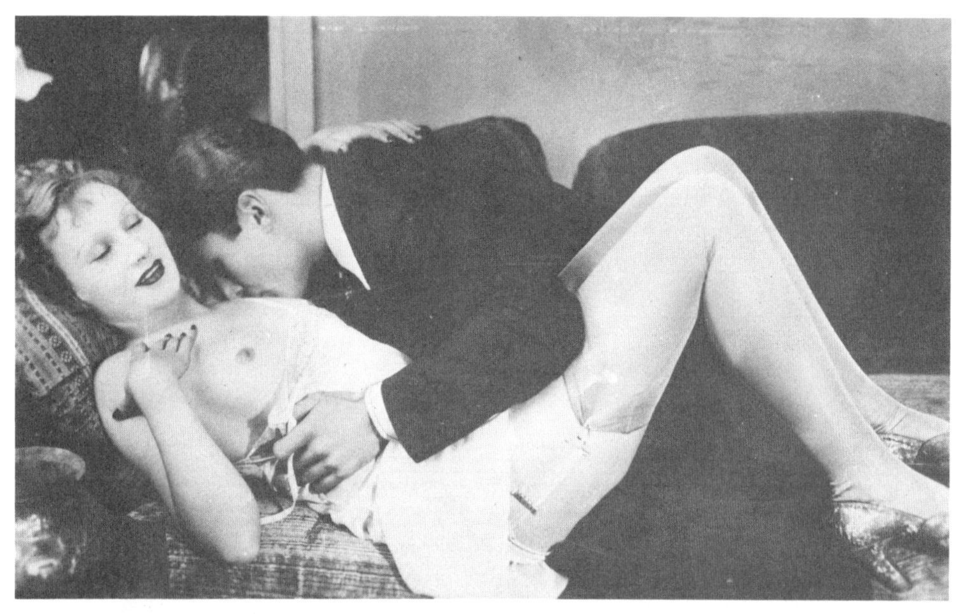

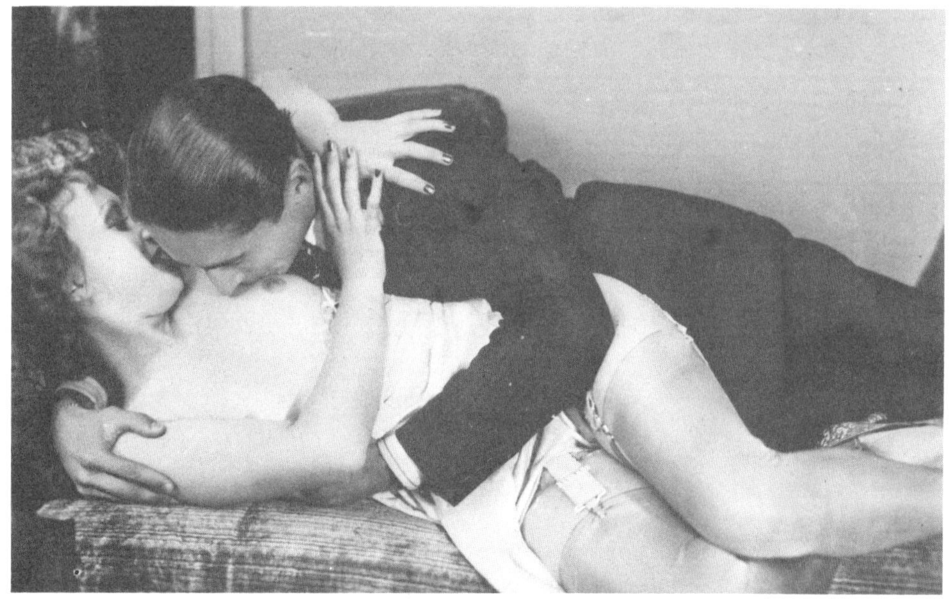

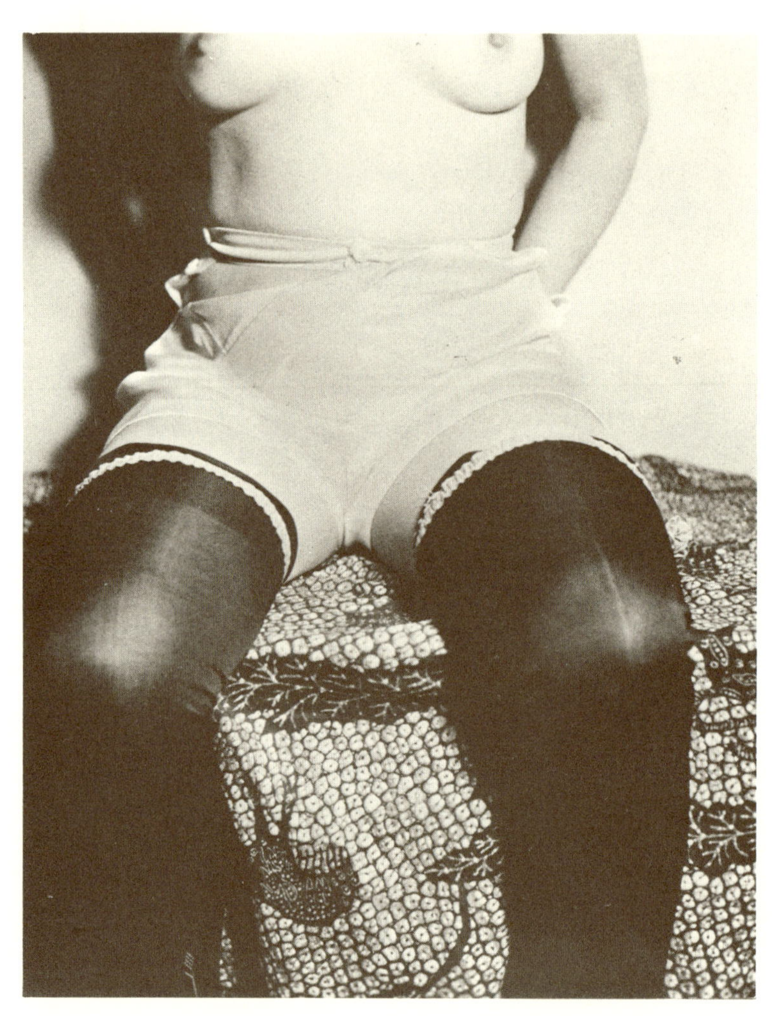

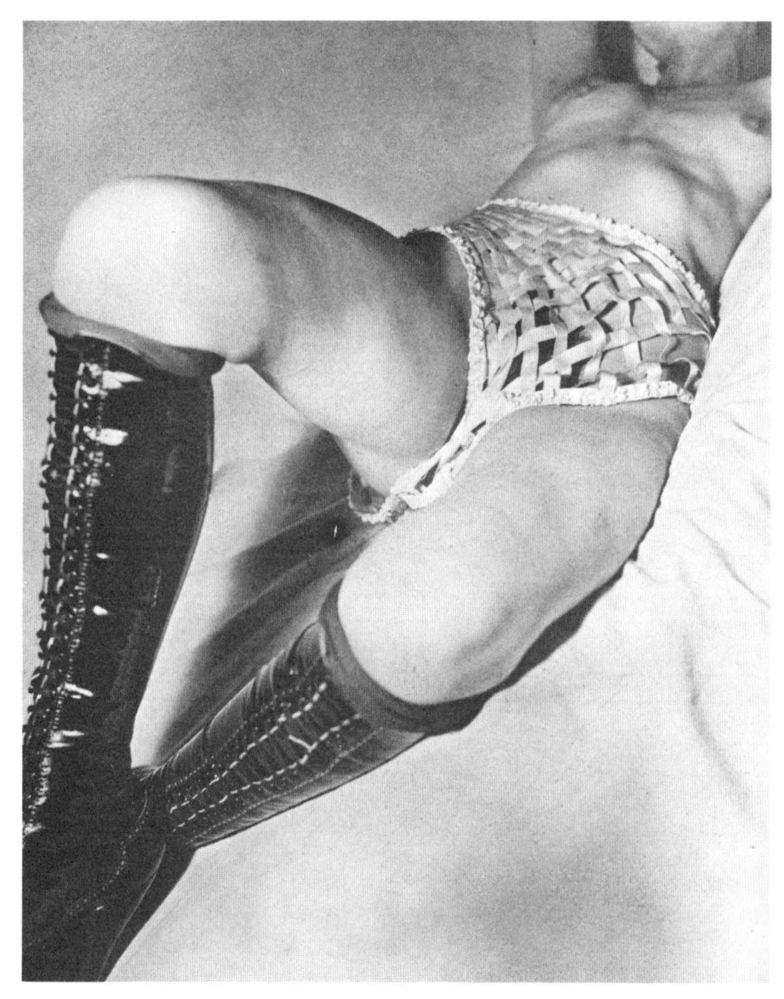

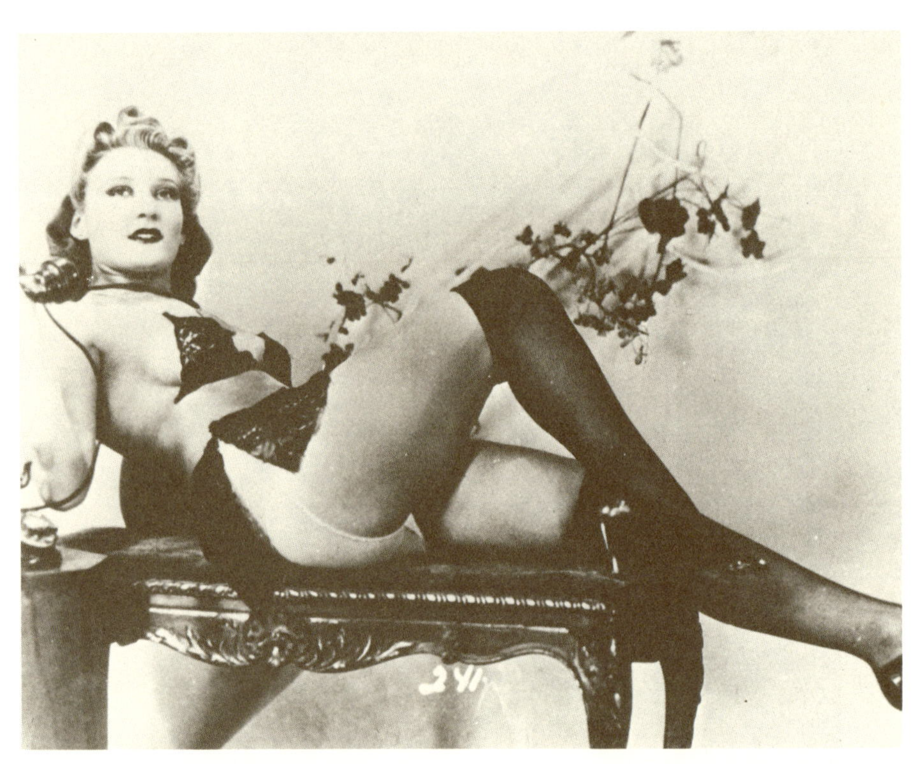
241

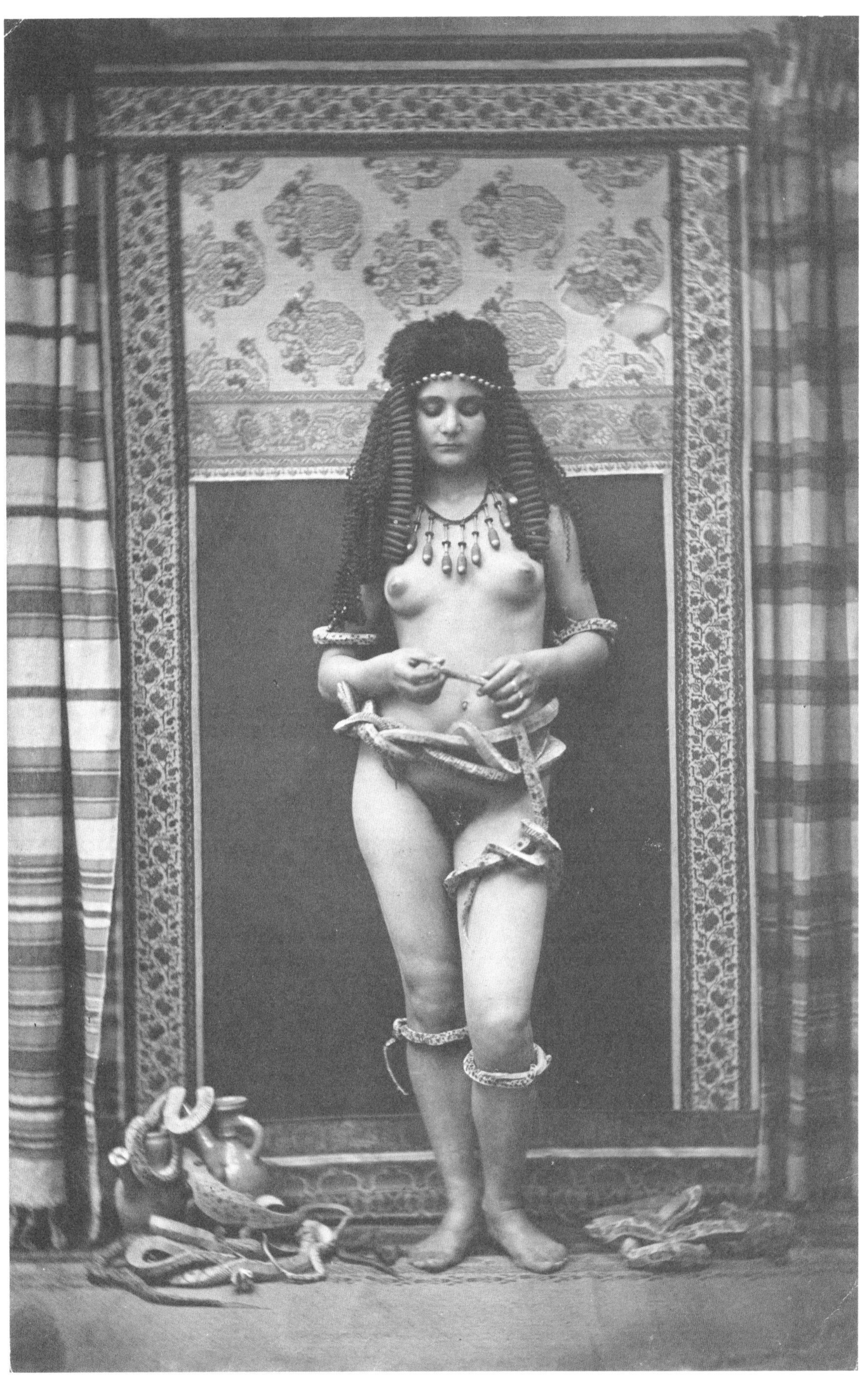

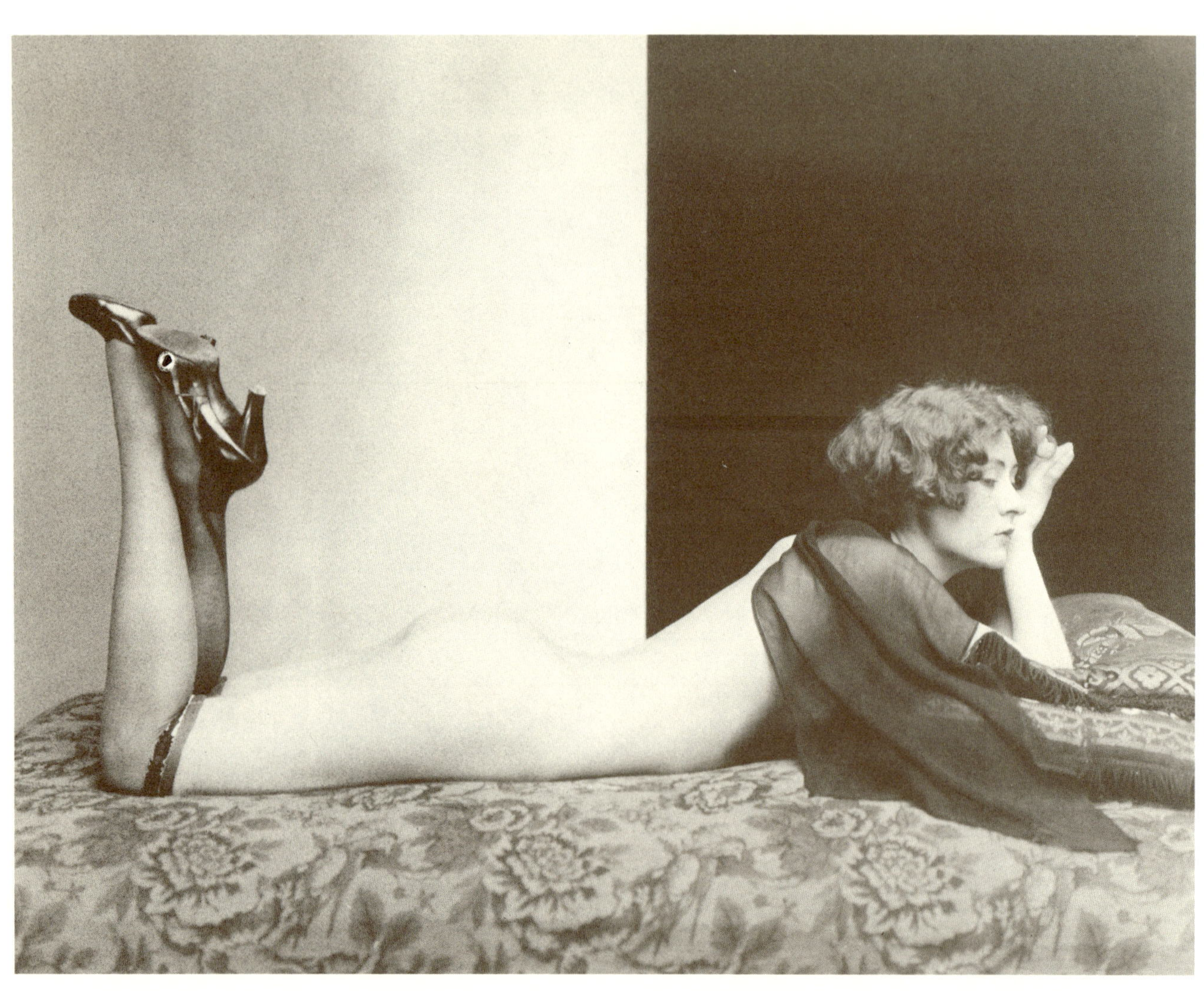

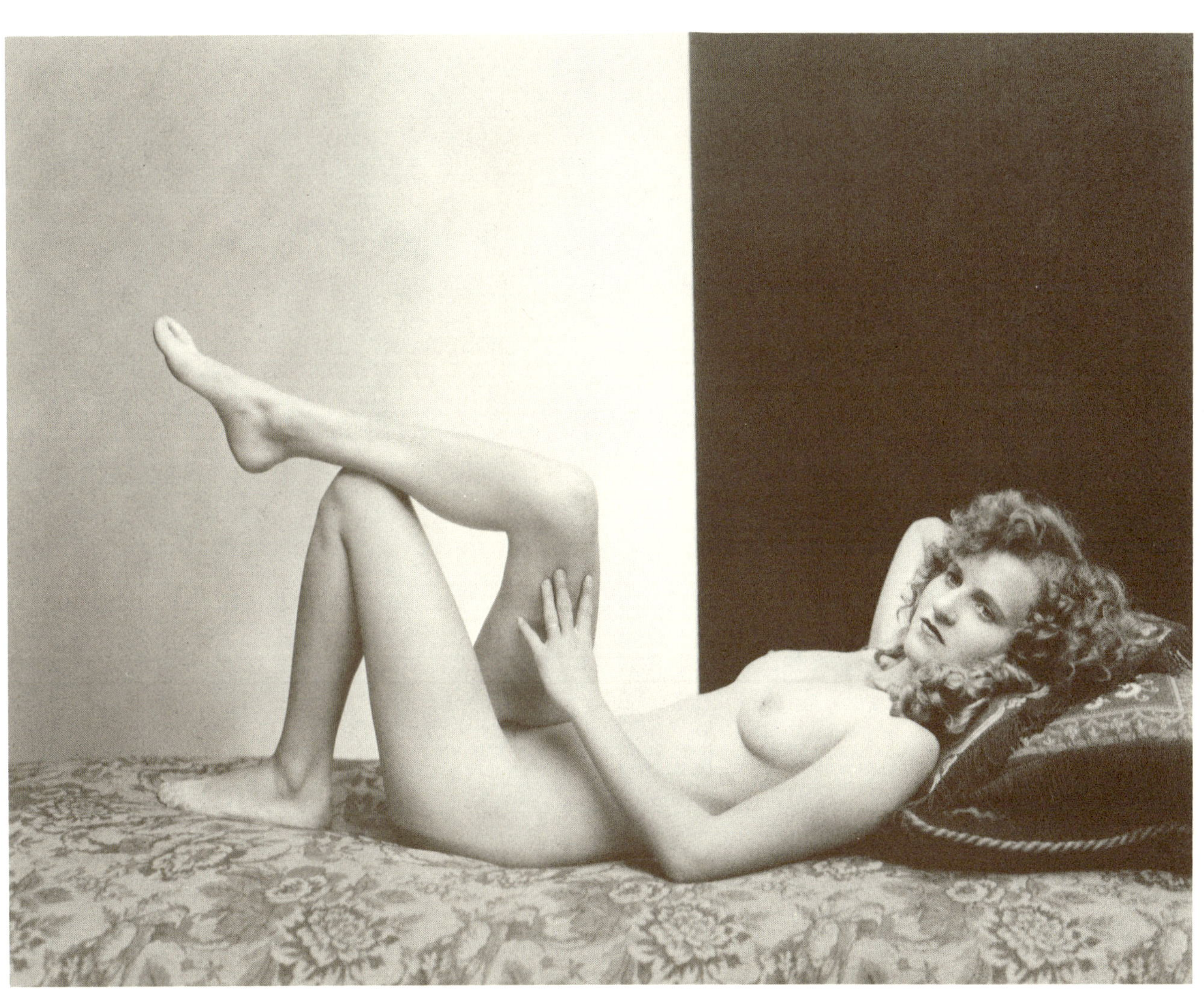

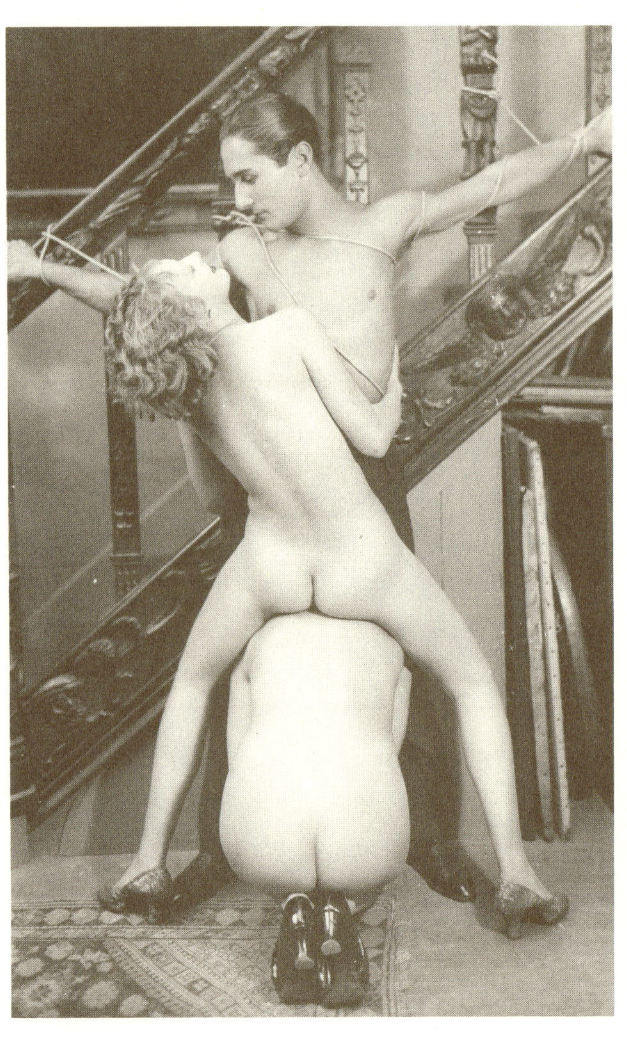

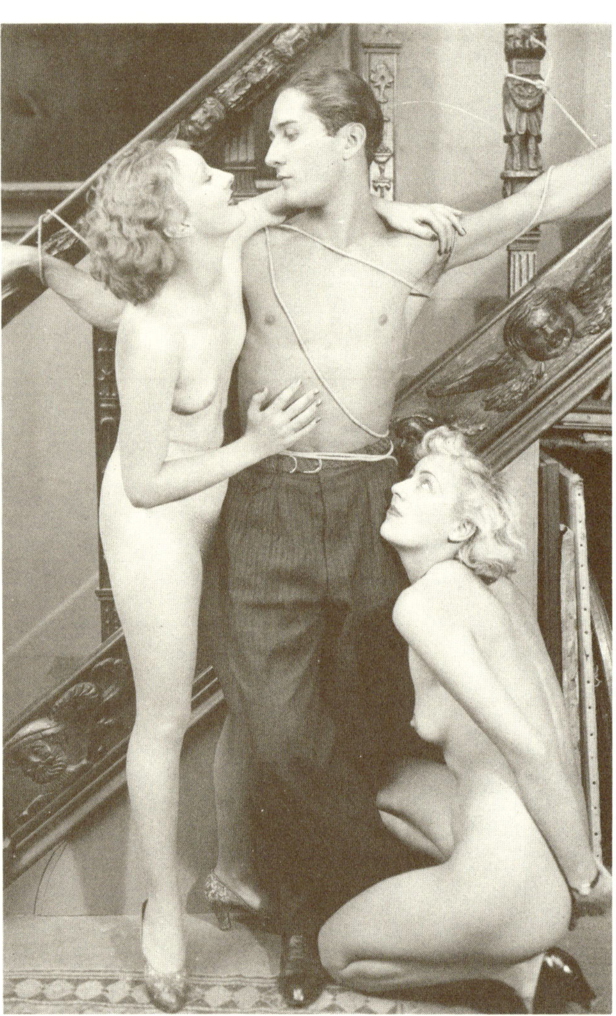

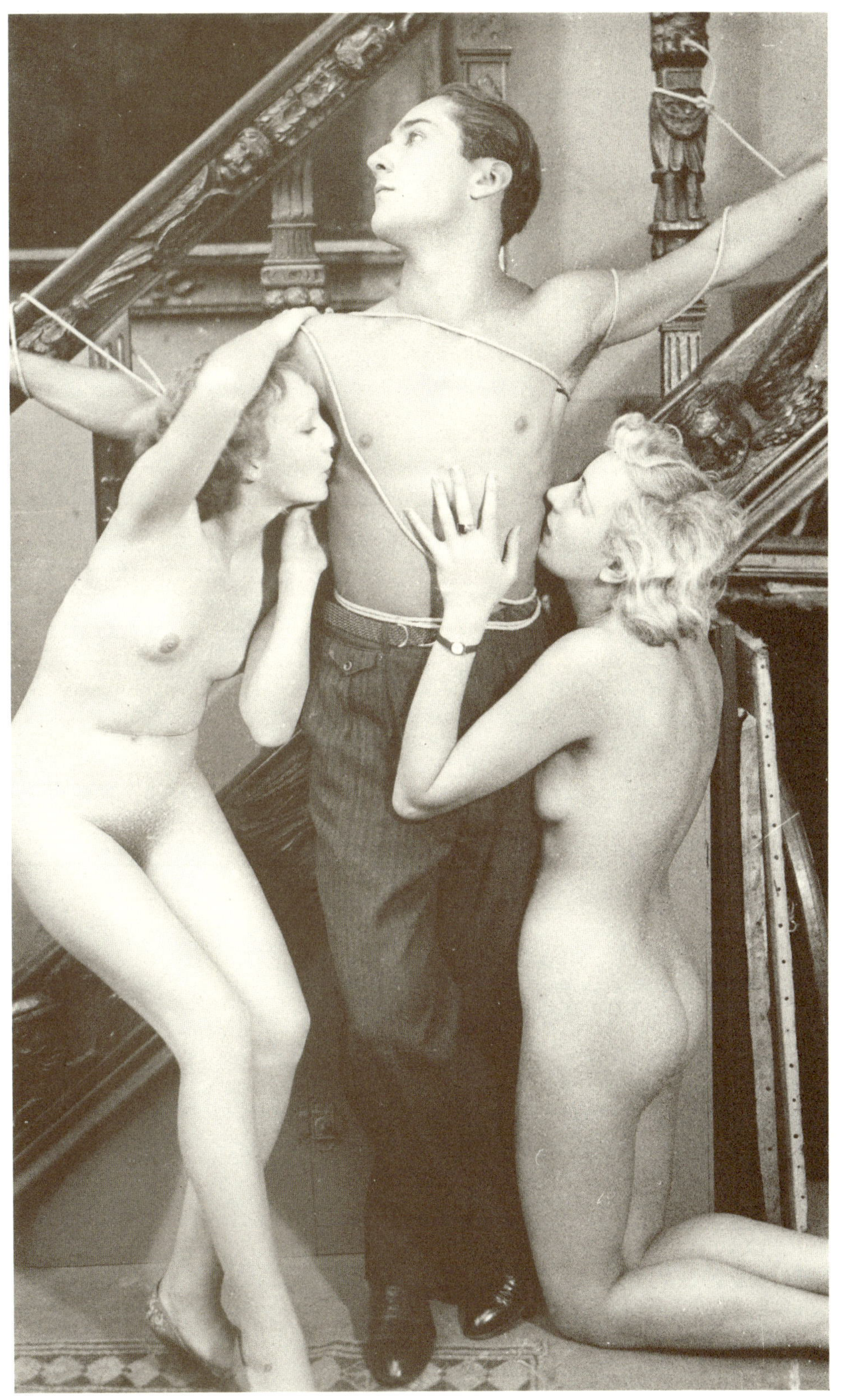

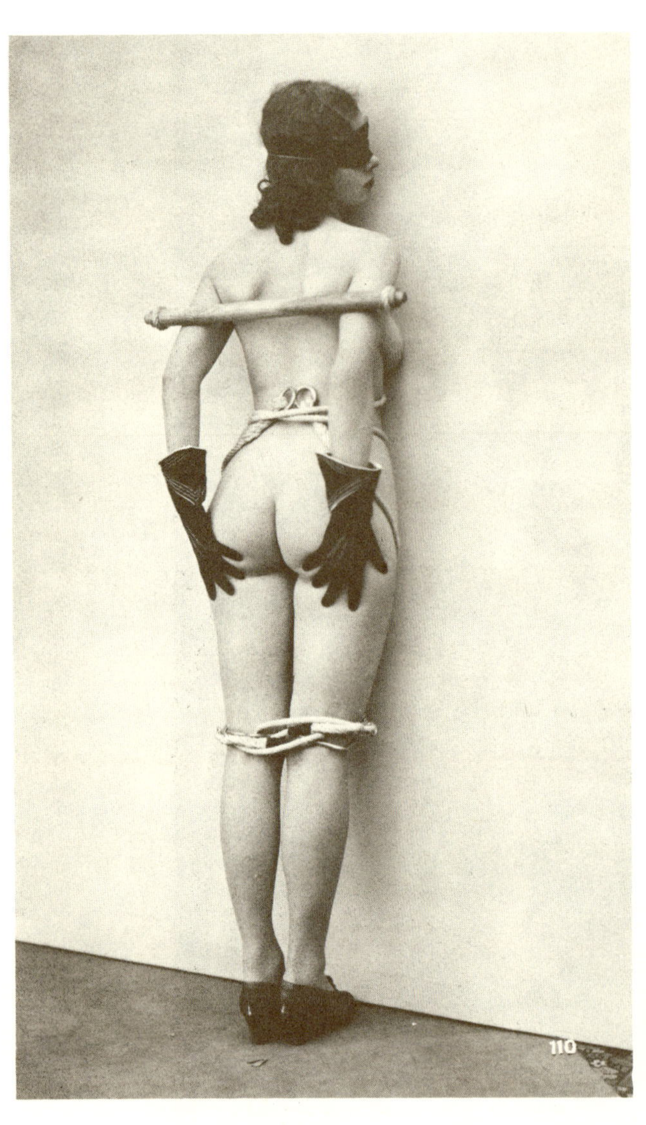
110

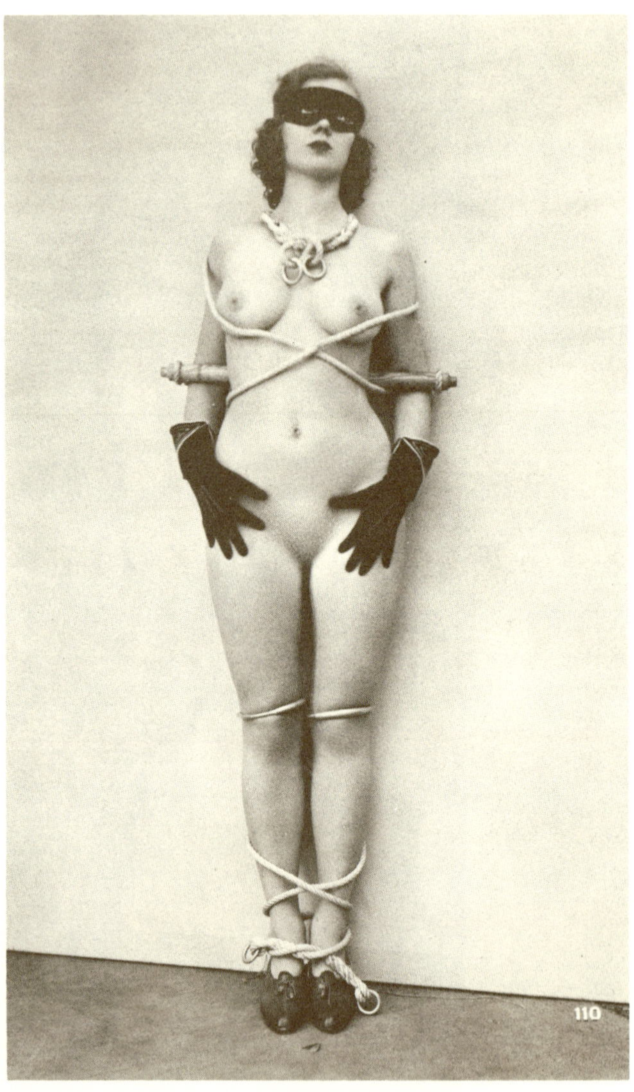
110

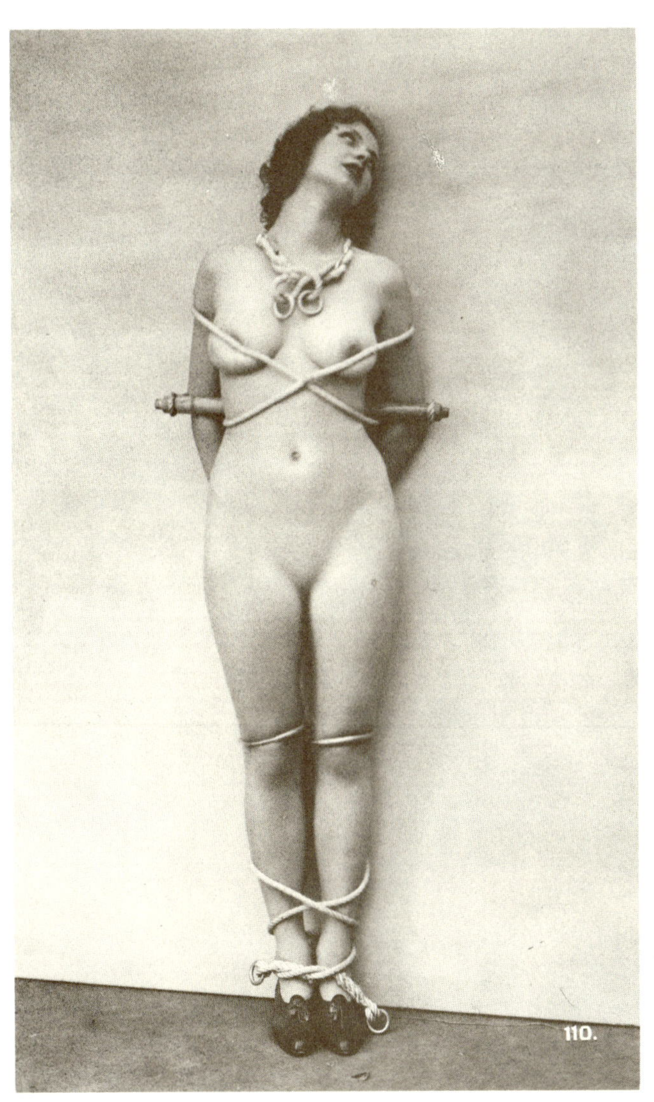
110.

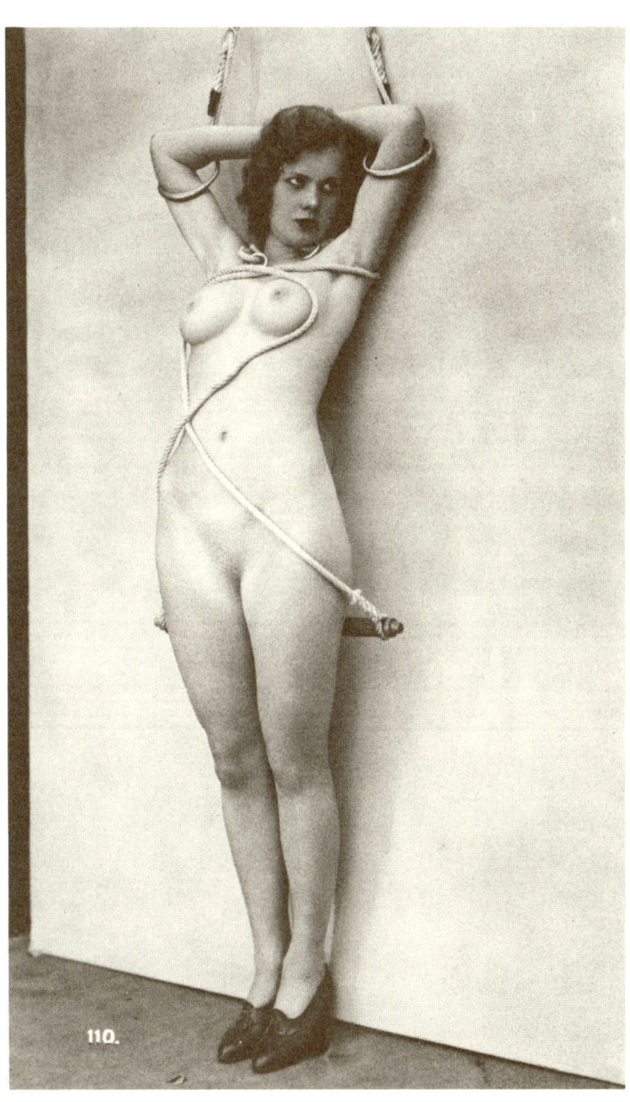
110.

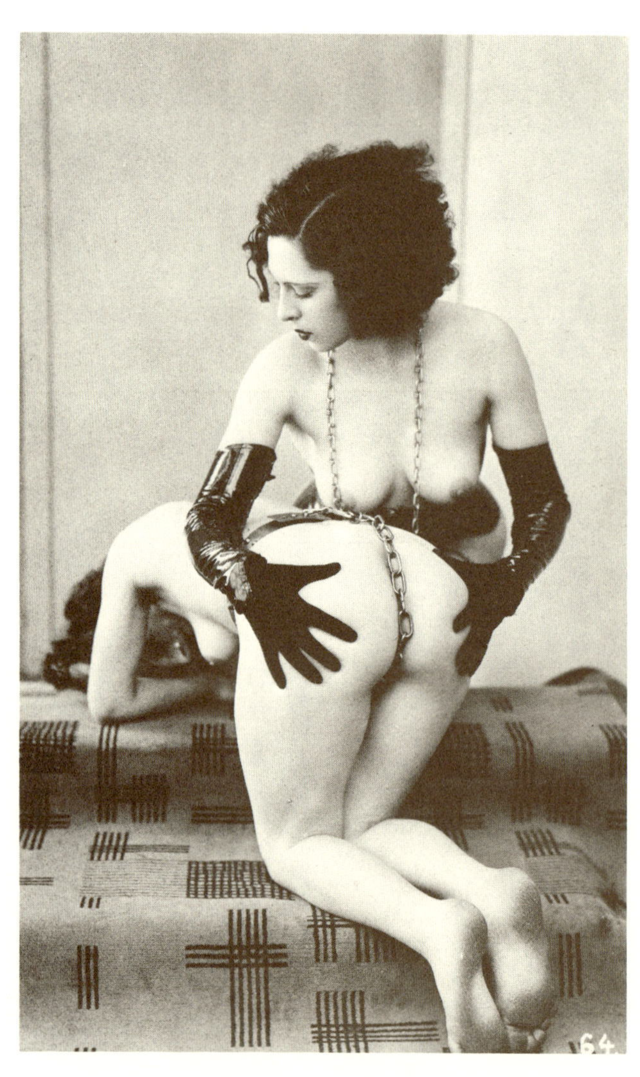
64

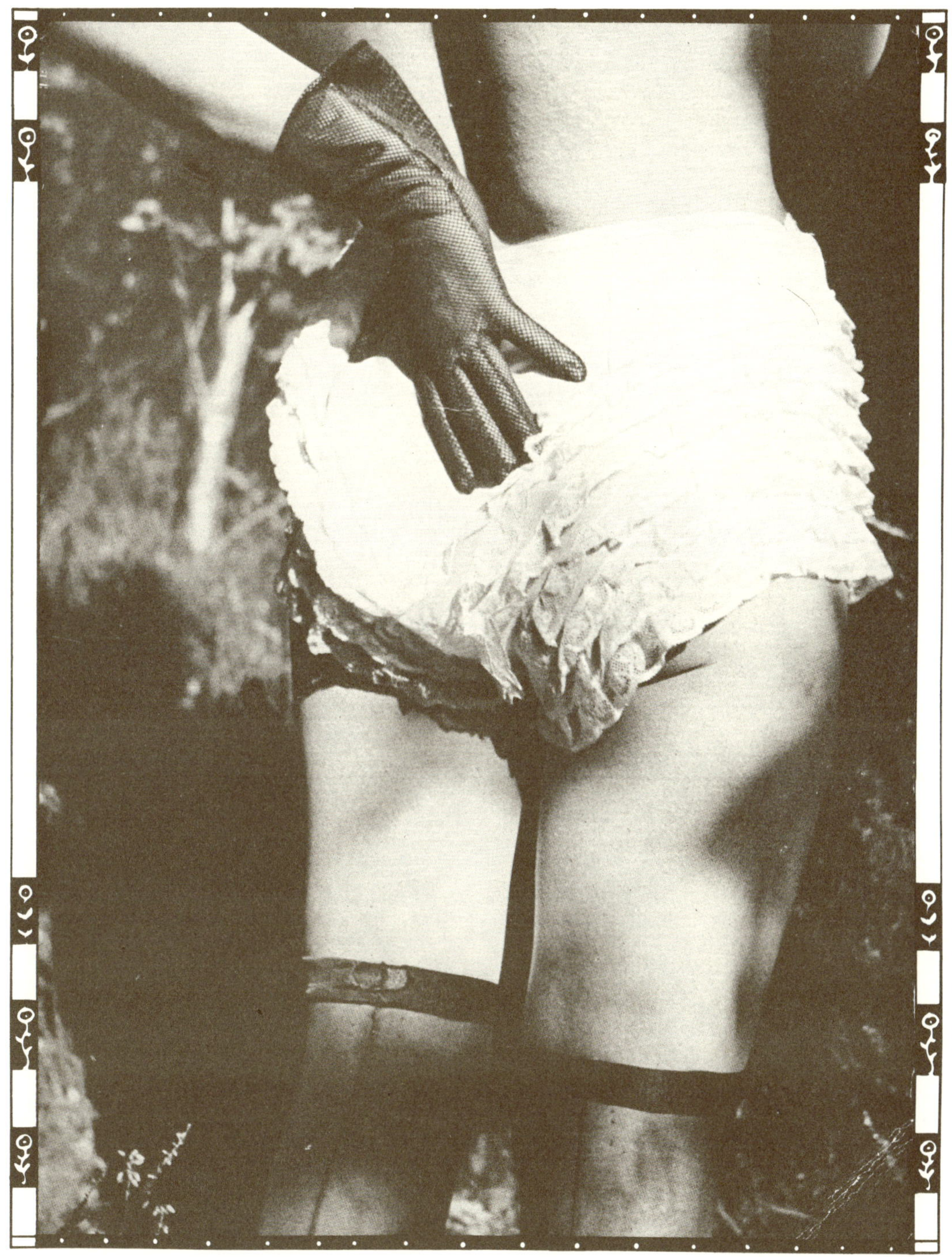

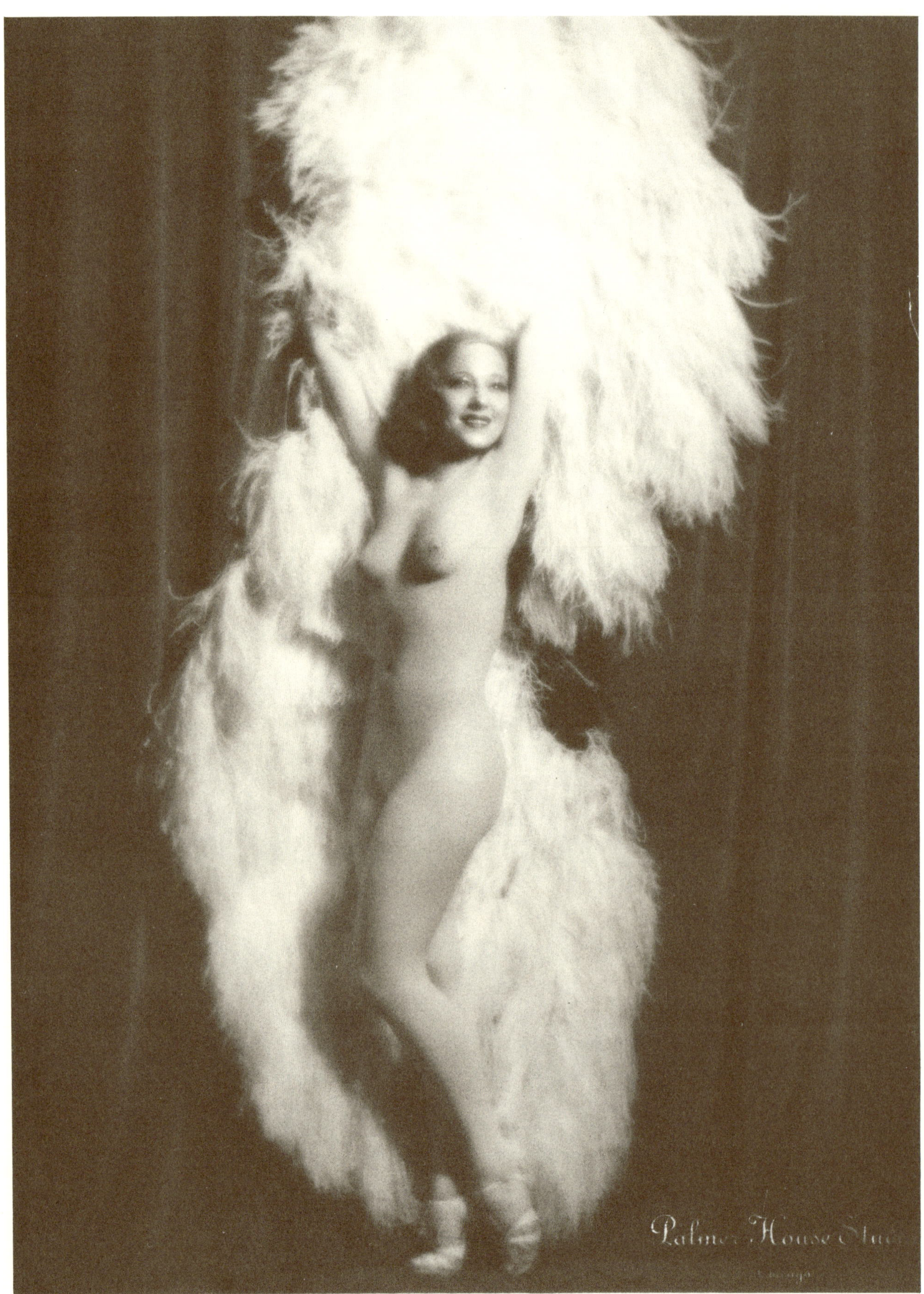
Palmer House

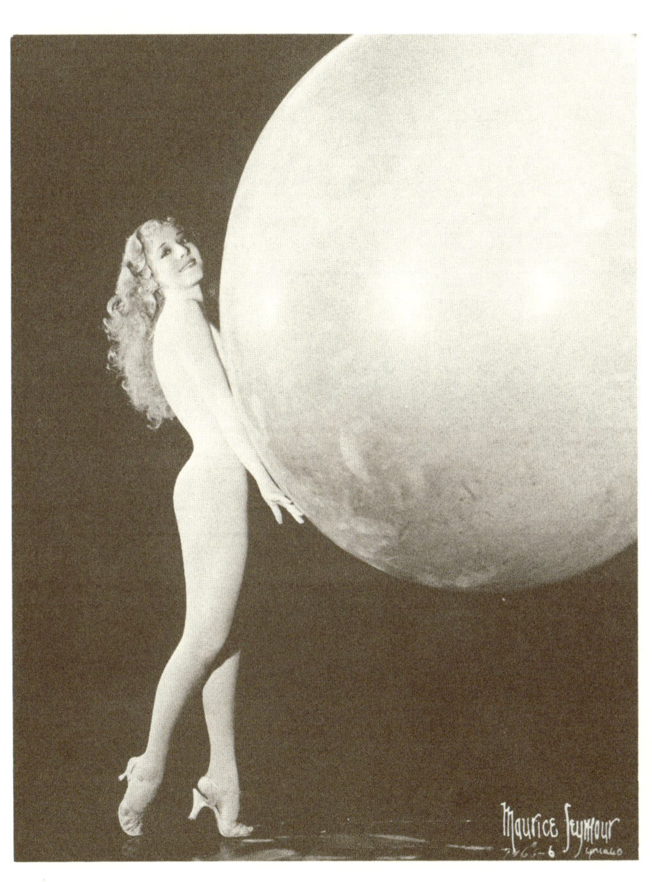
Maurice Seymour

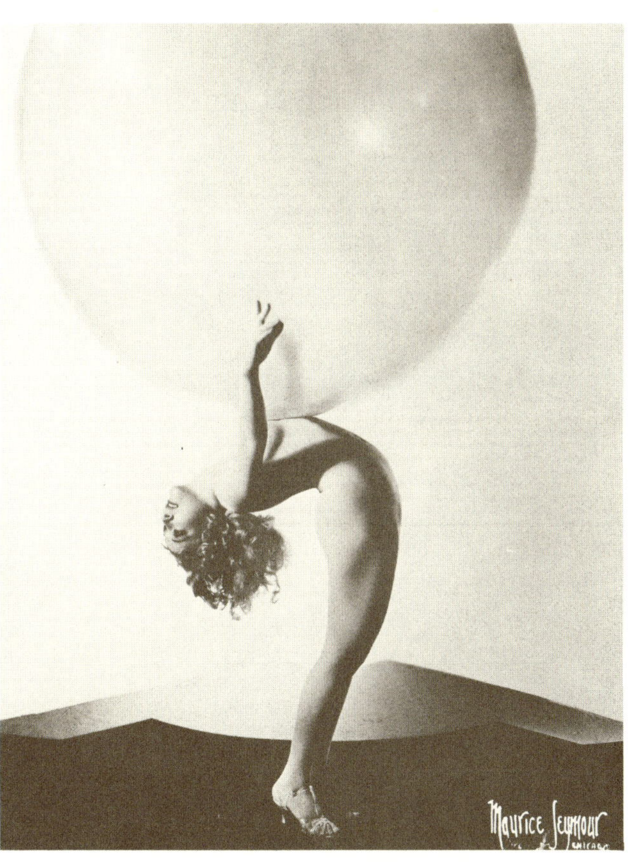
Maurice Seymour

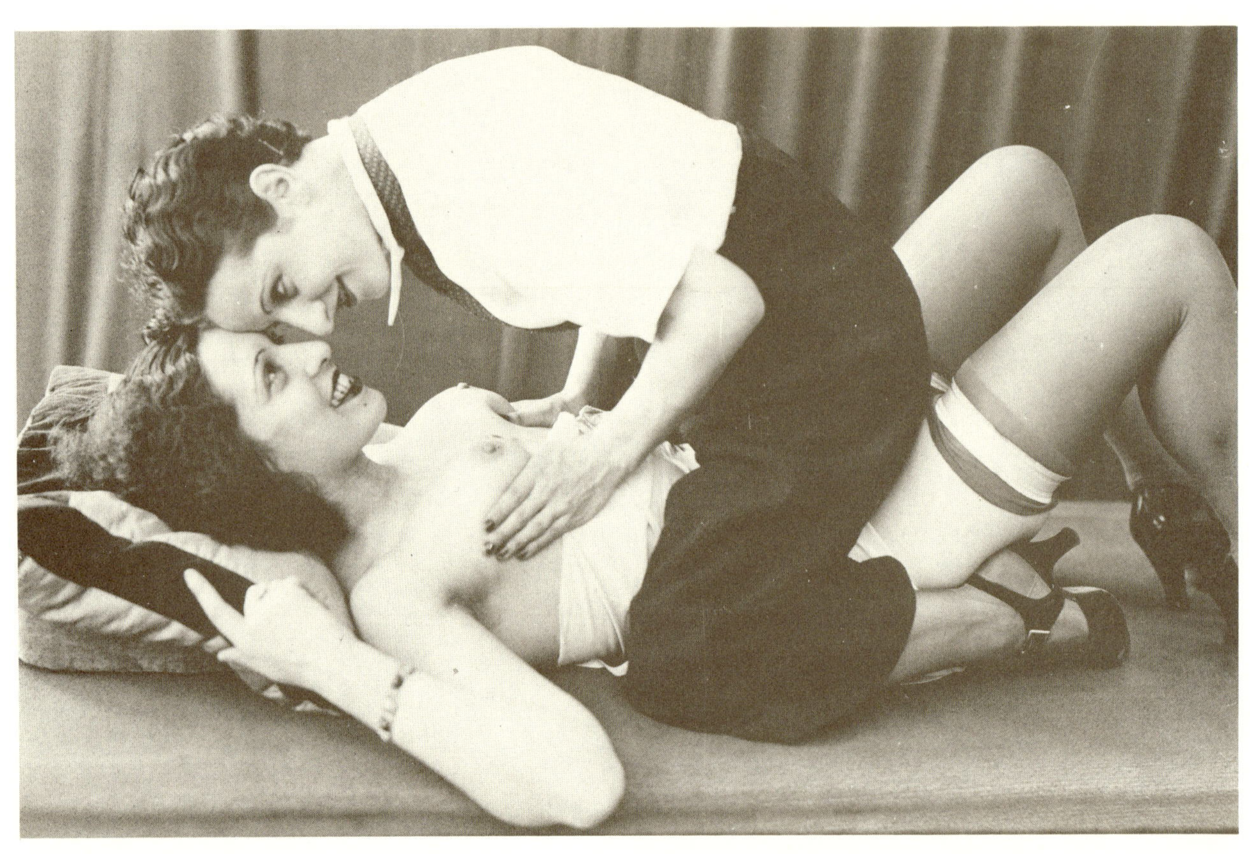

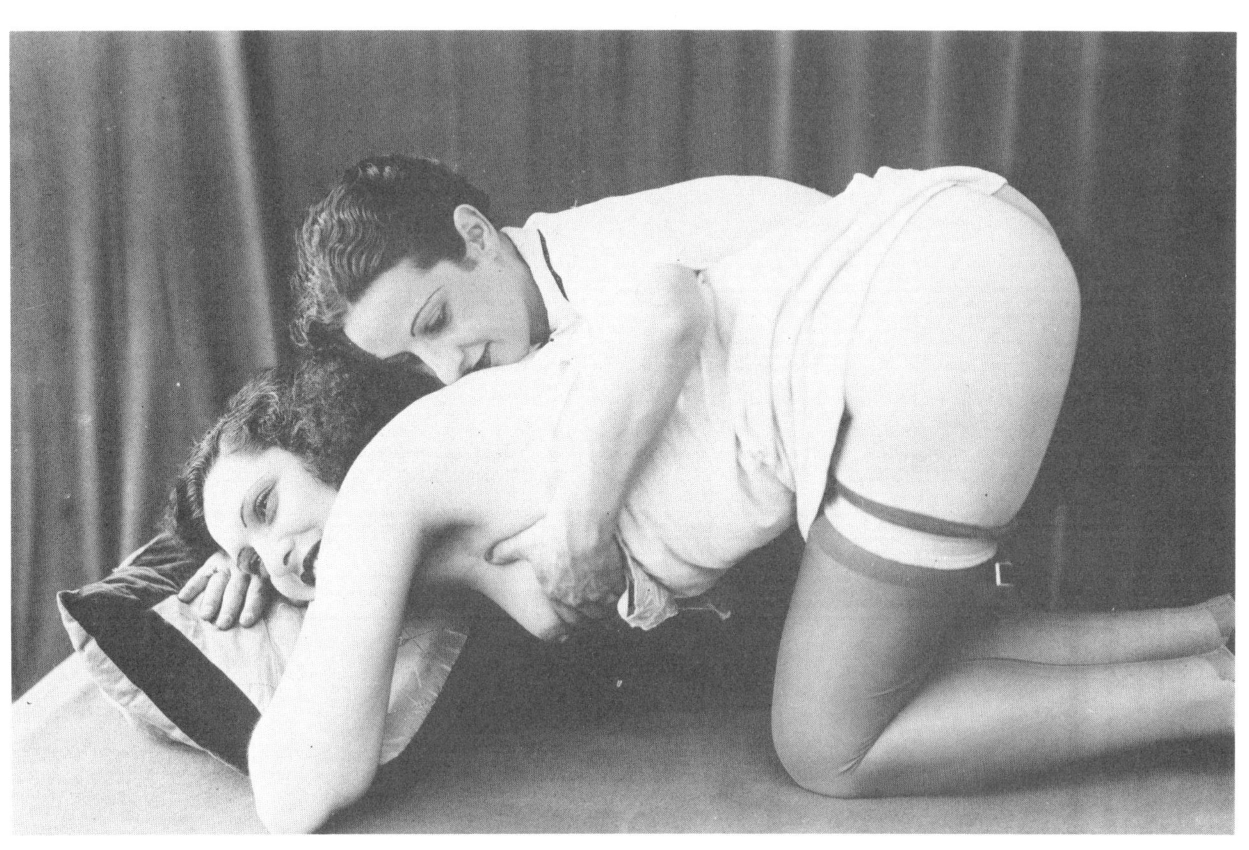

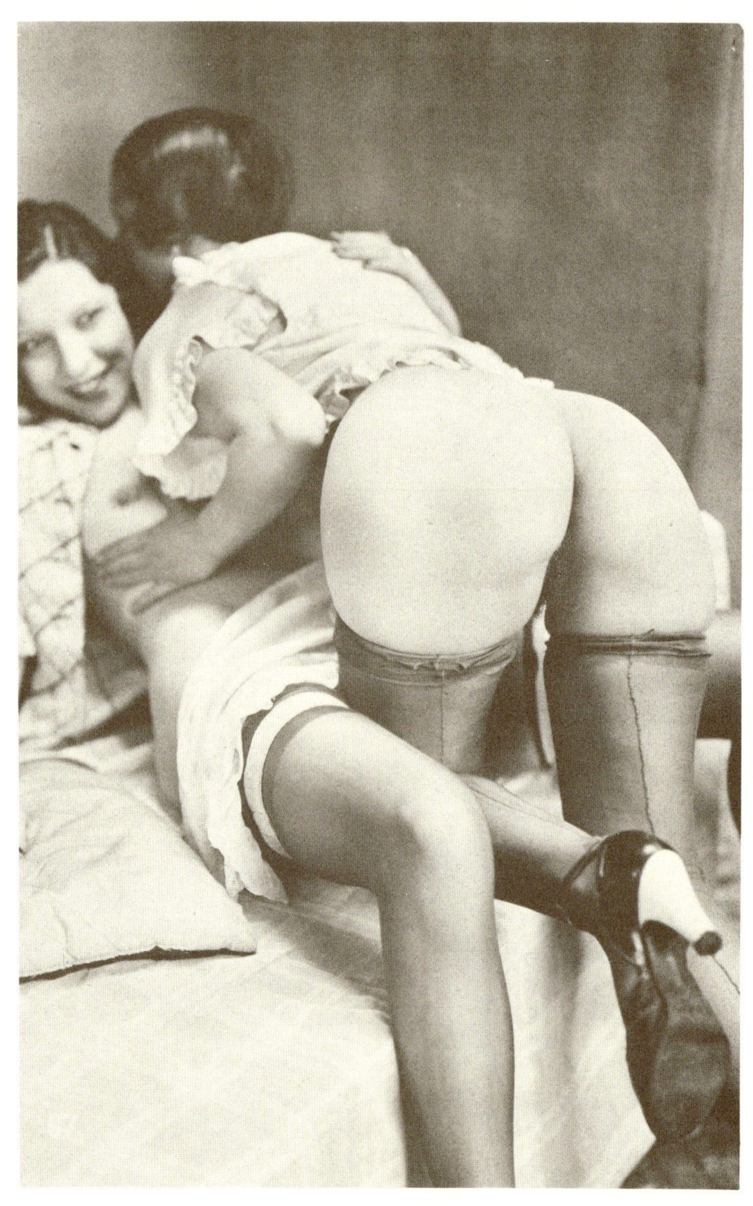

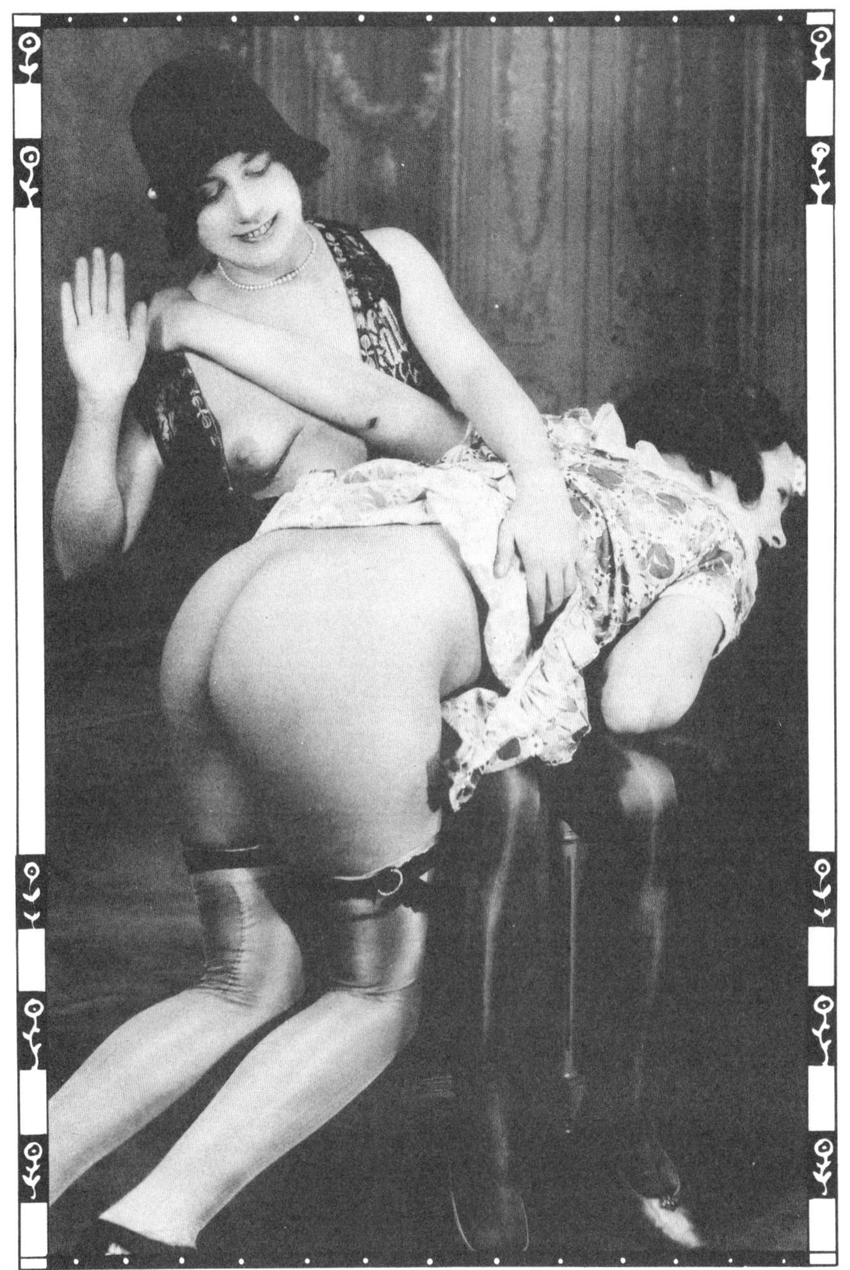

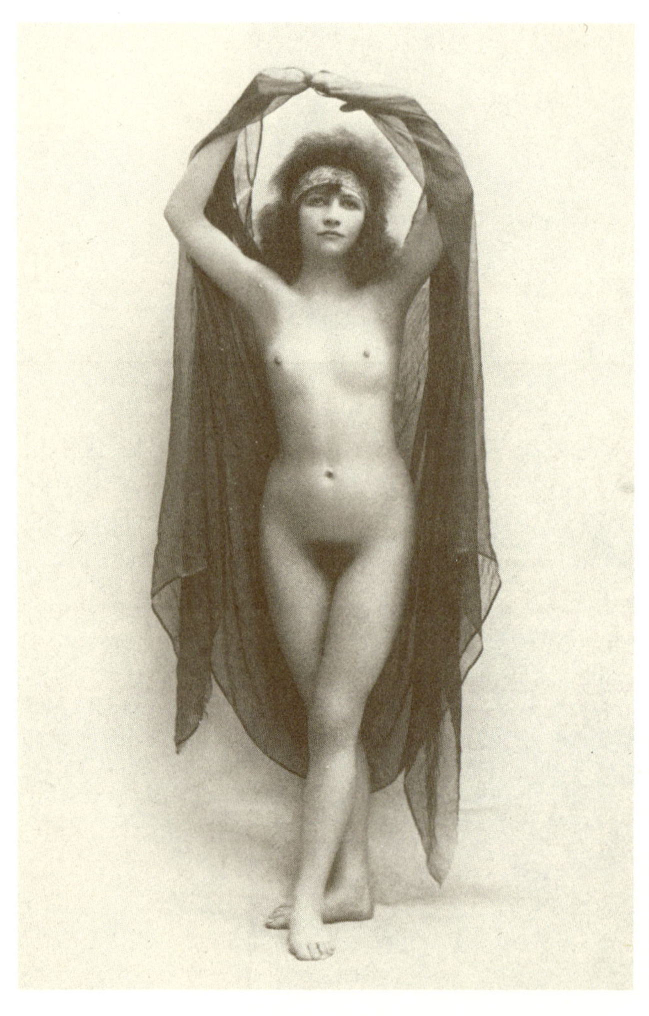

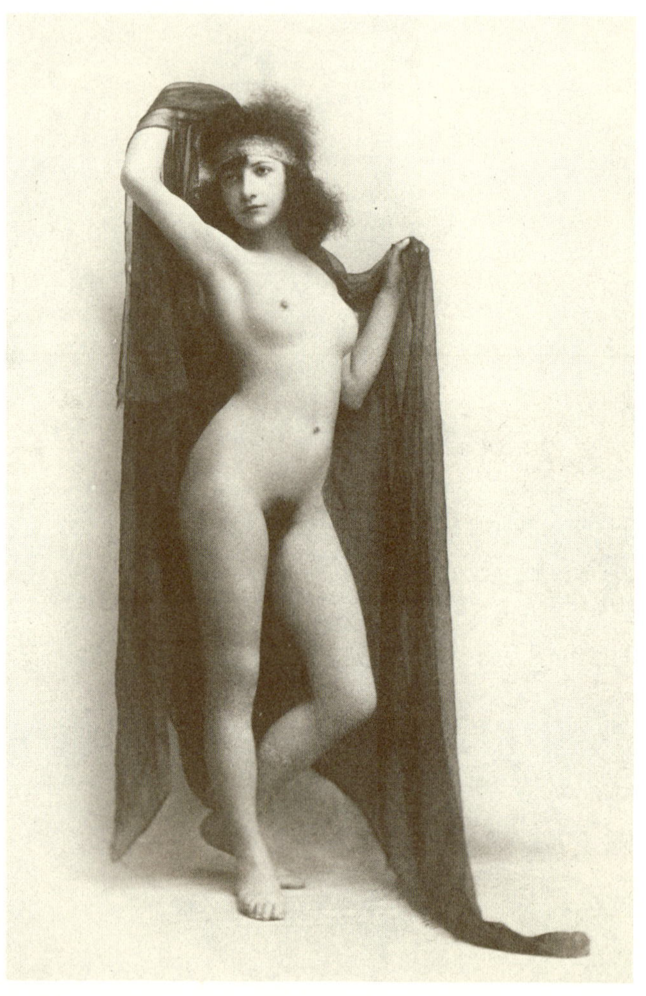

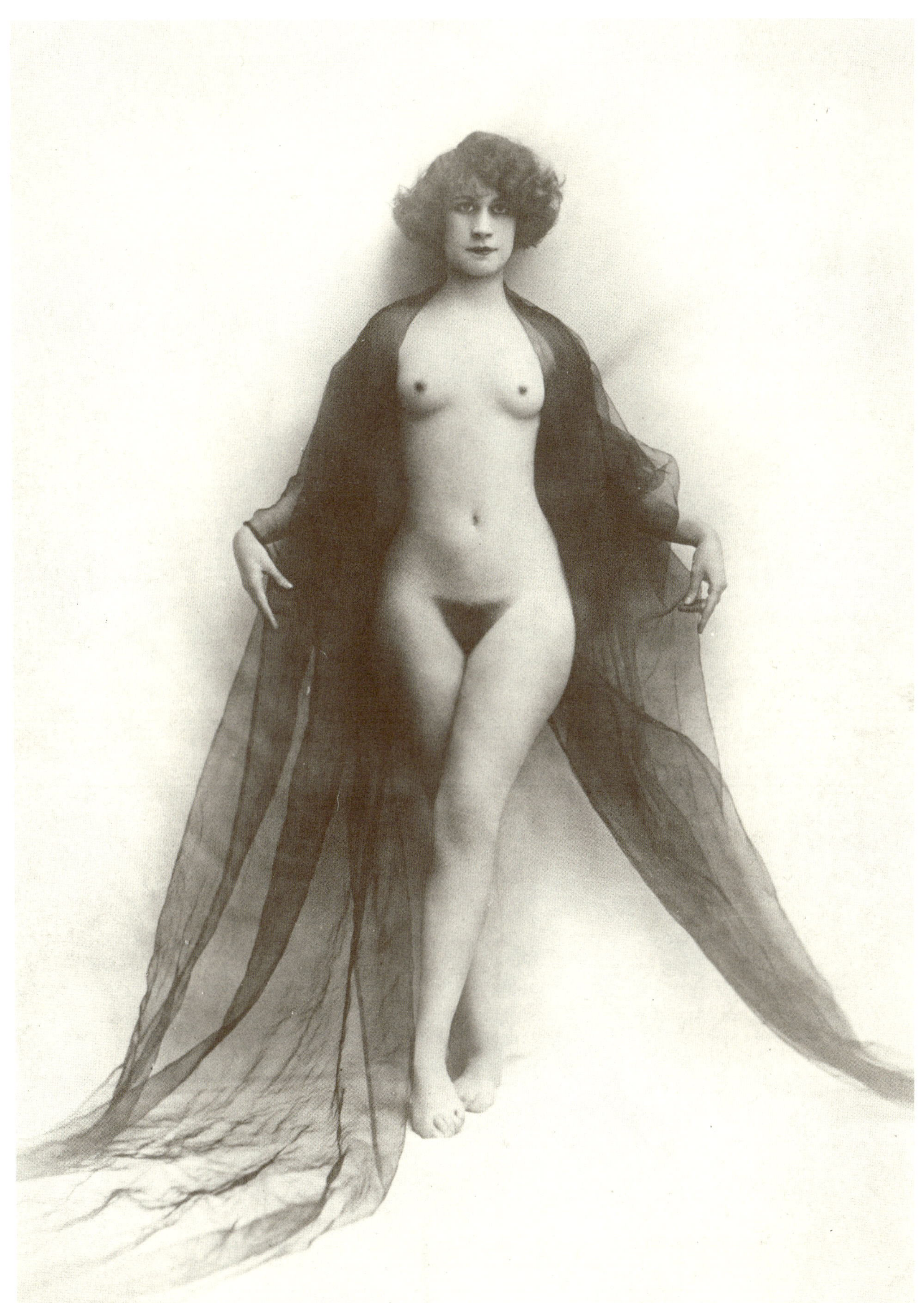

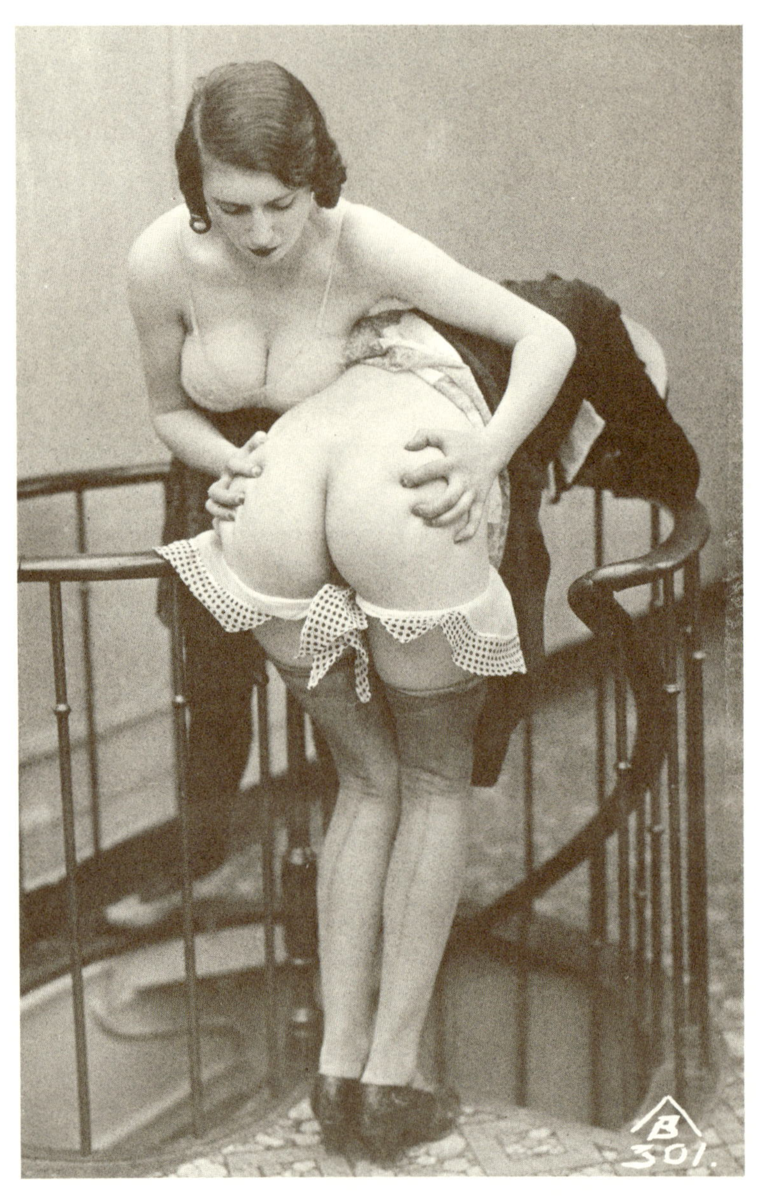
B
301.

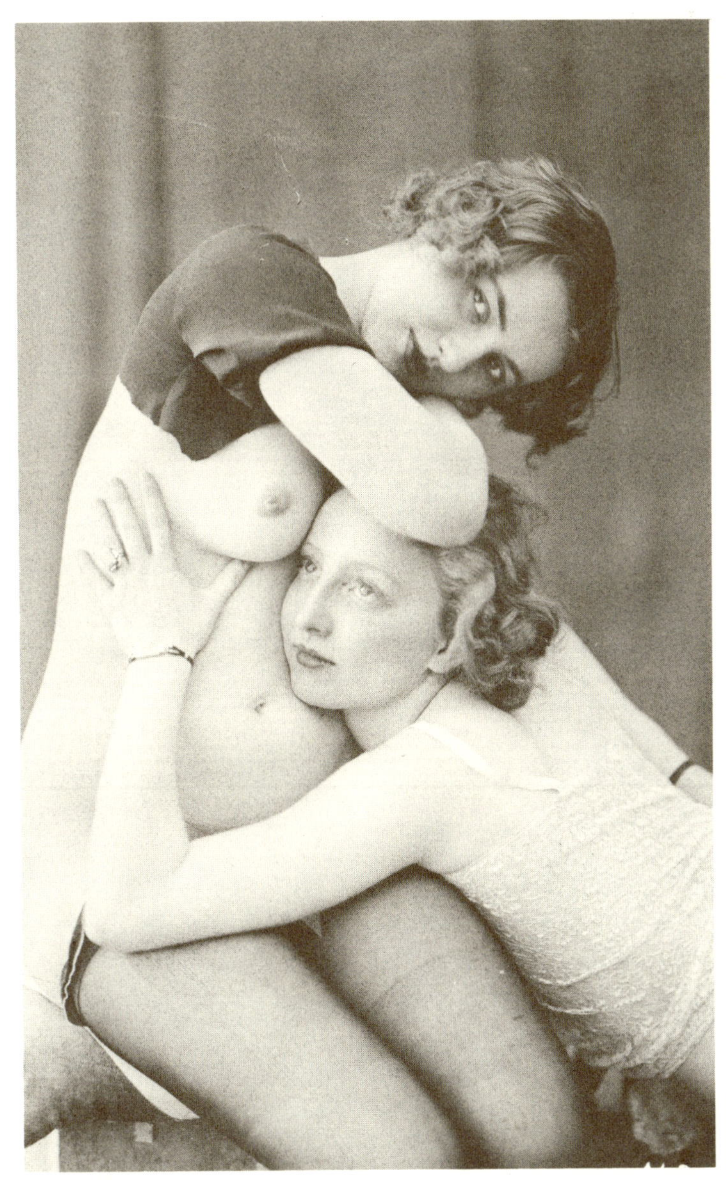

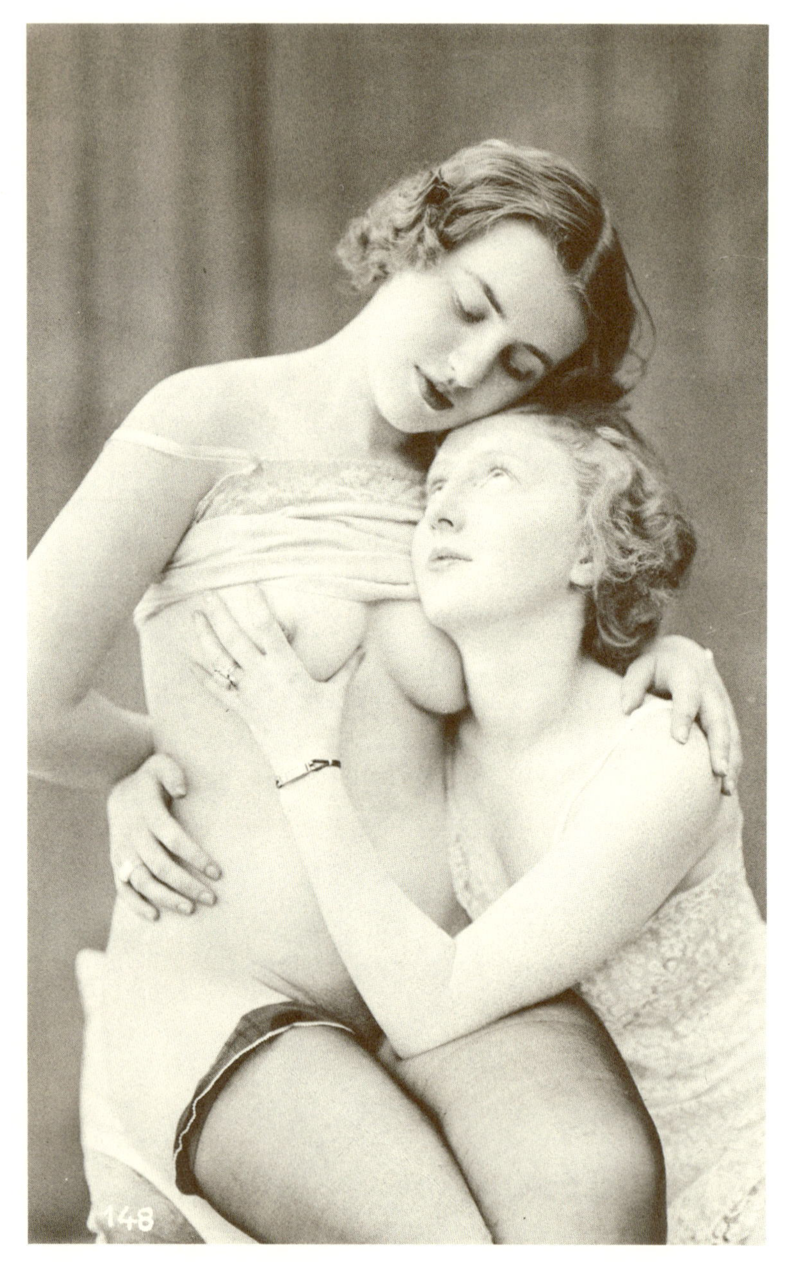
148

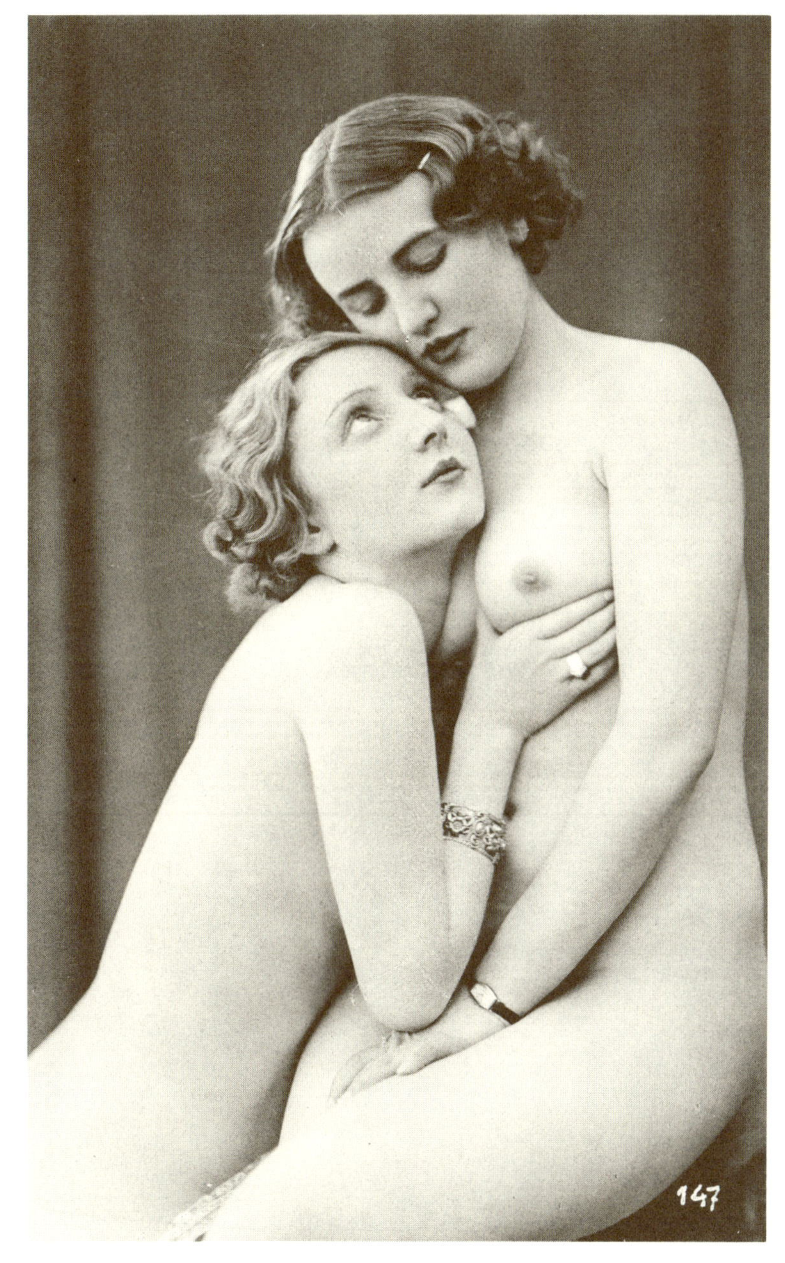
147

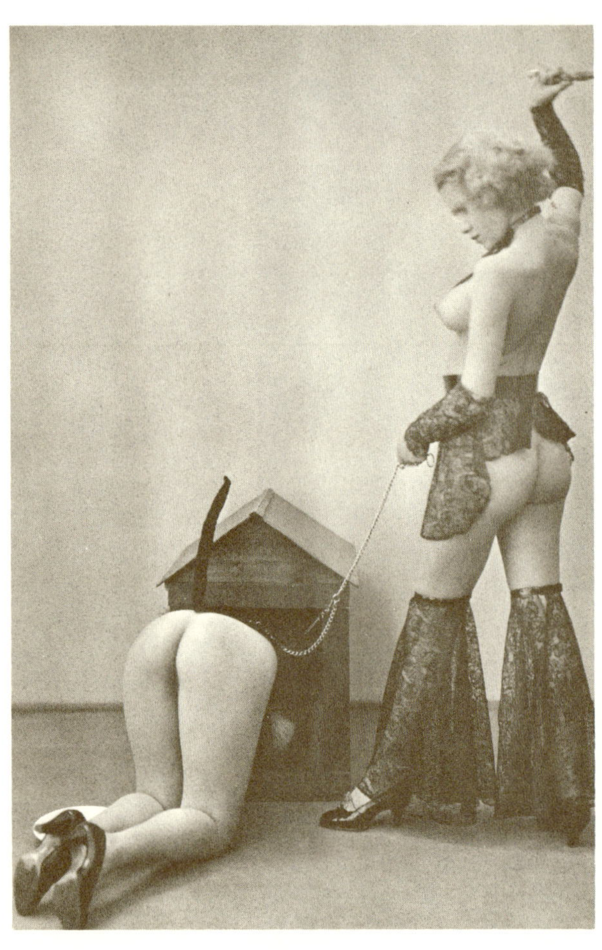
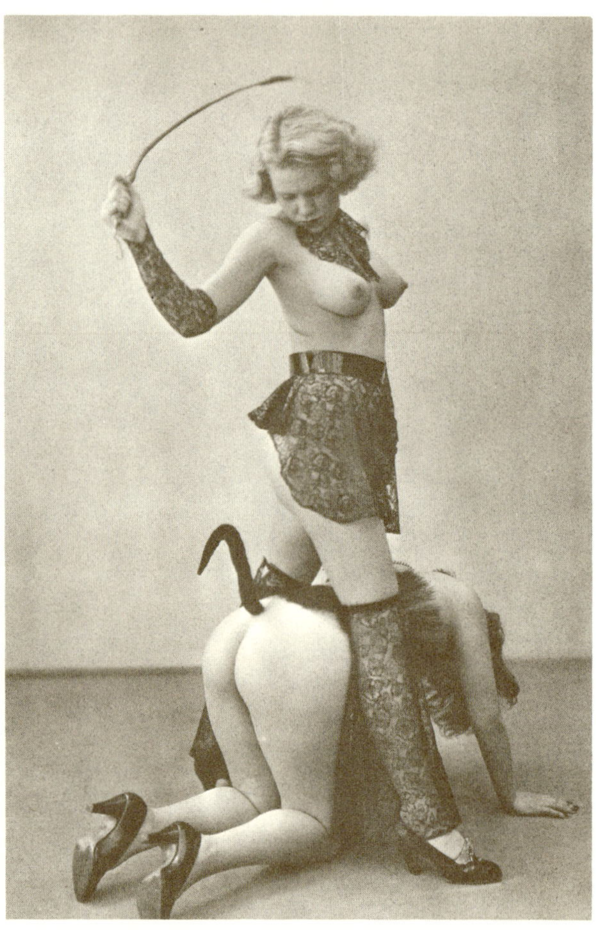

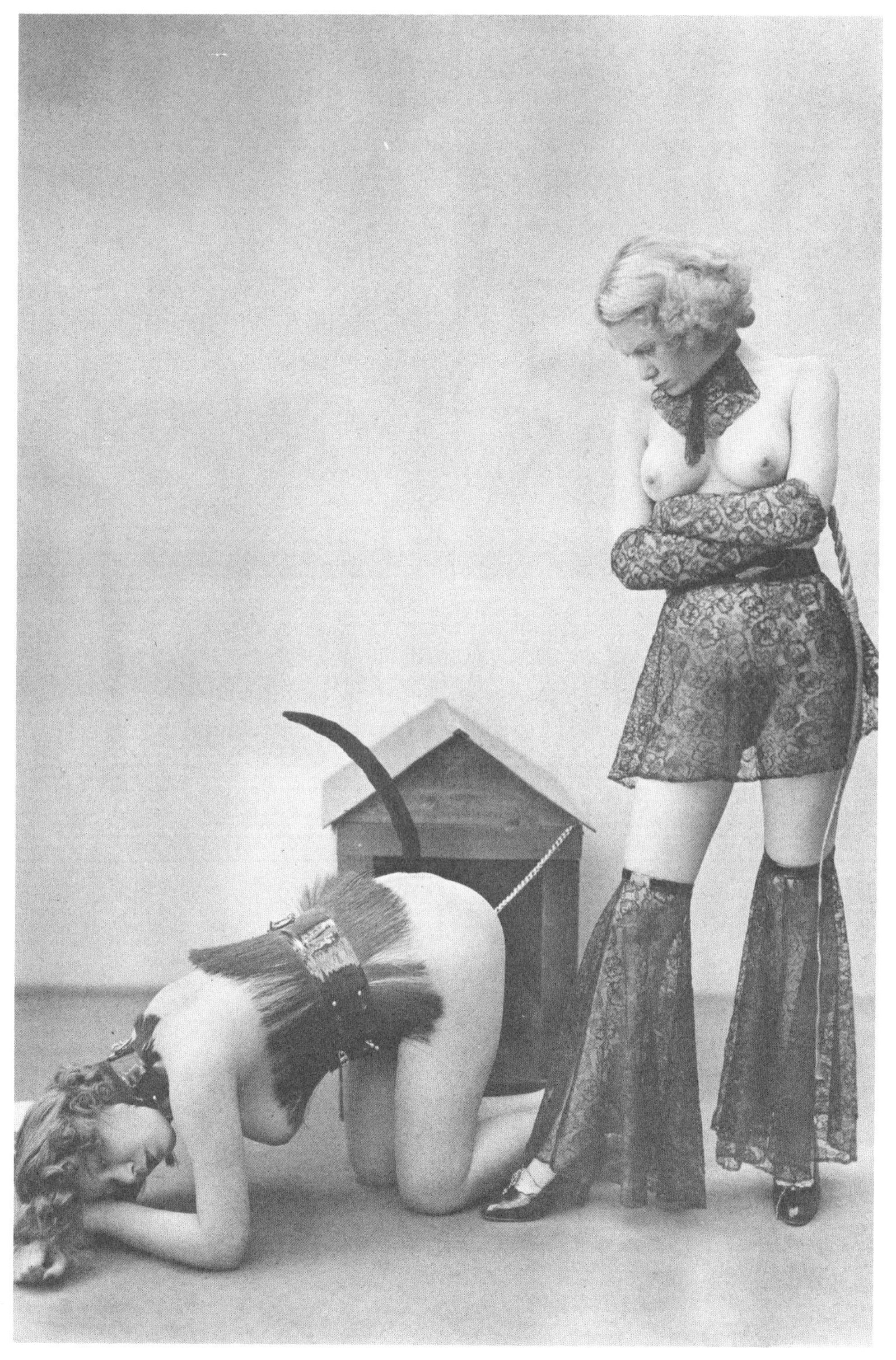

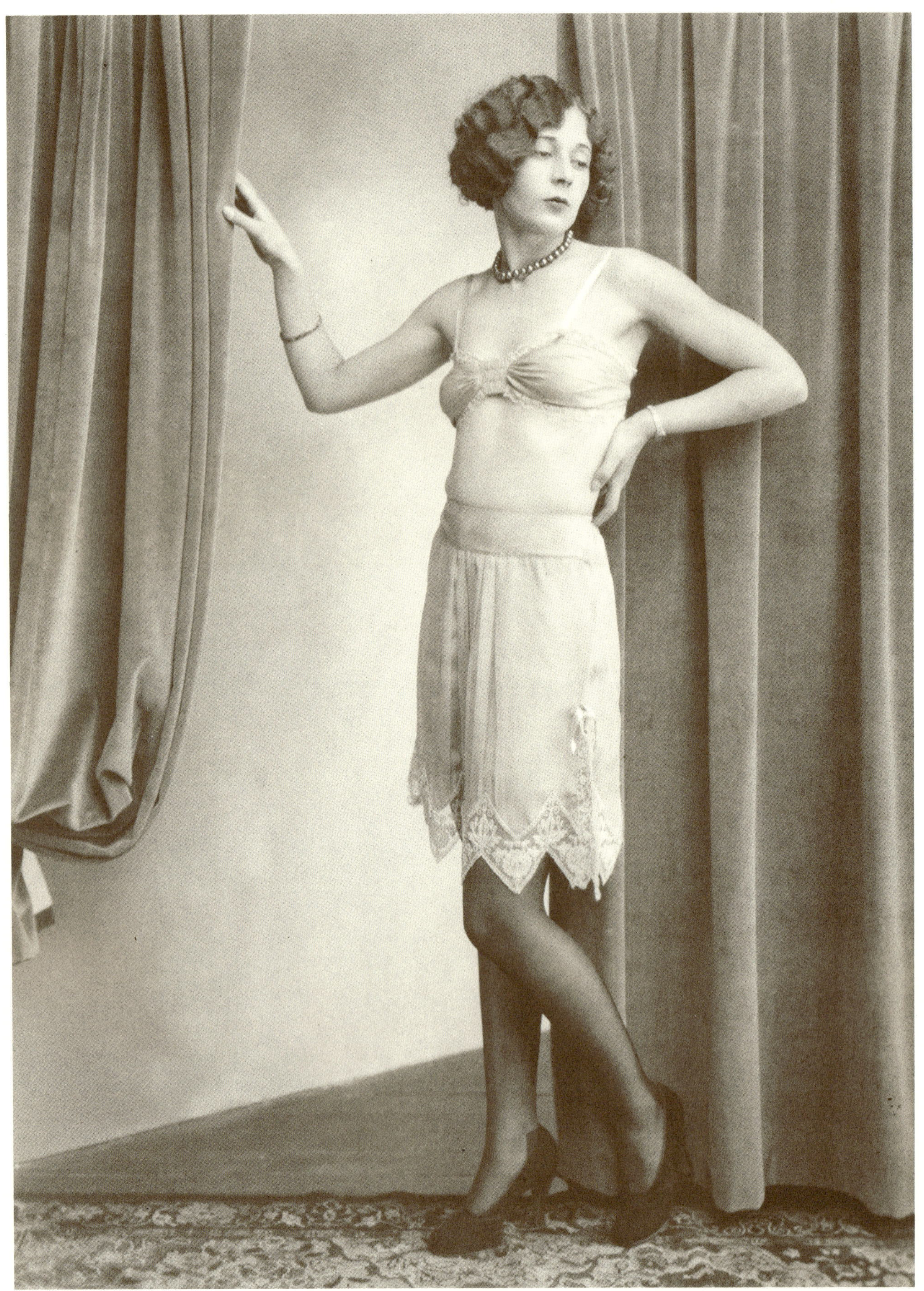

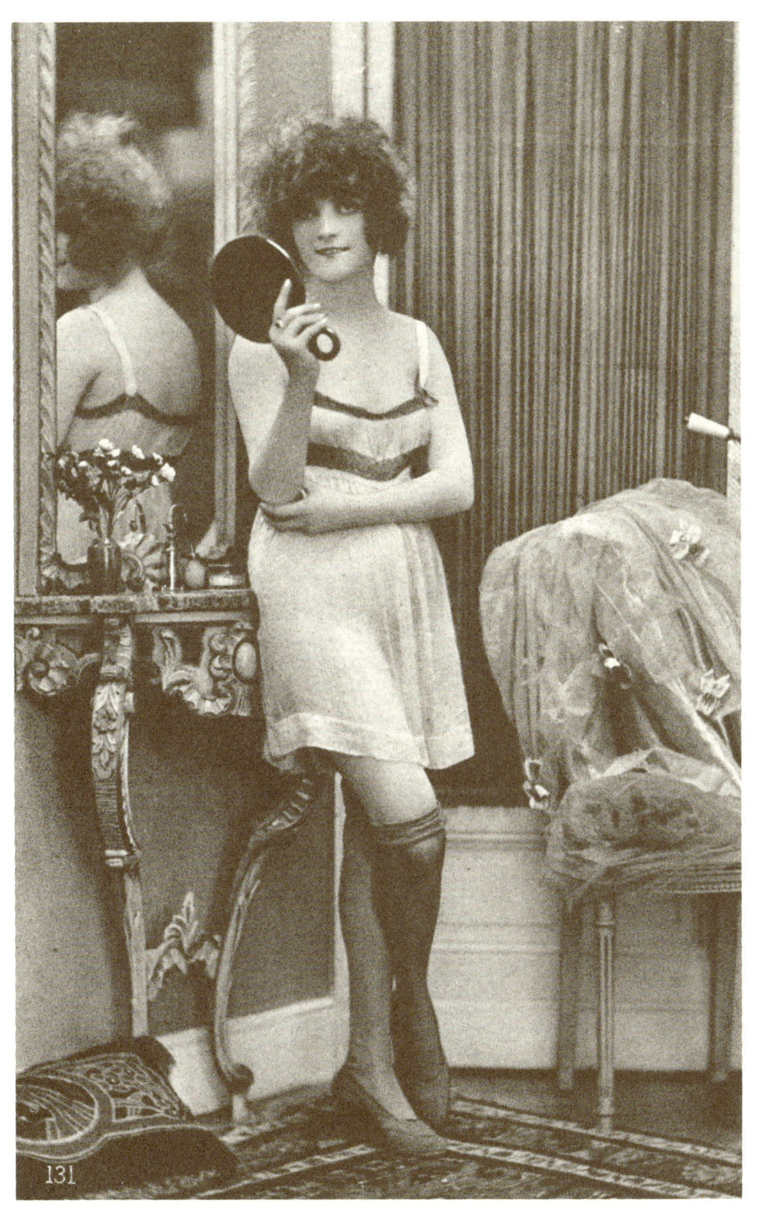
131

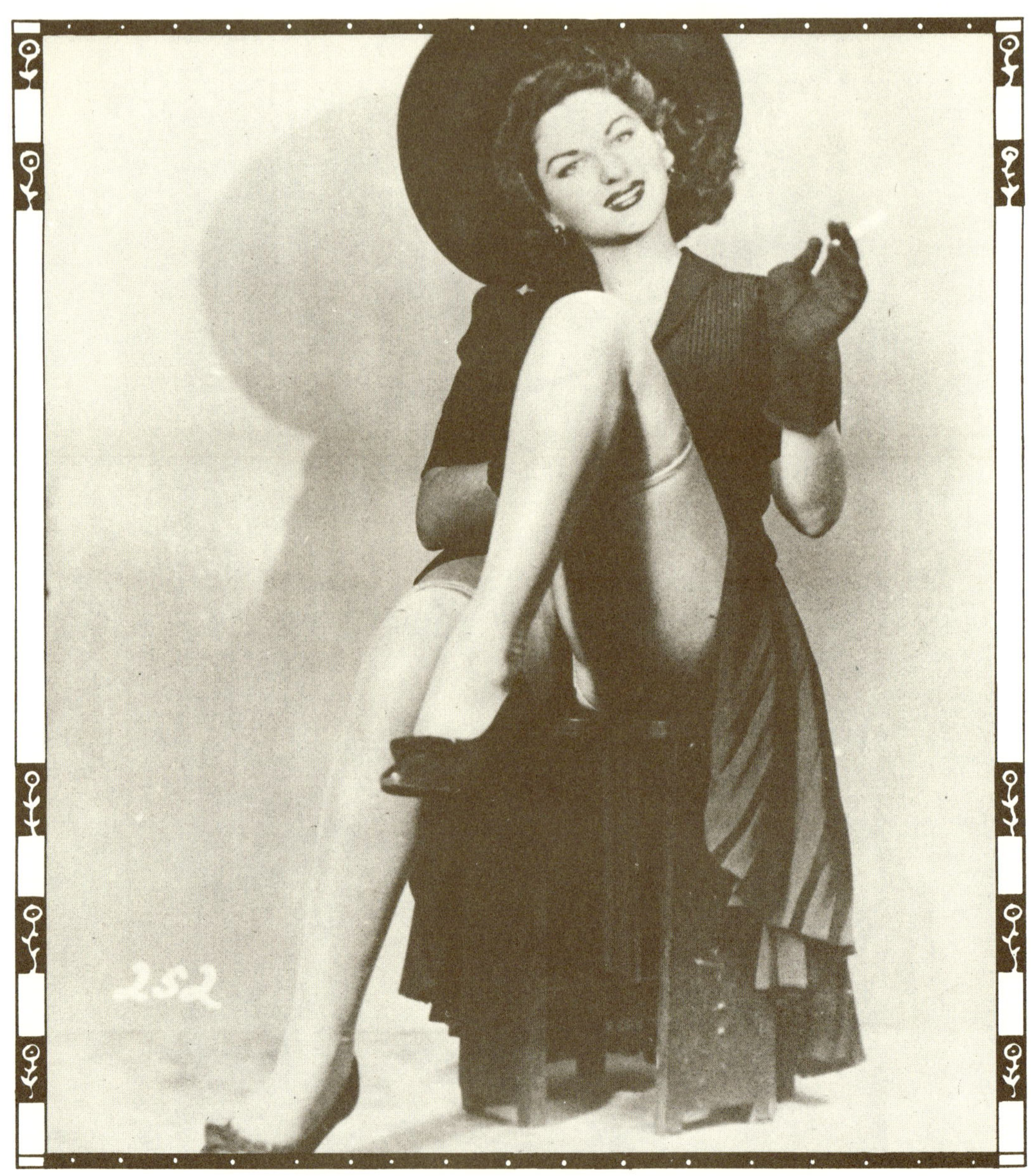
252

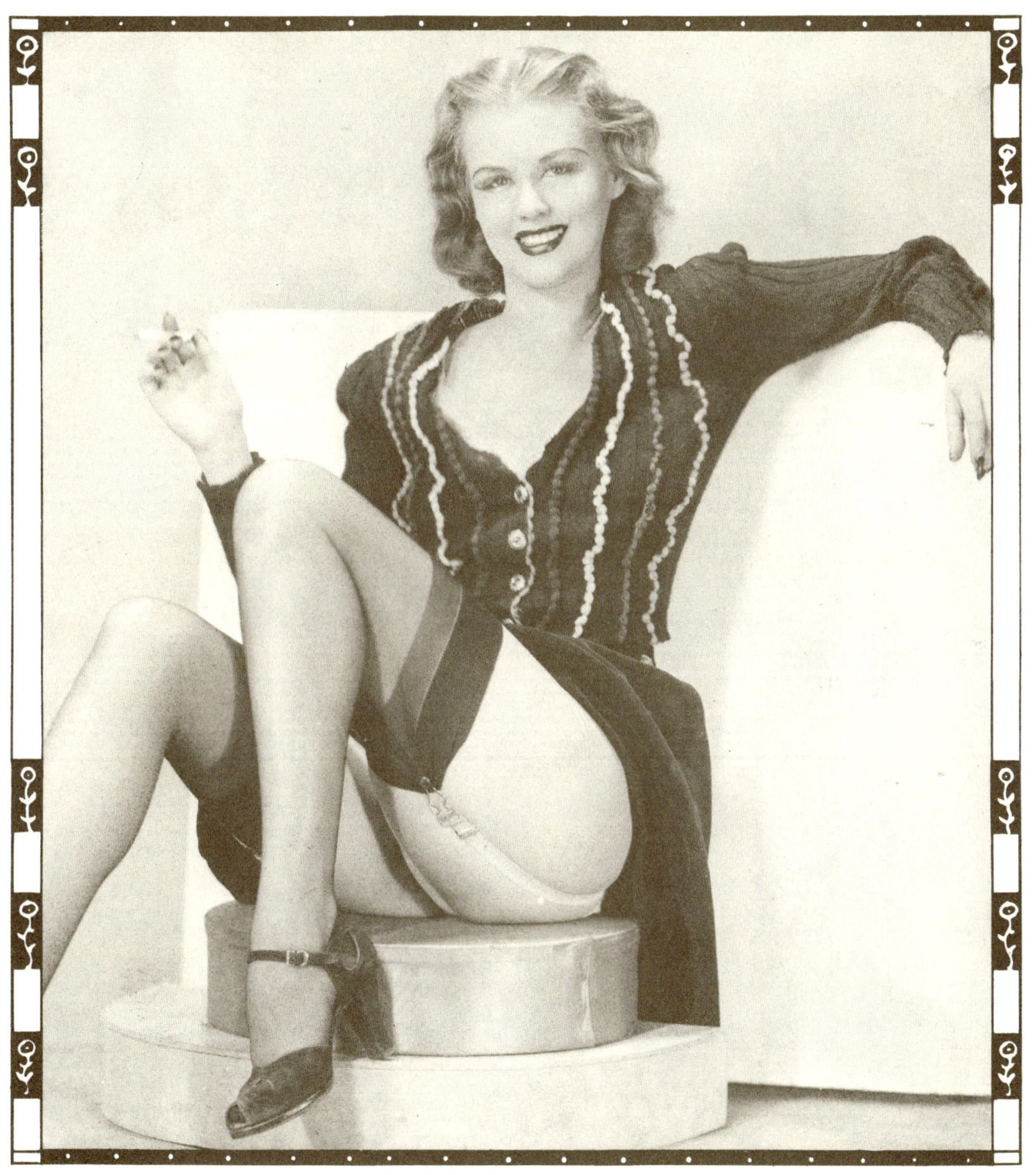

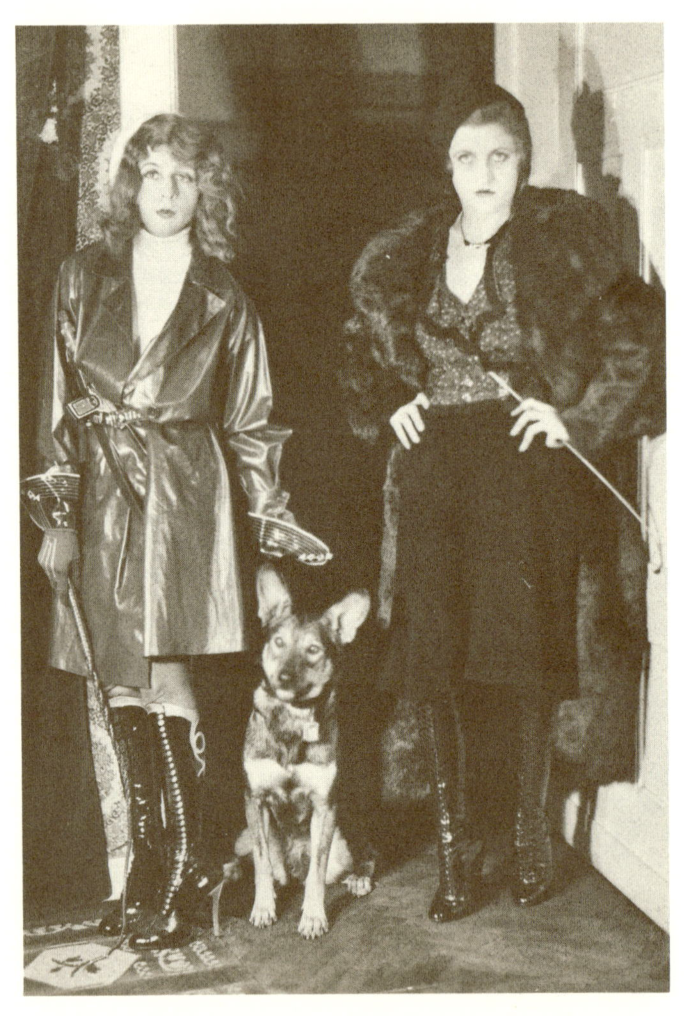

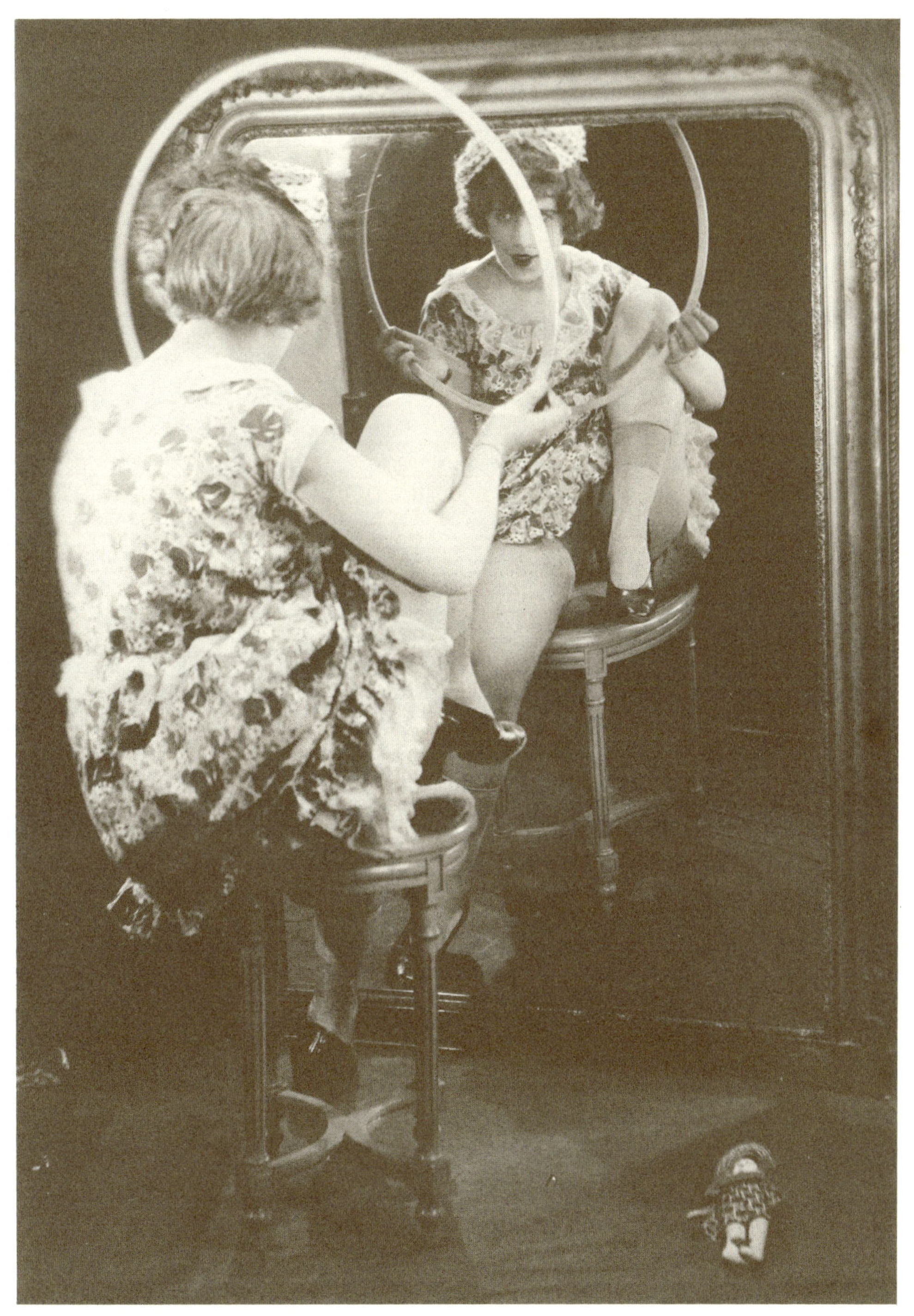

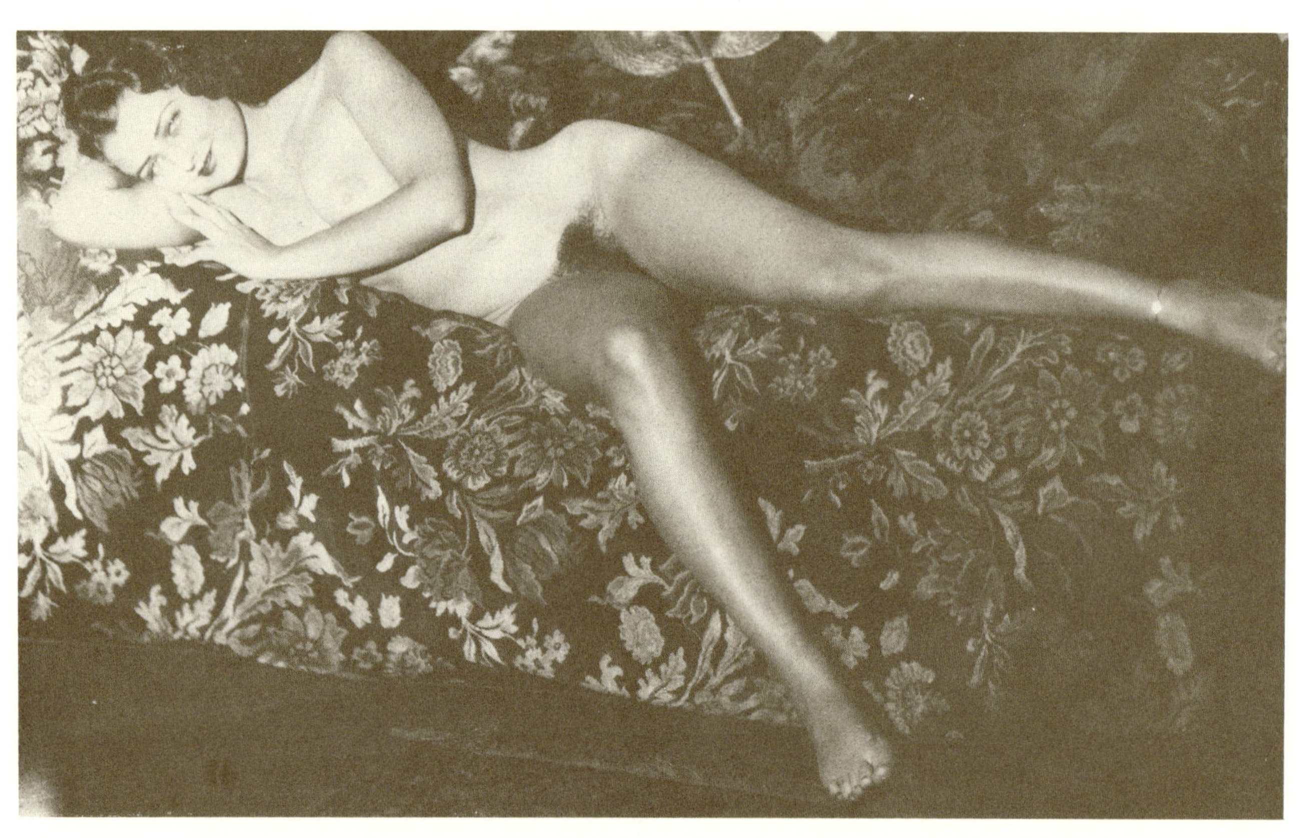

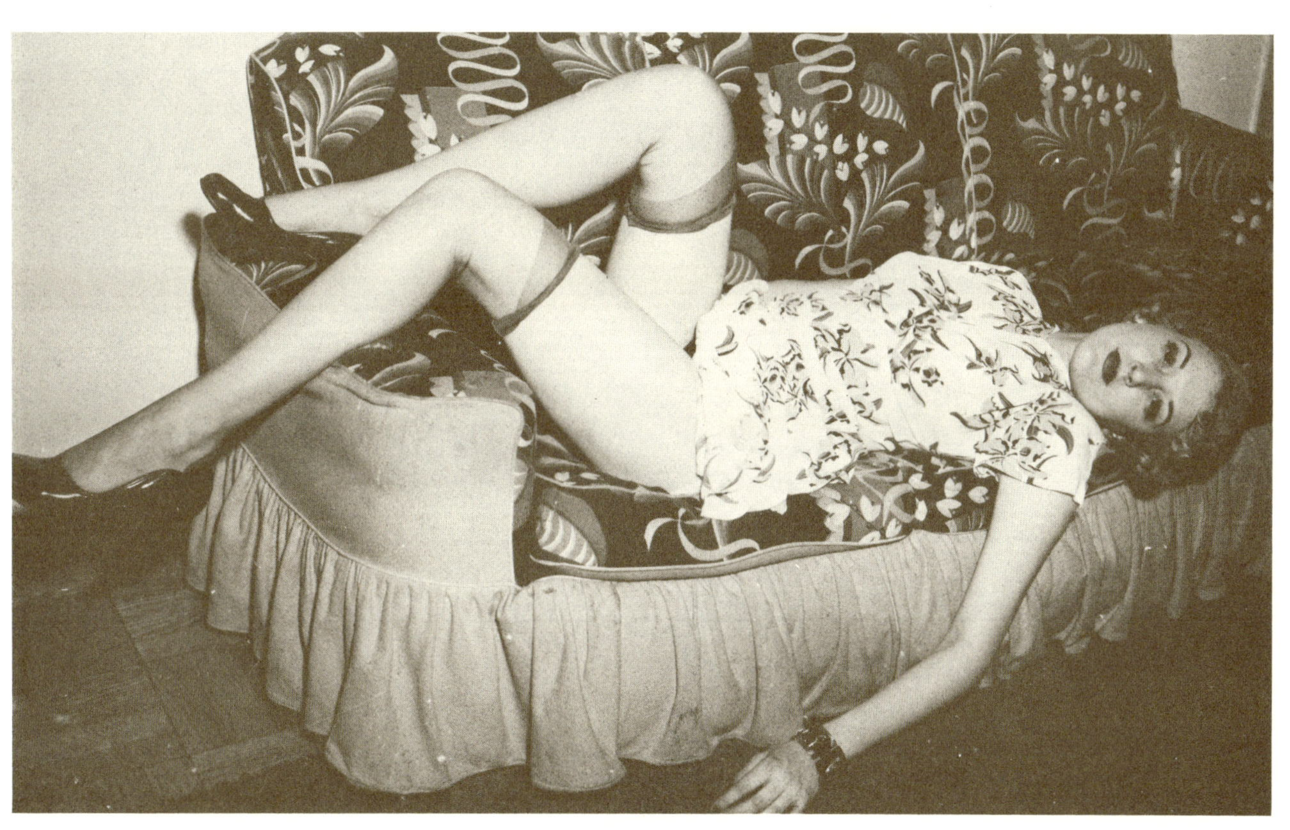

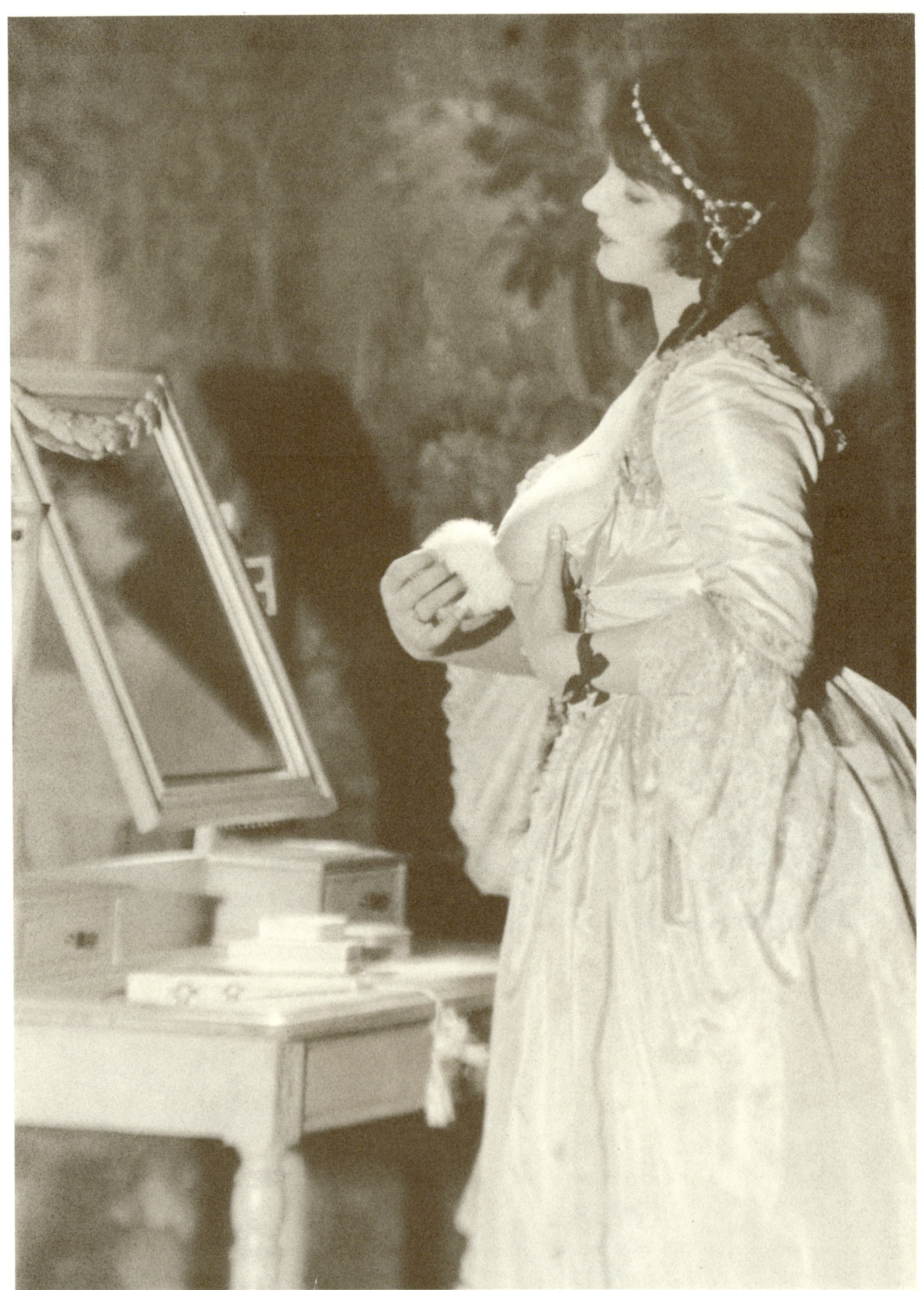

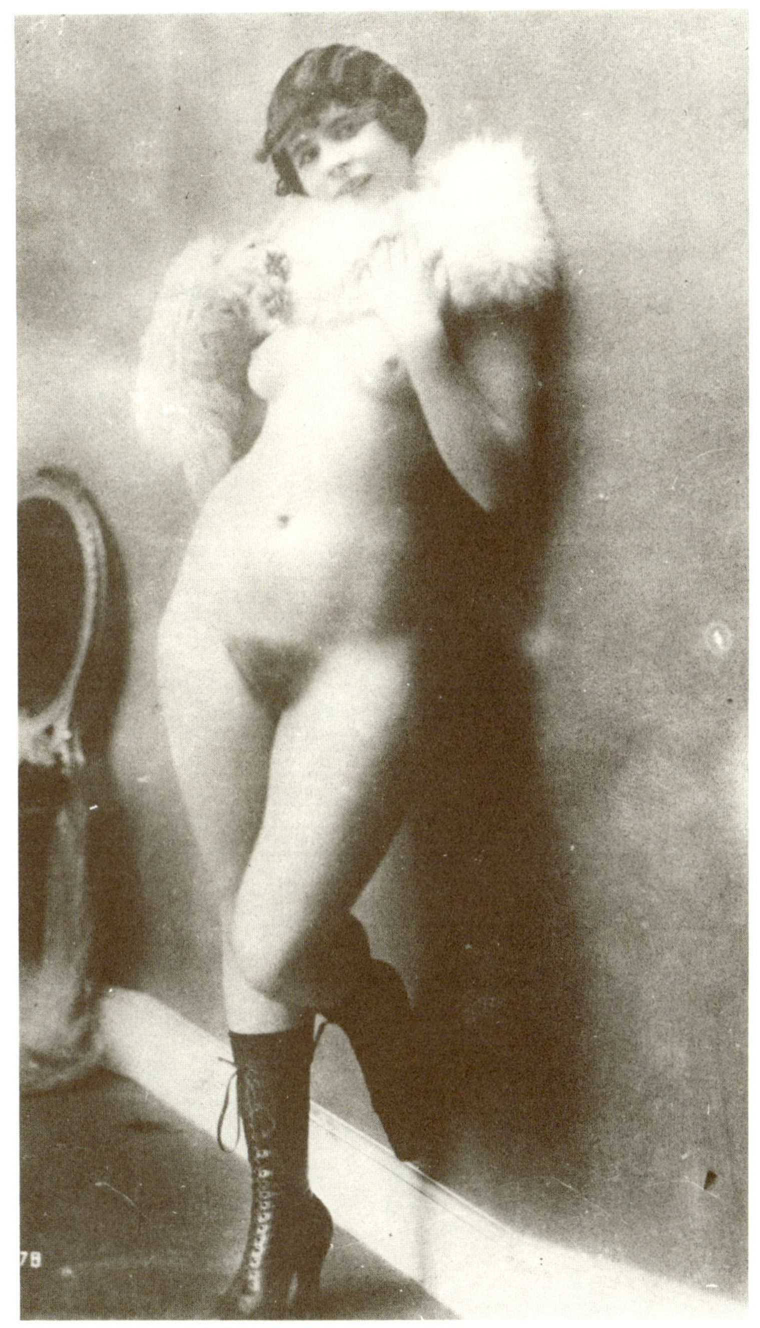

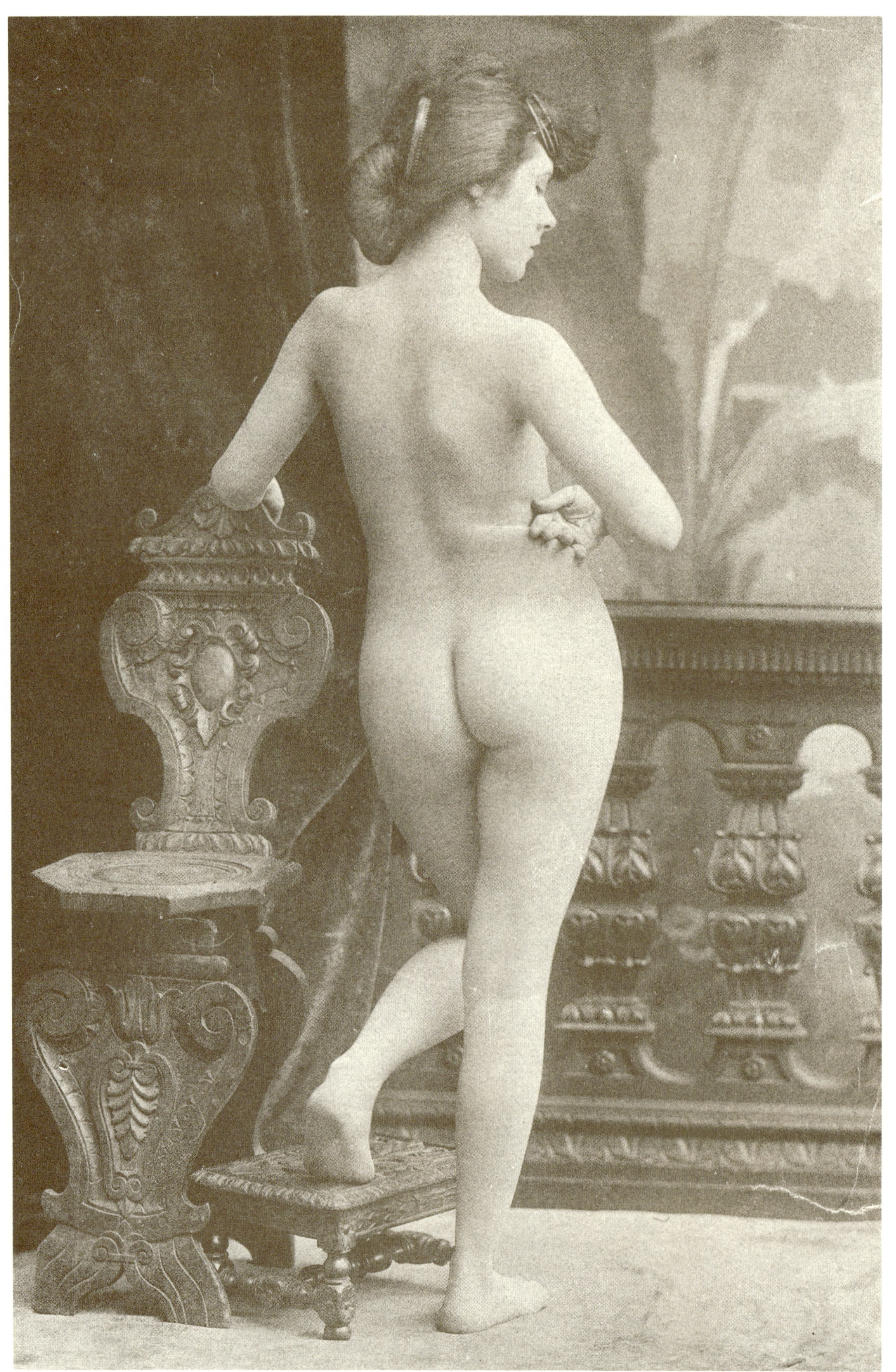

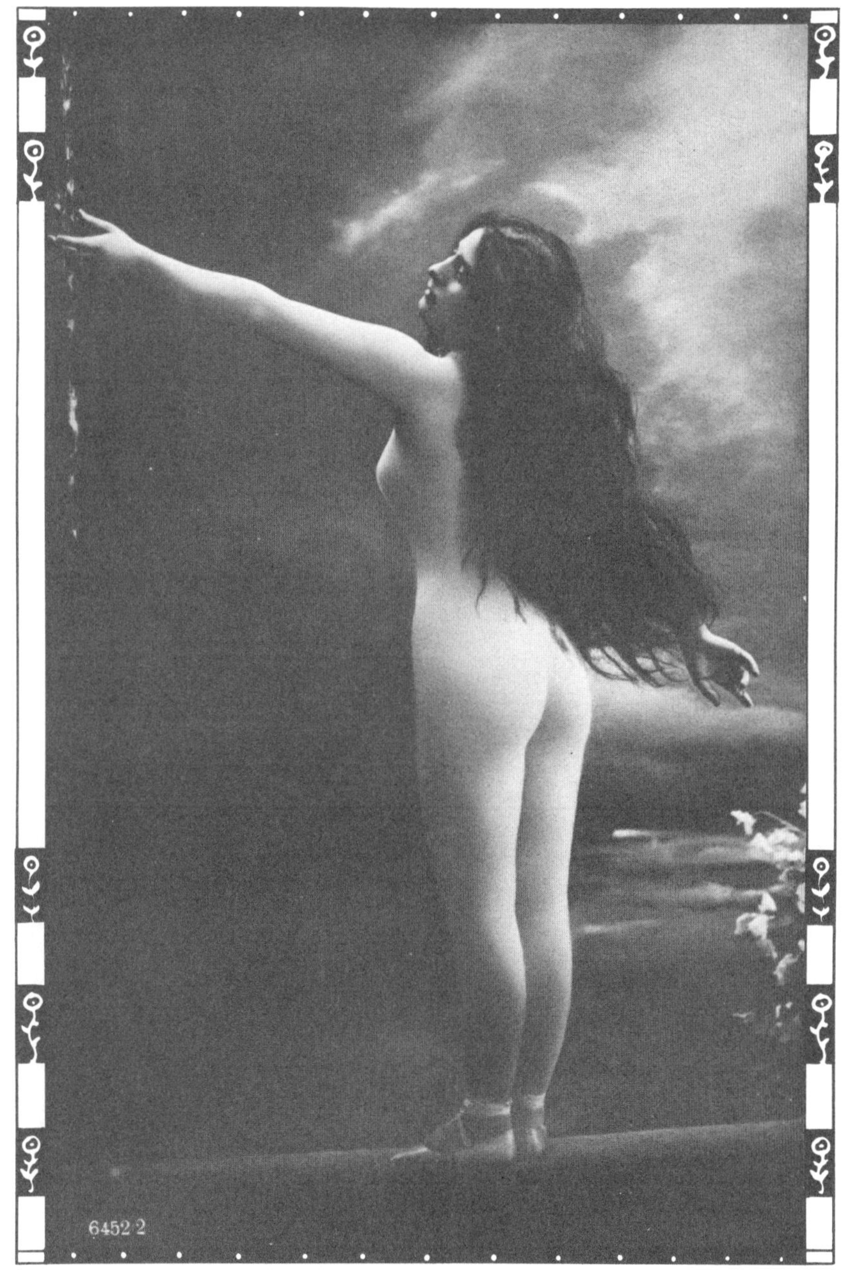
6452 2

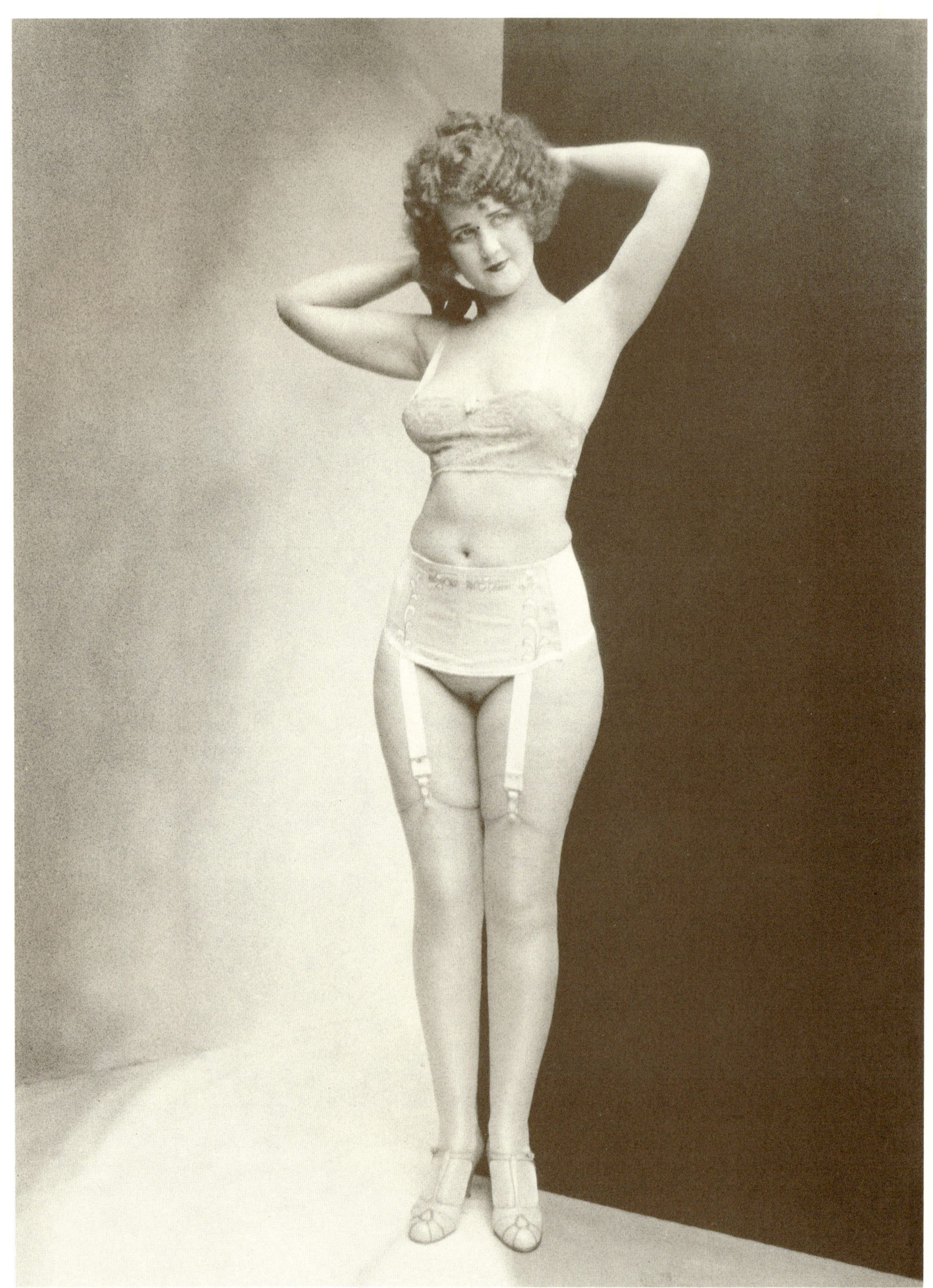

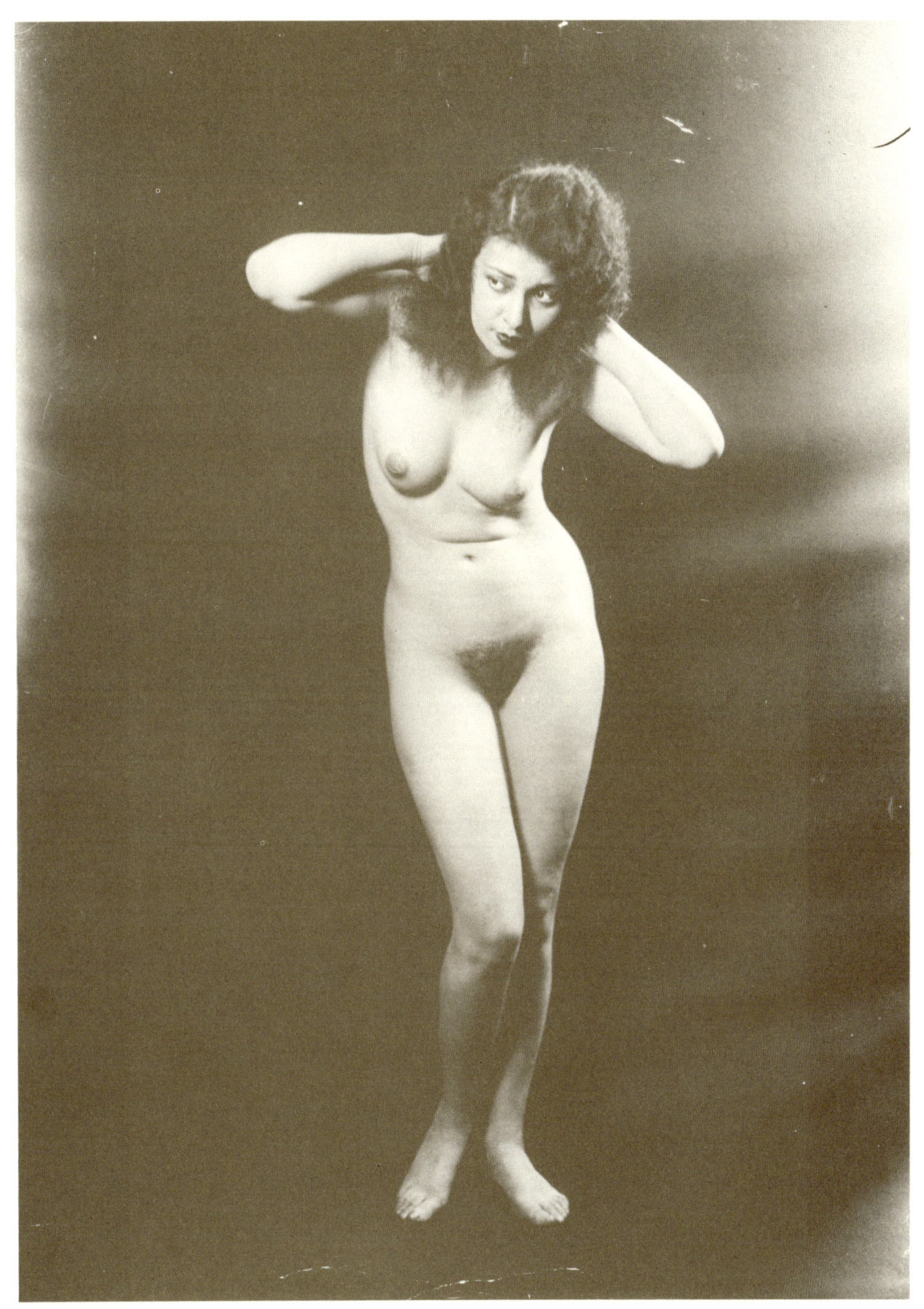

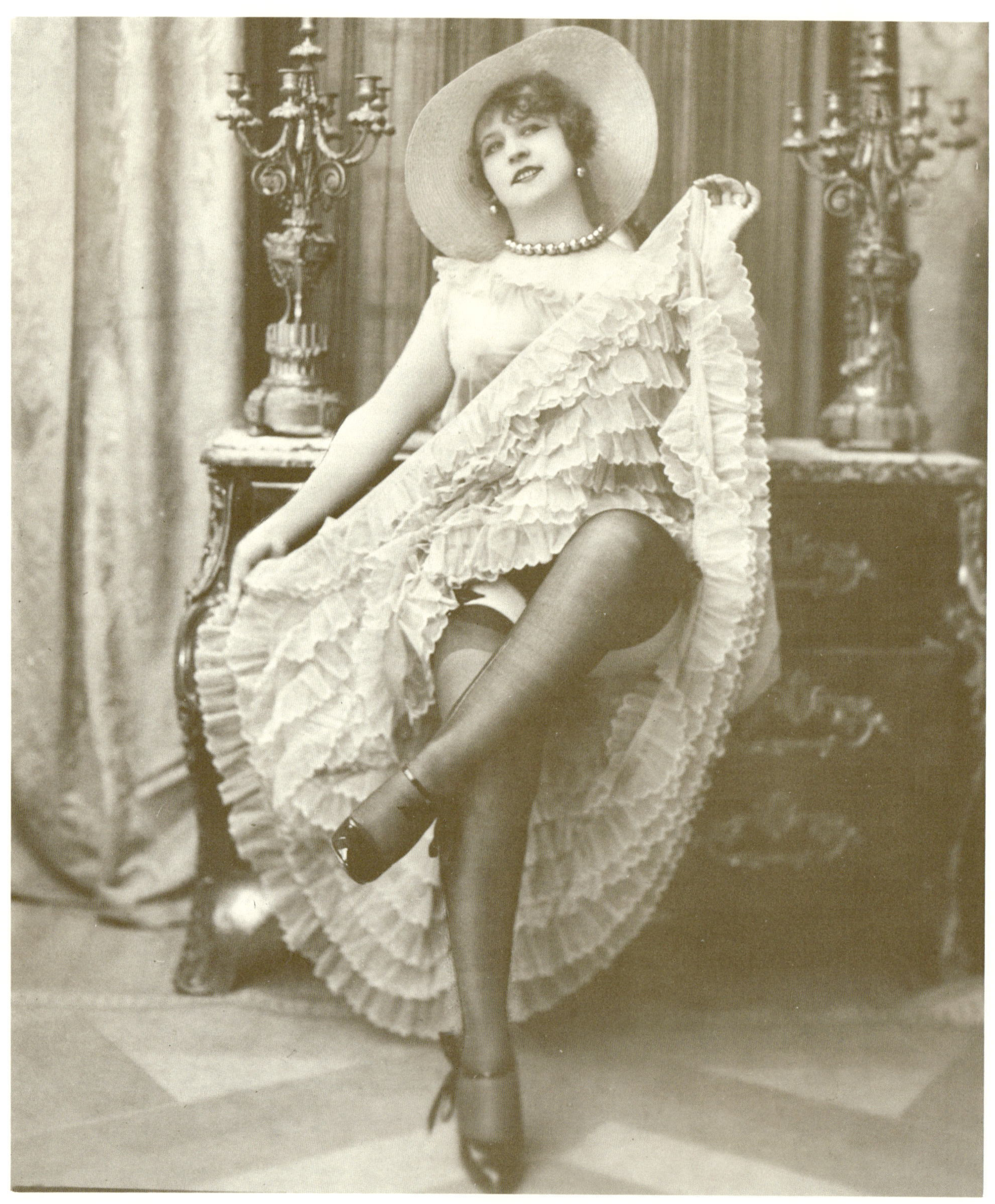

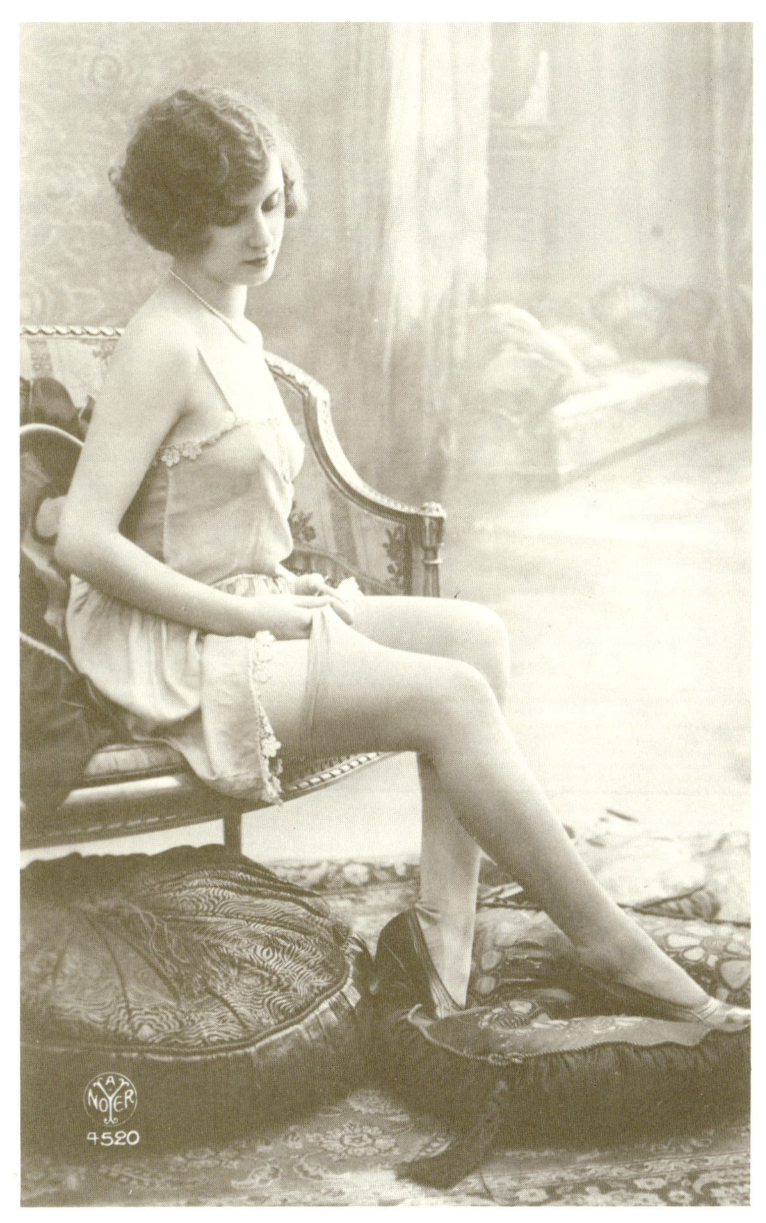
NOYER
4520

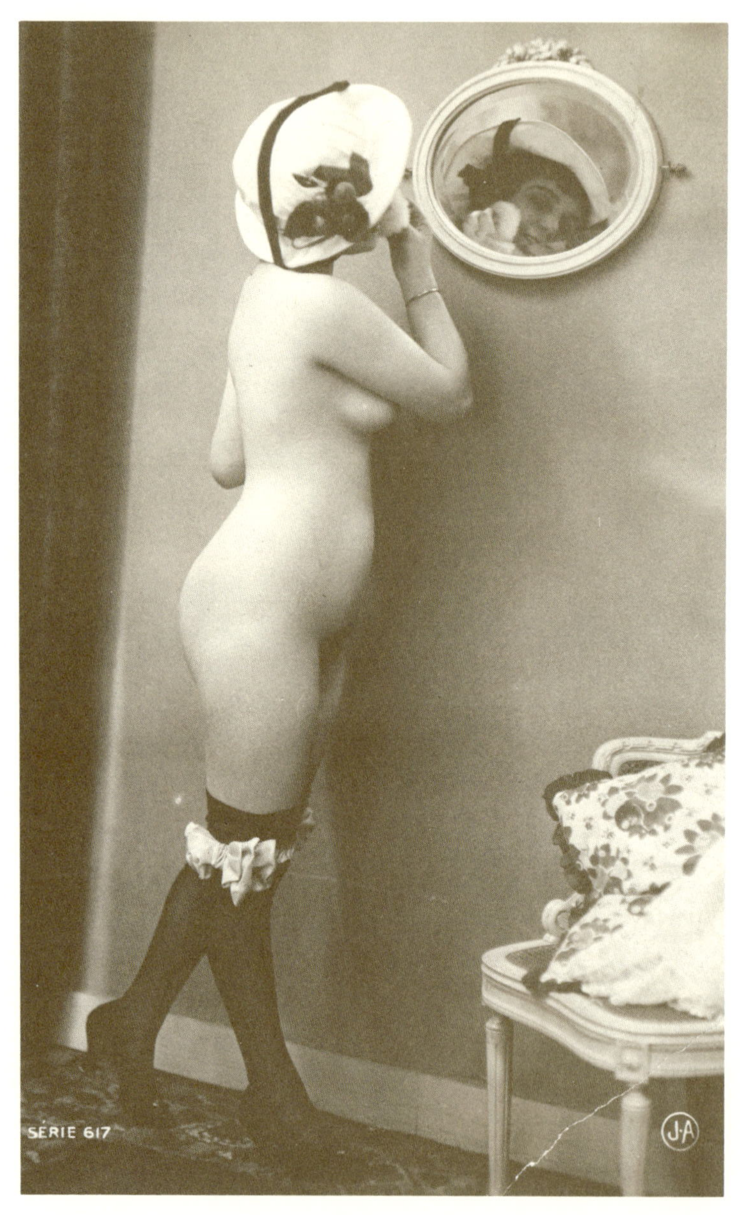
SERIE 617
J·A

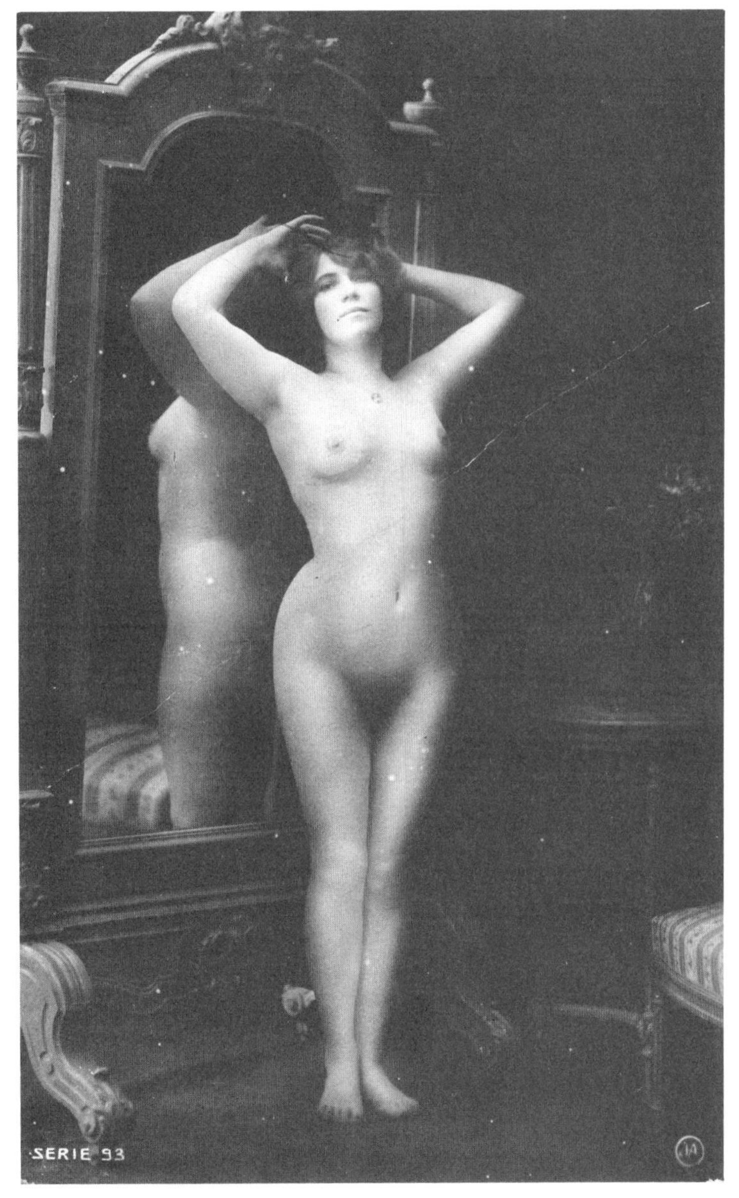
SERIE 93

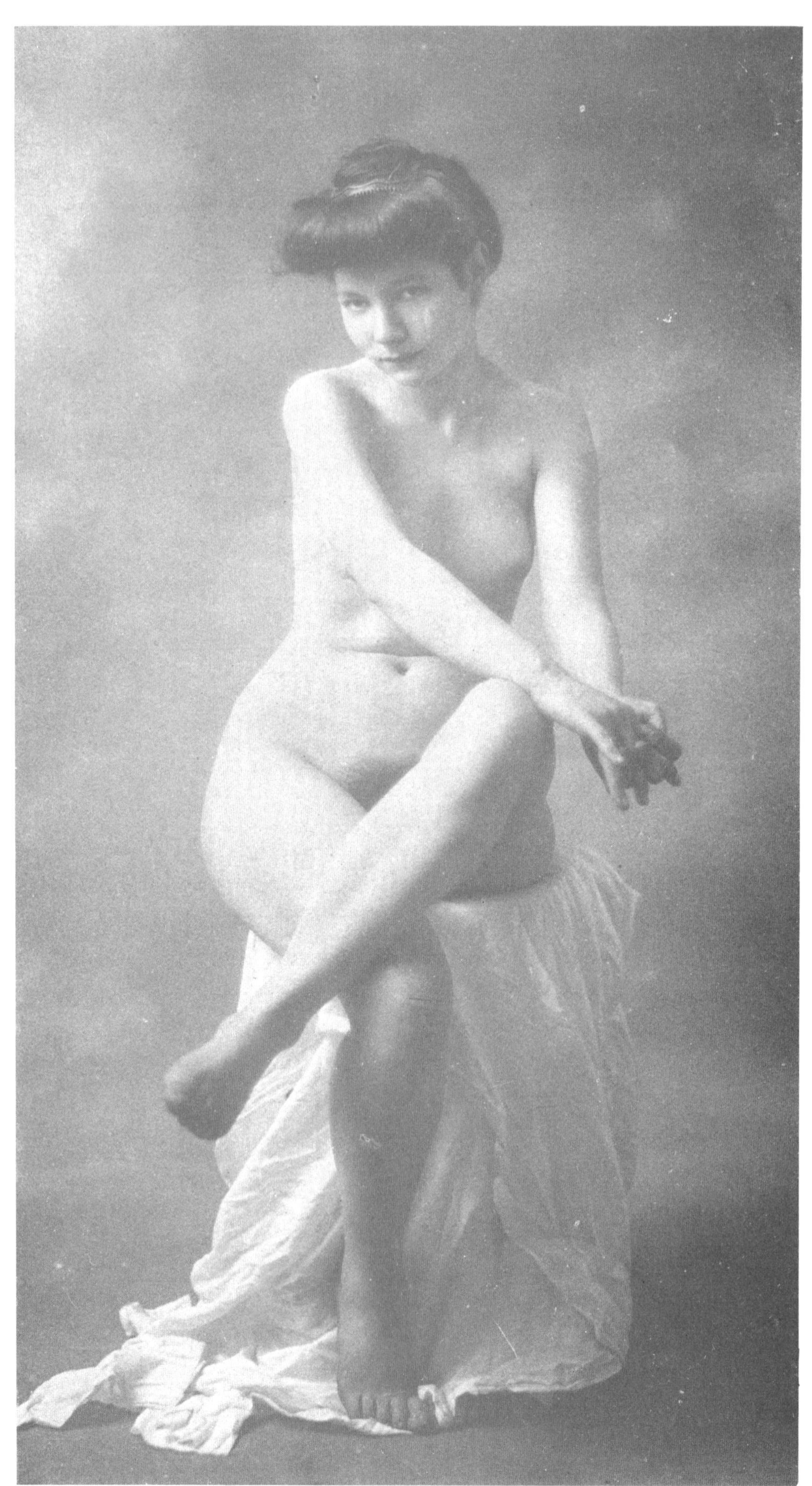

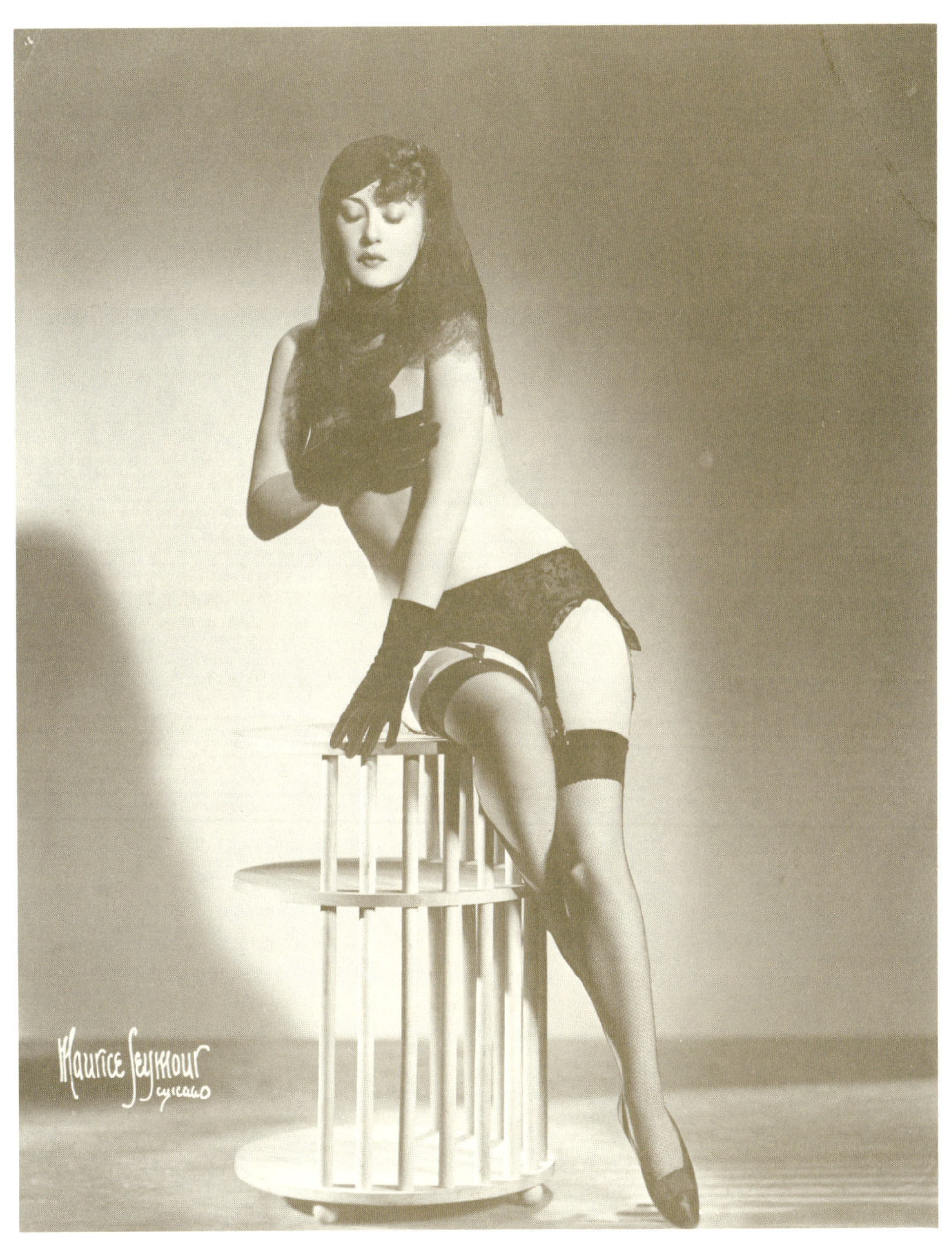
Maurice Seymour
Chicago

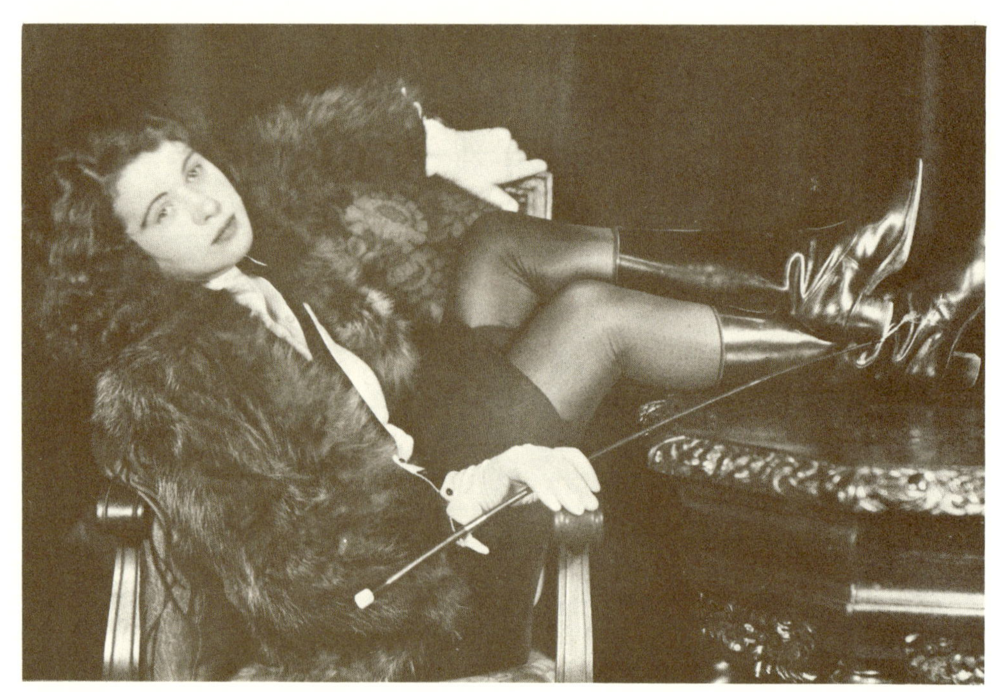

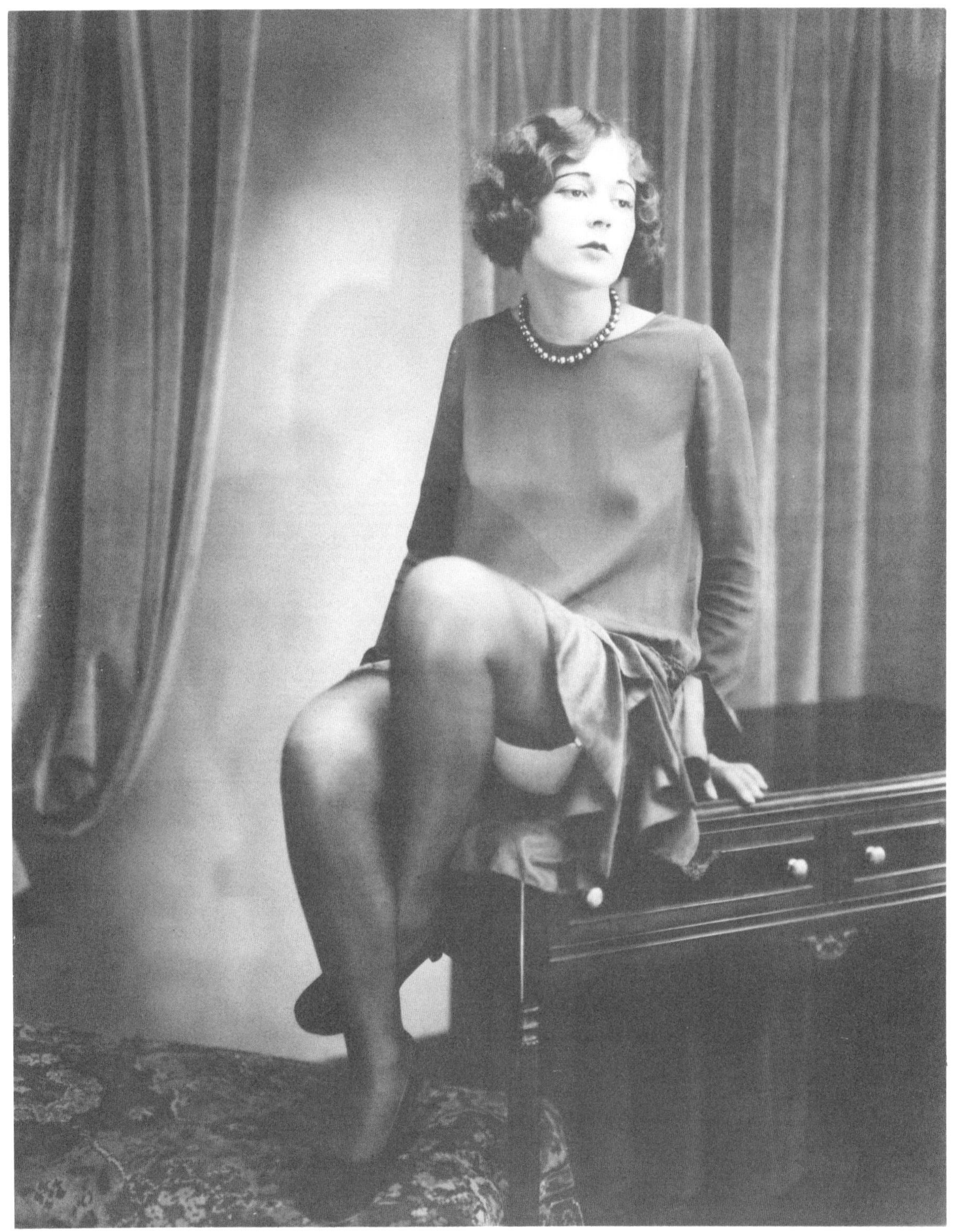

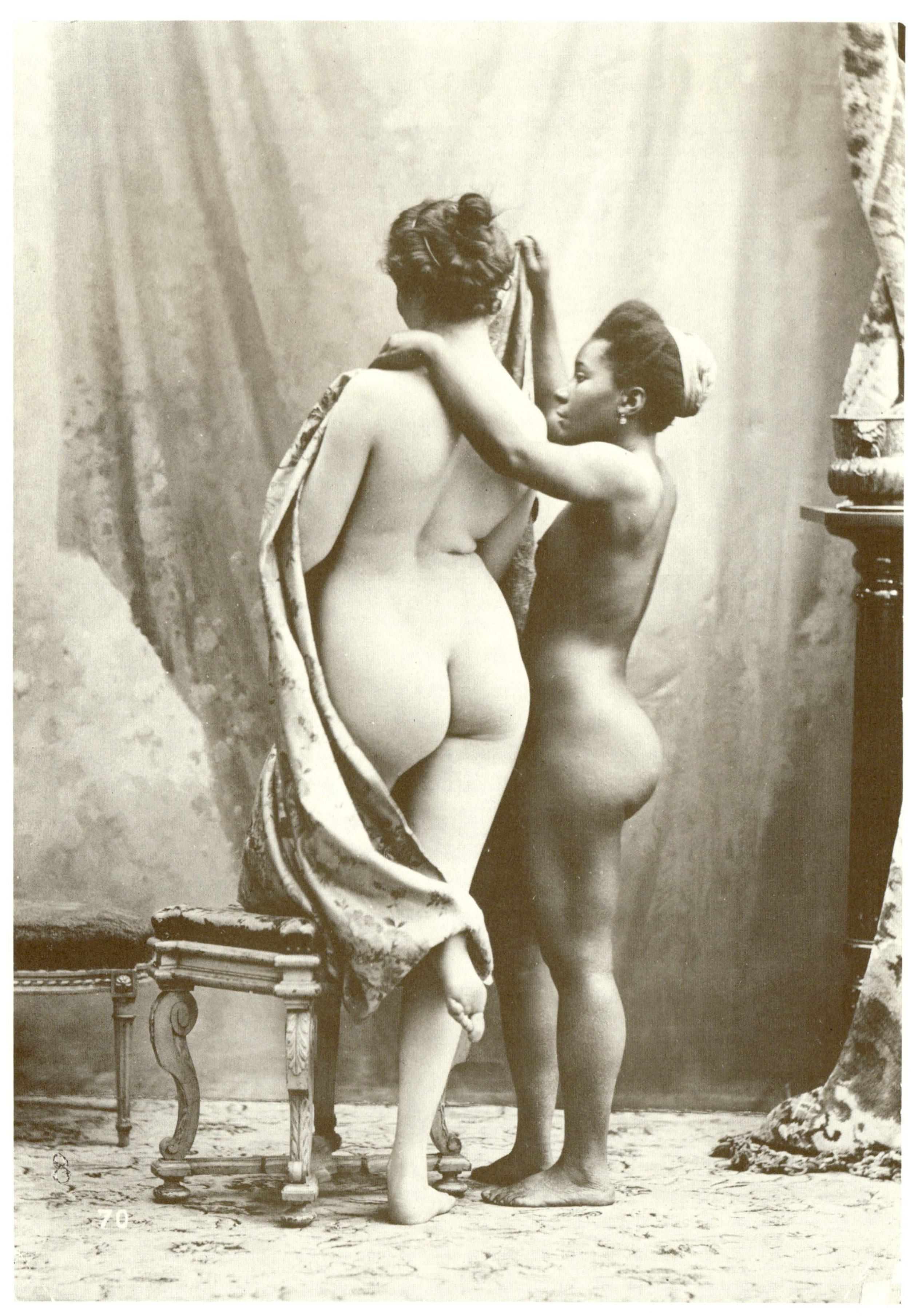
70

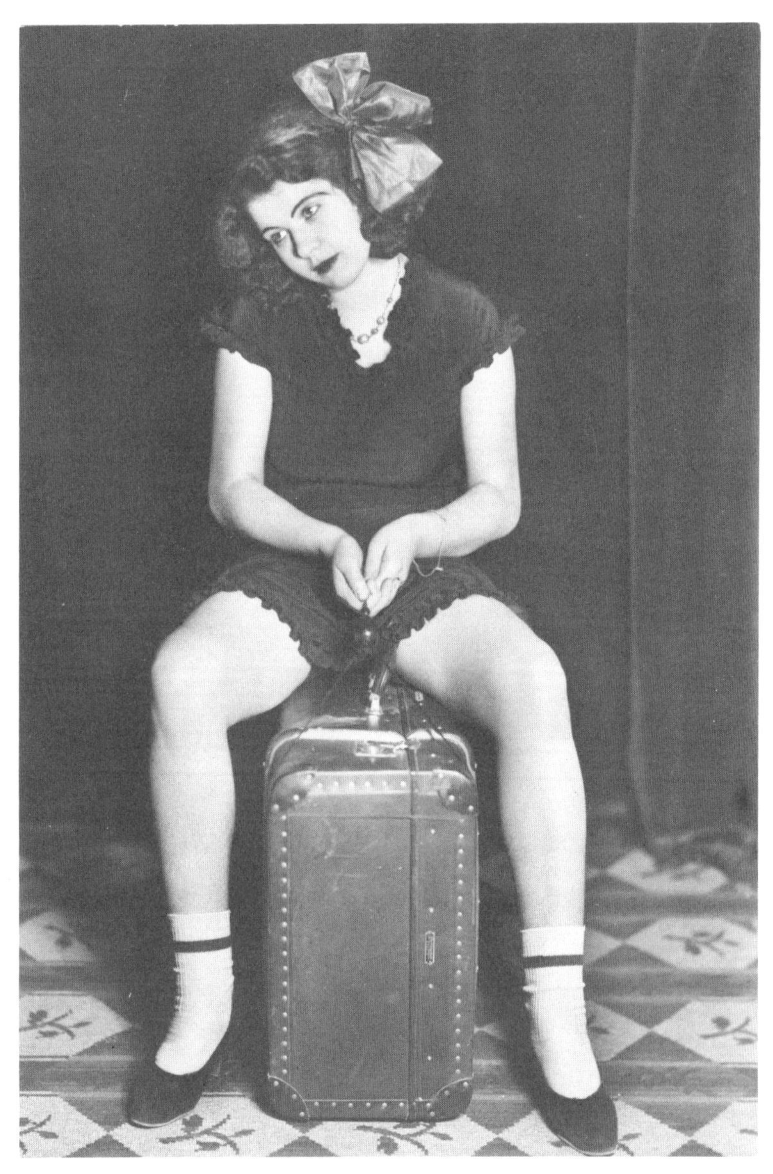

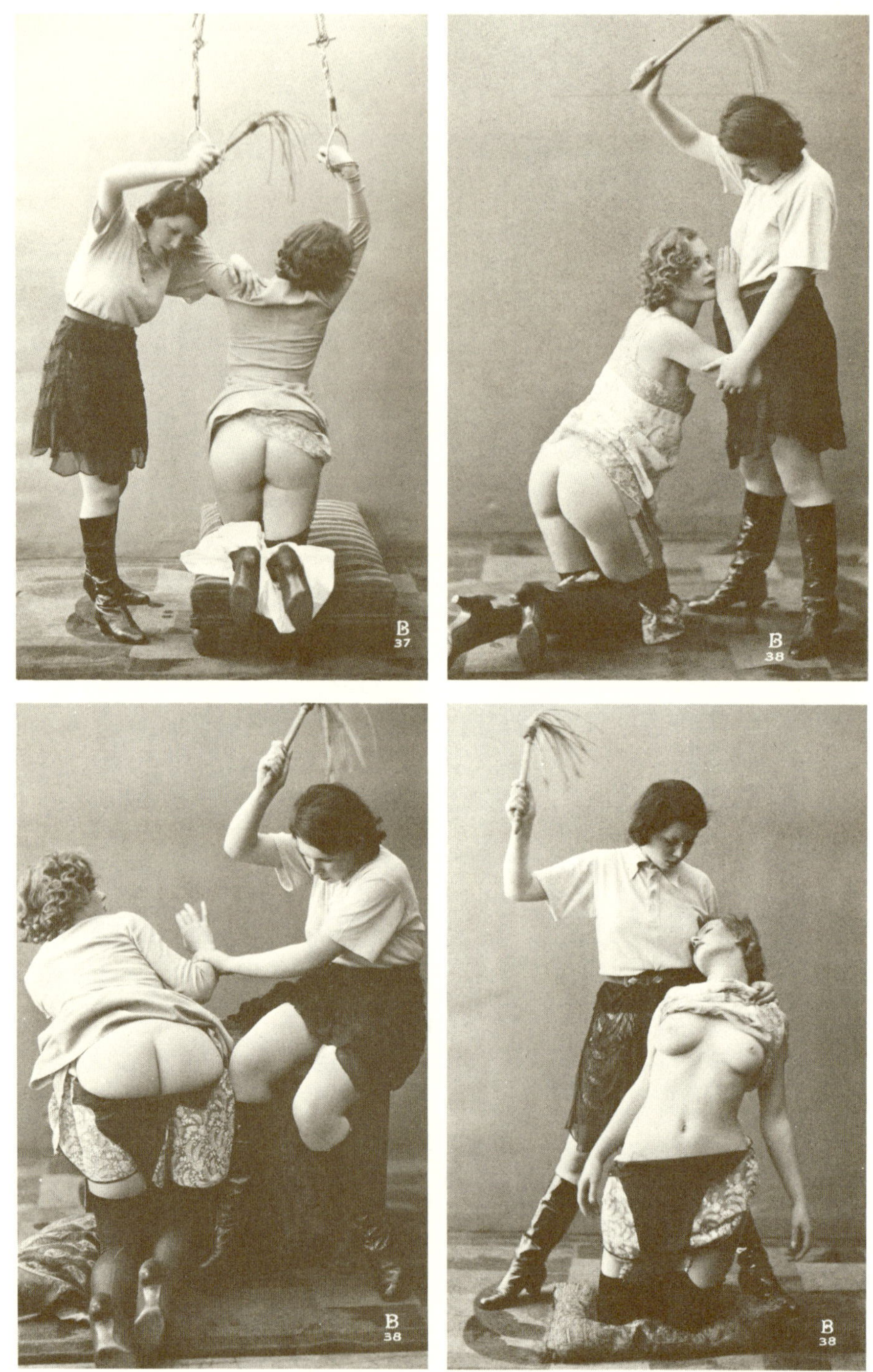
B
37
B
38
B
38
B
38

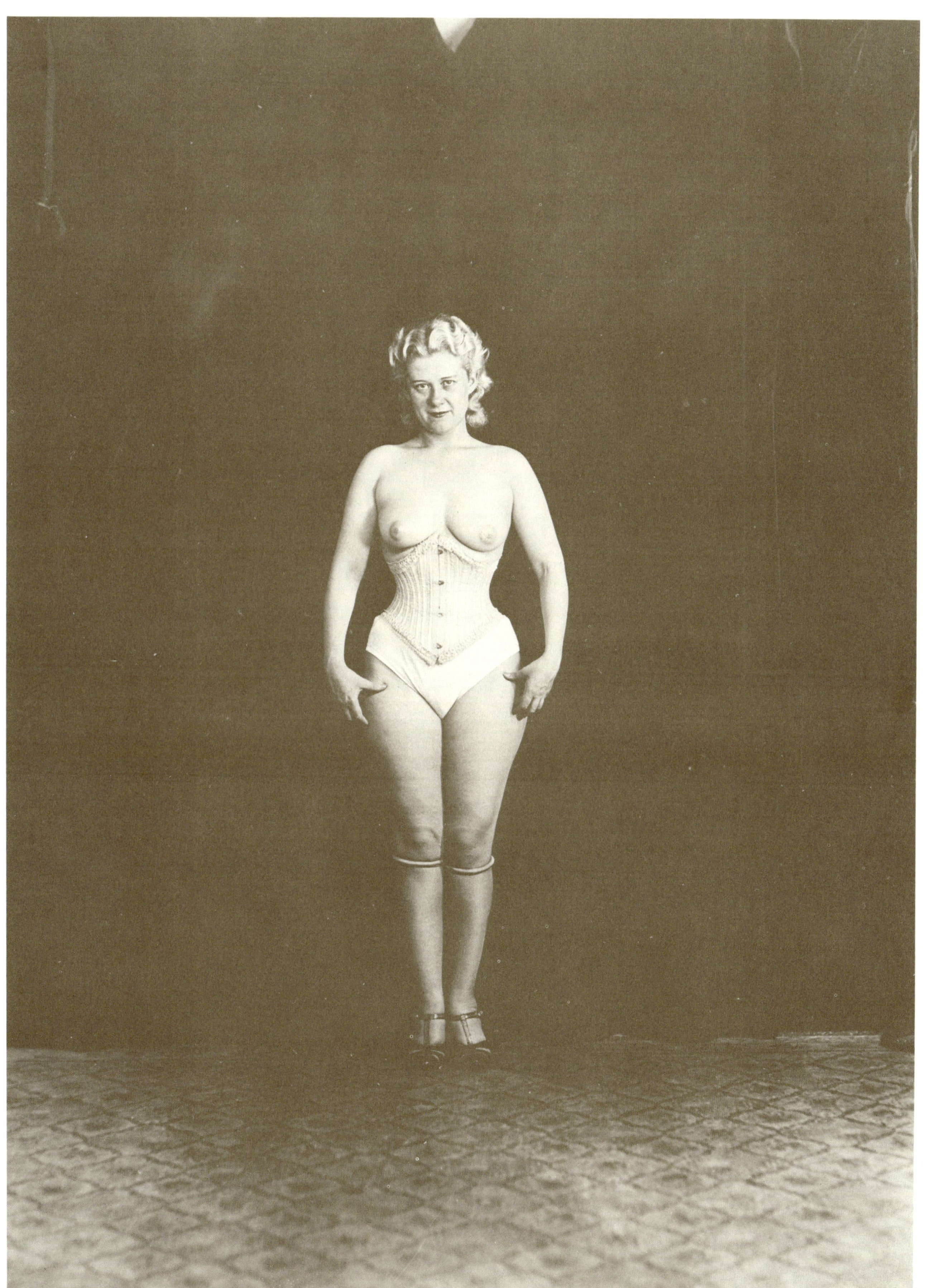

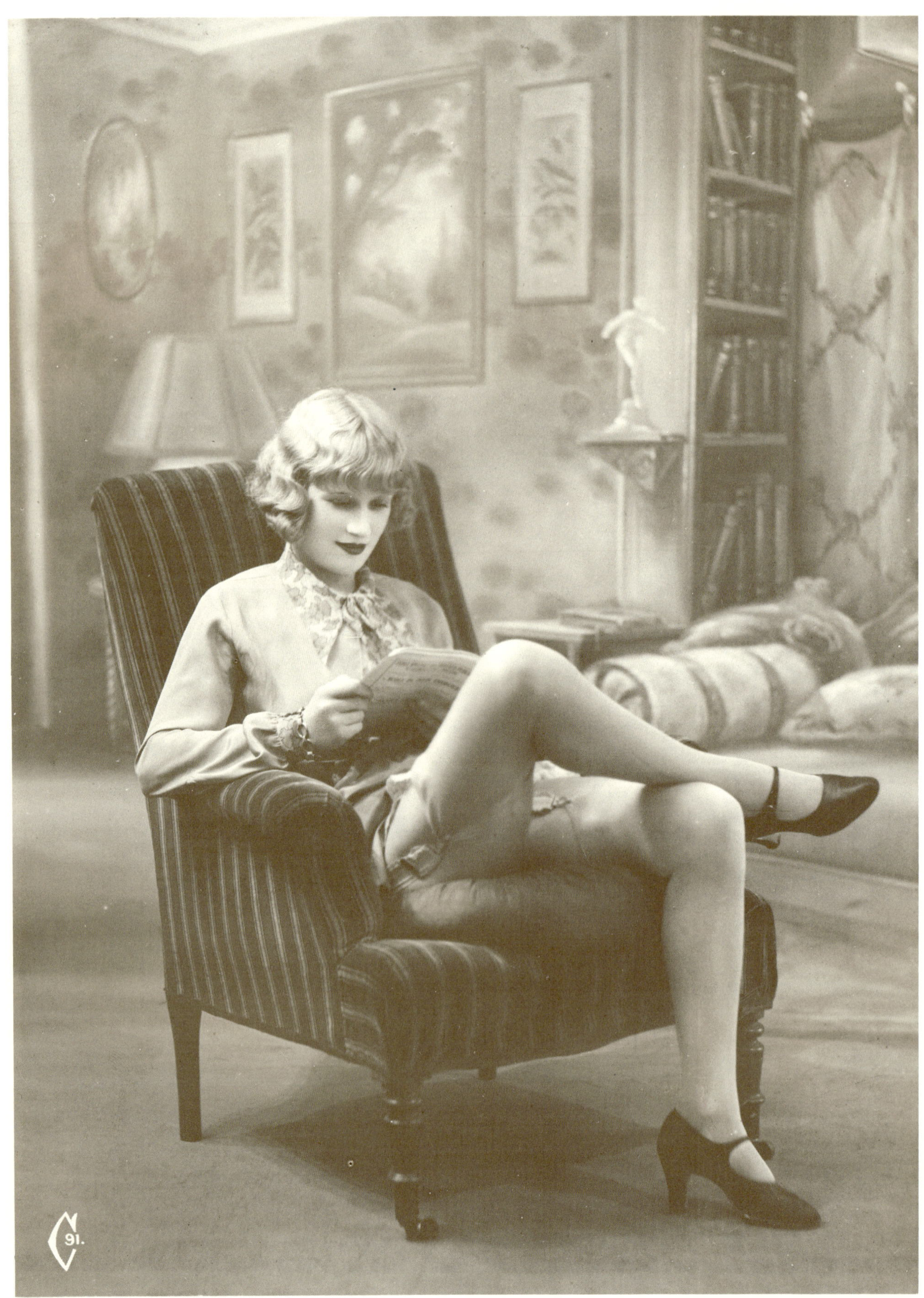

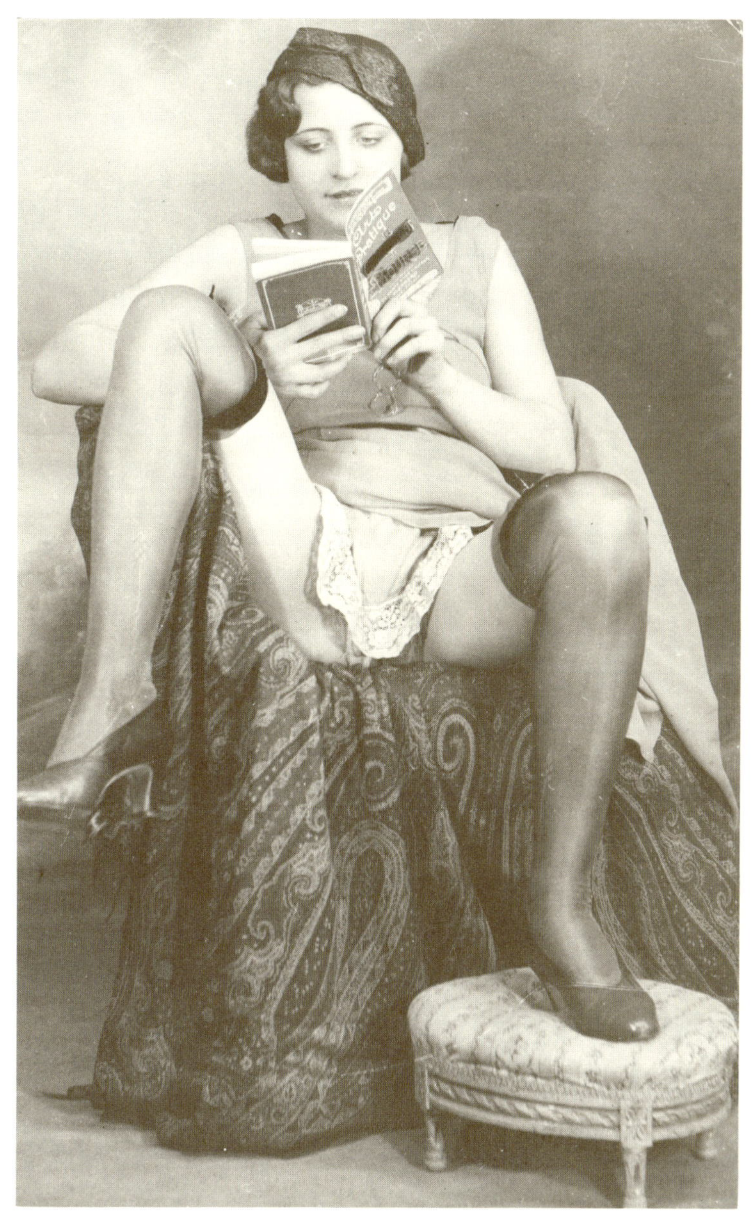

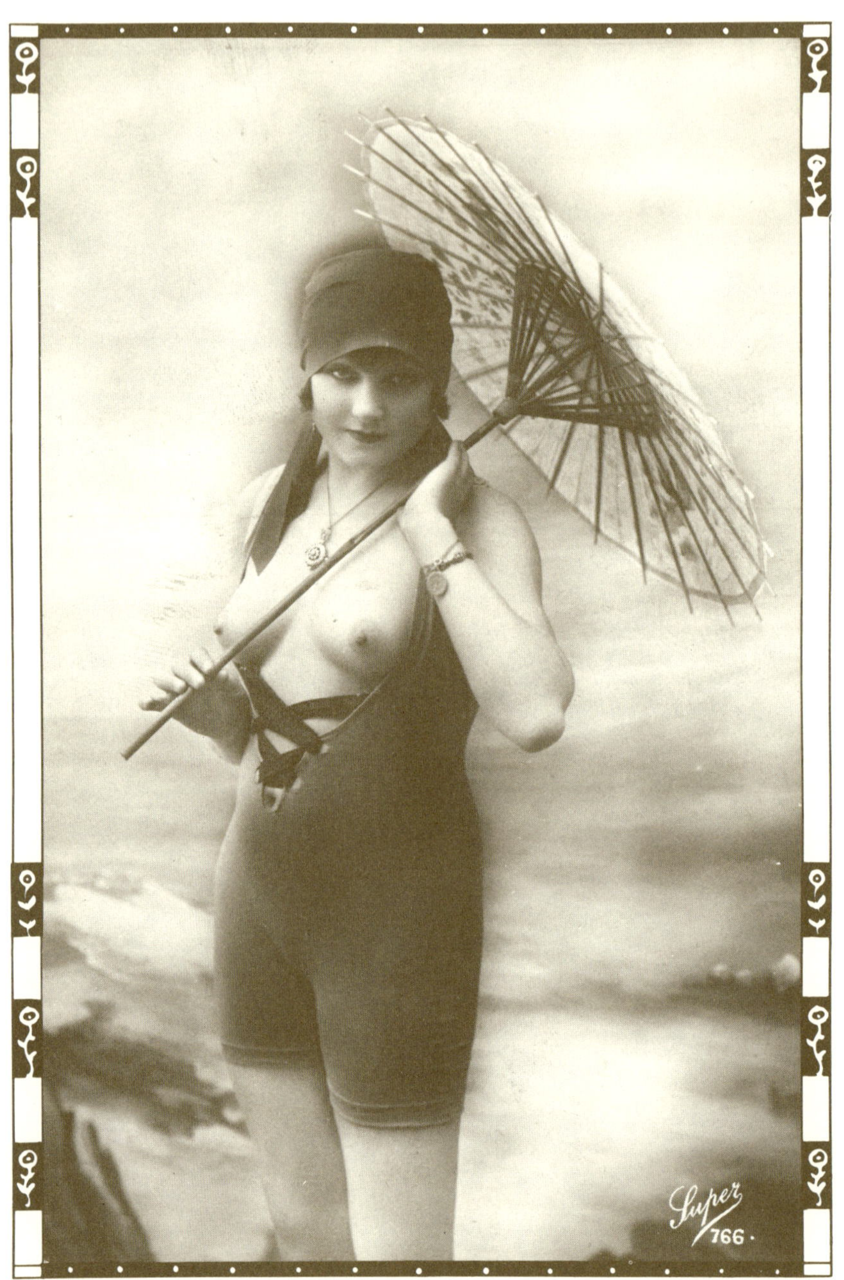
Super
766.

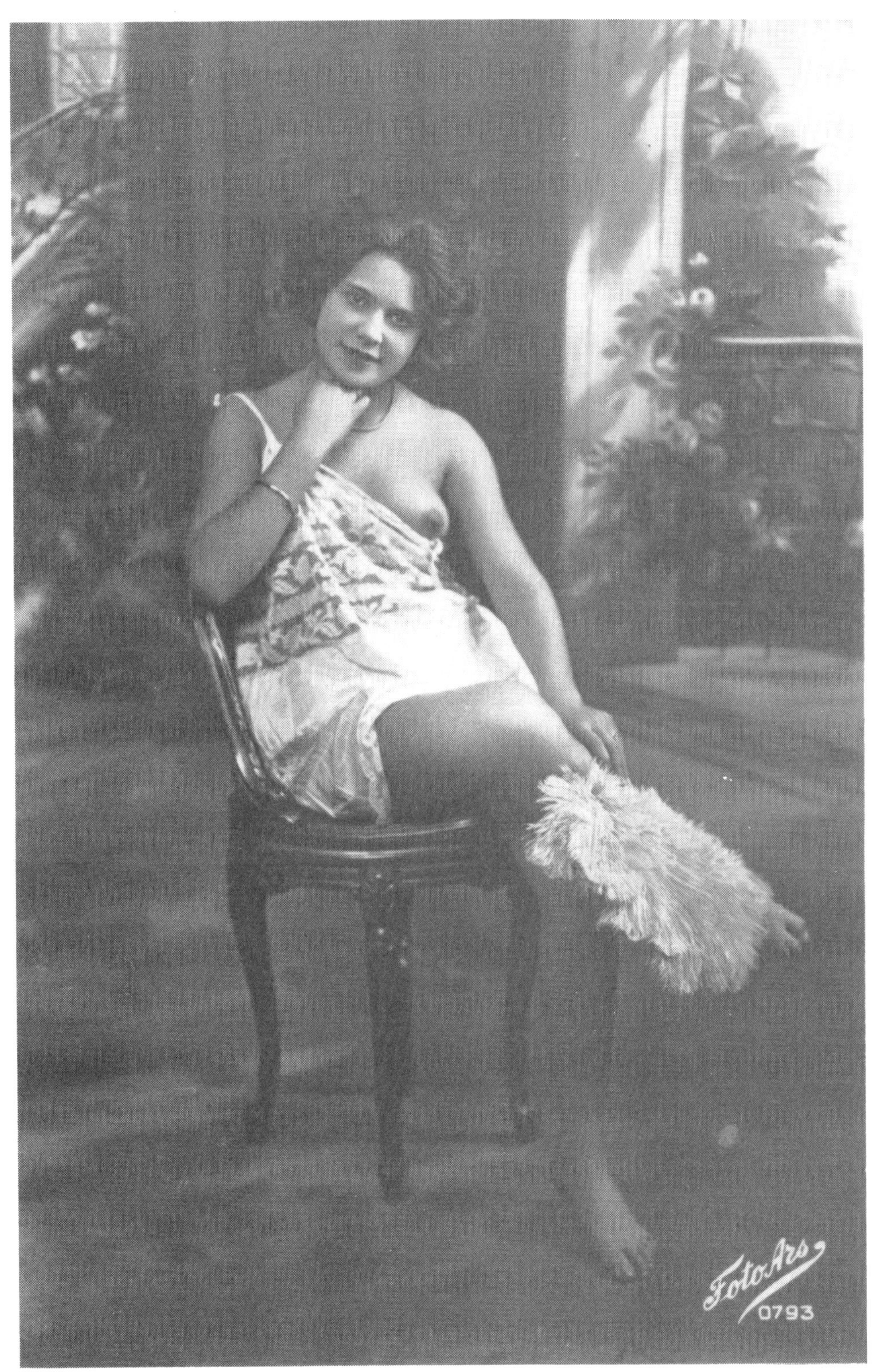
Foto Ars
0793

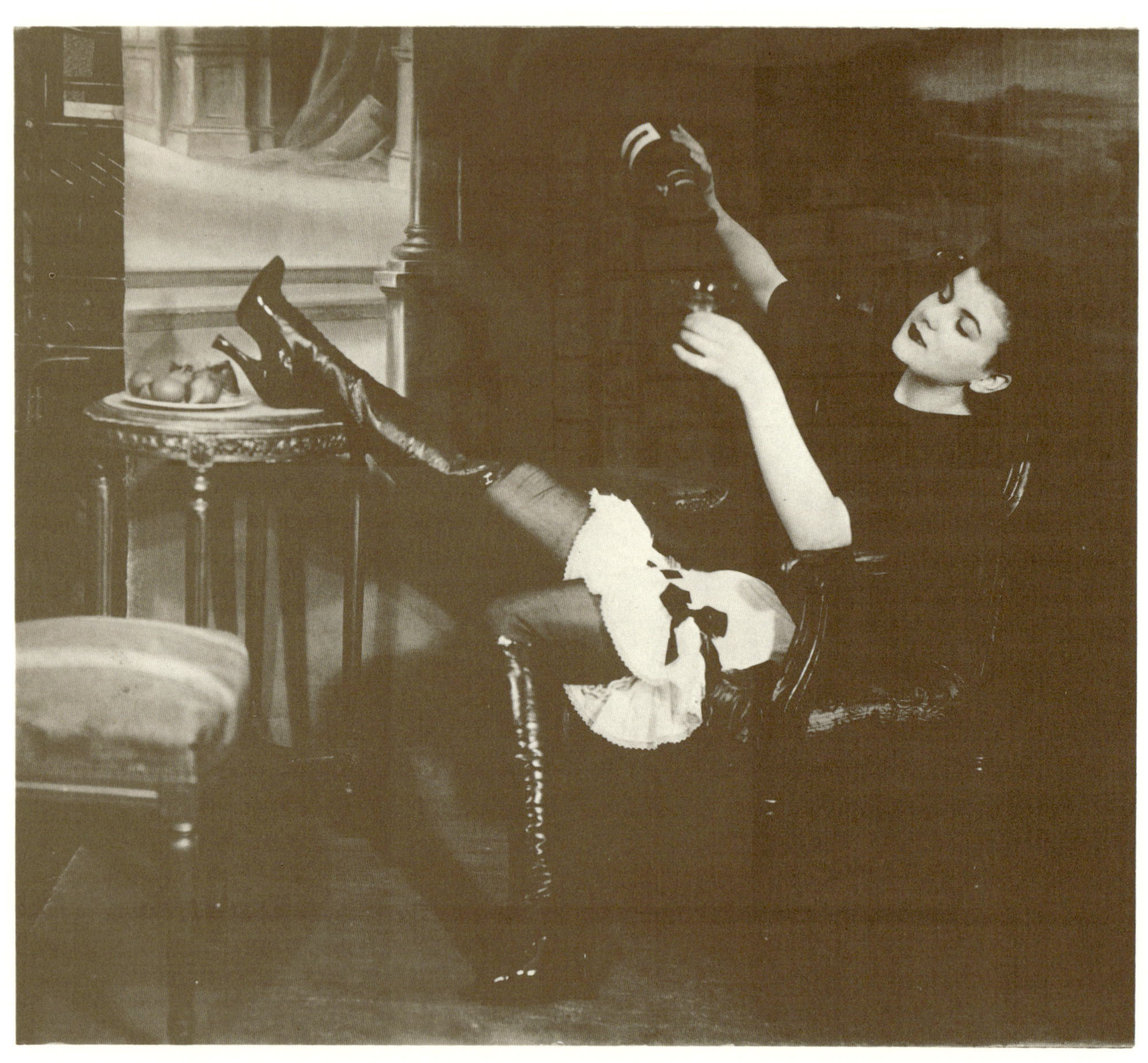

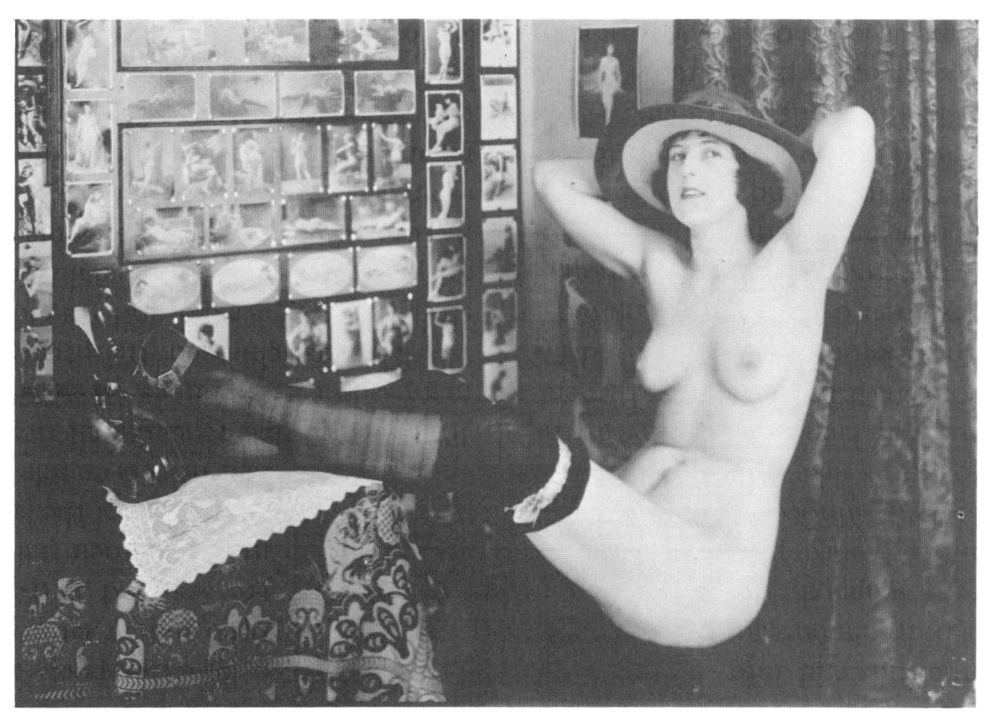

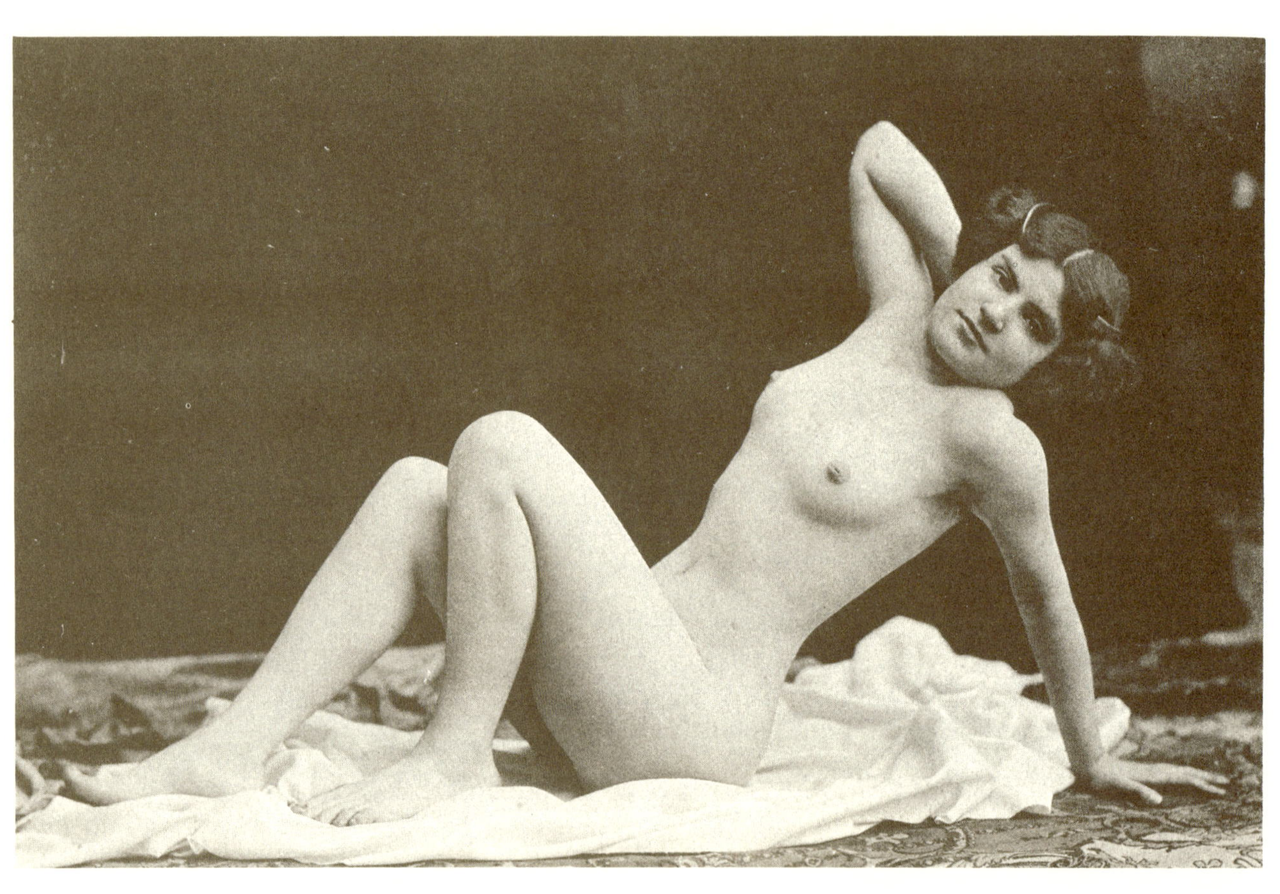

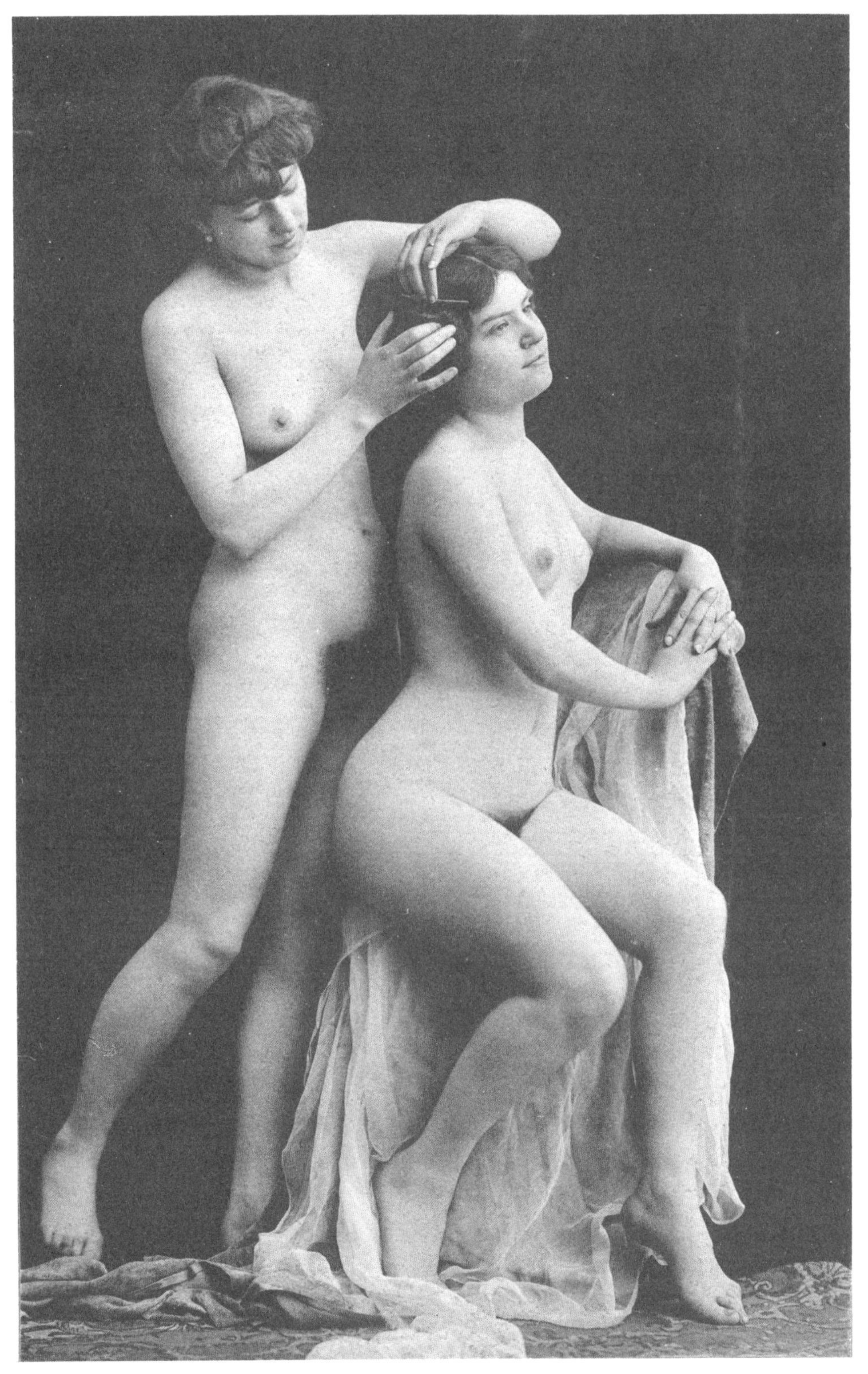

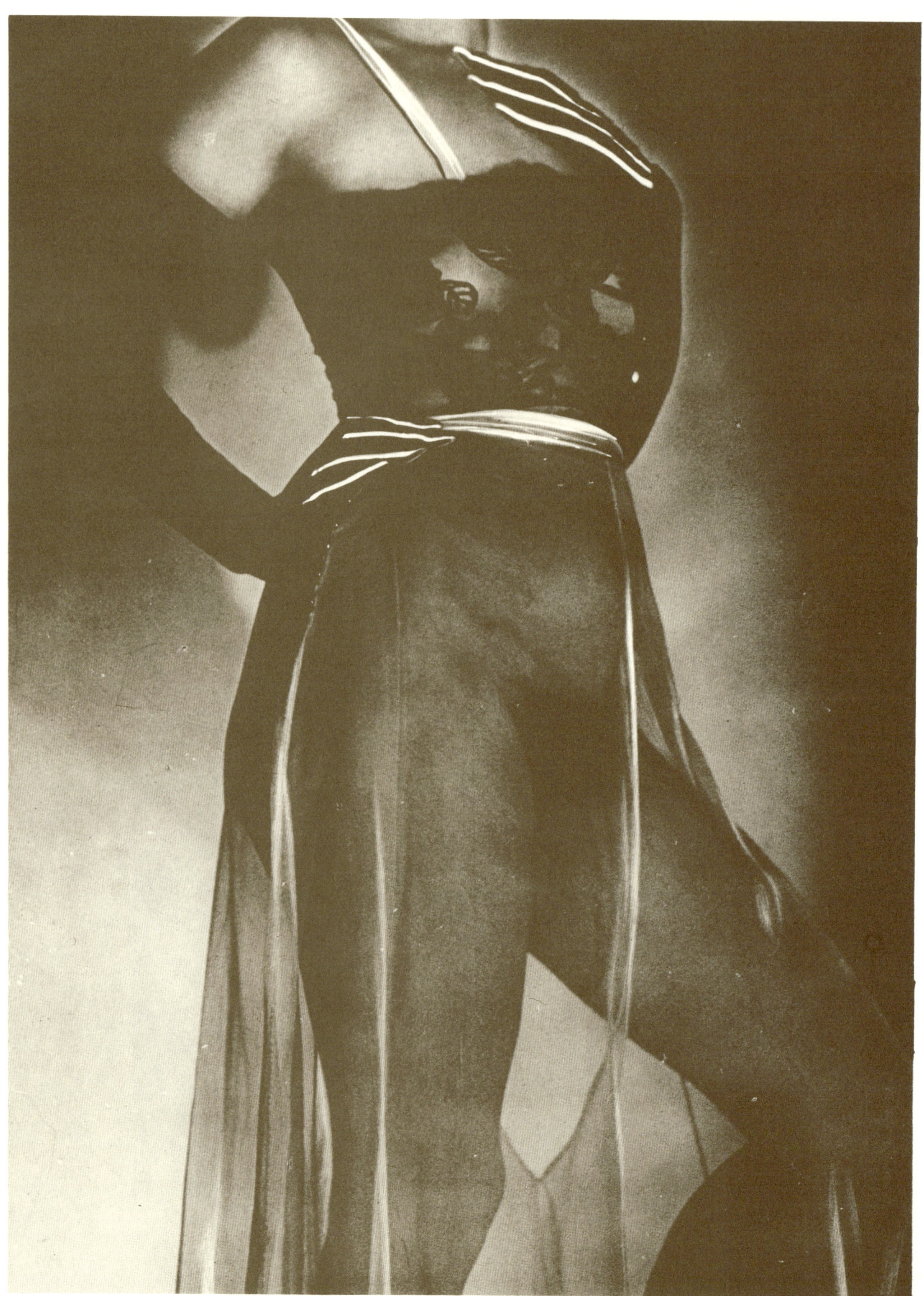

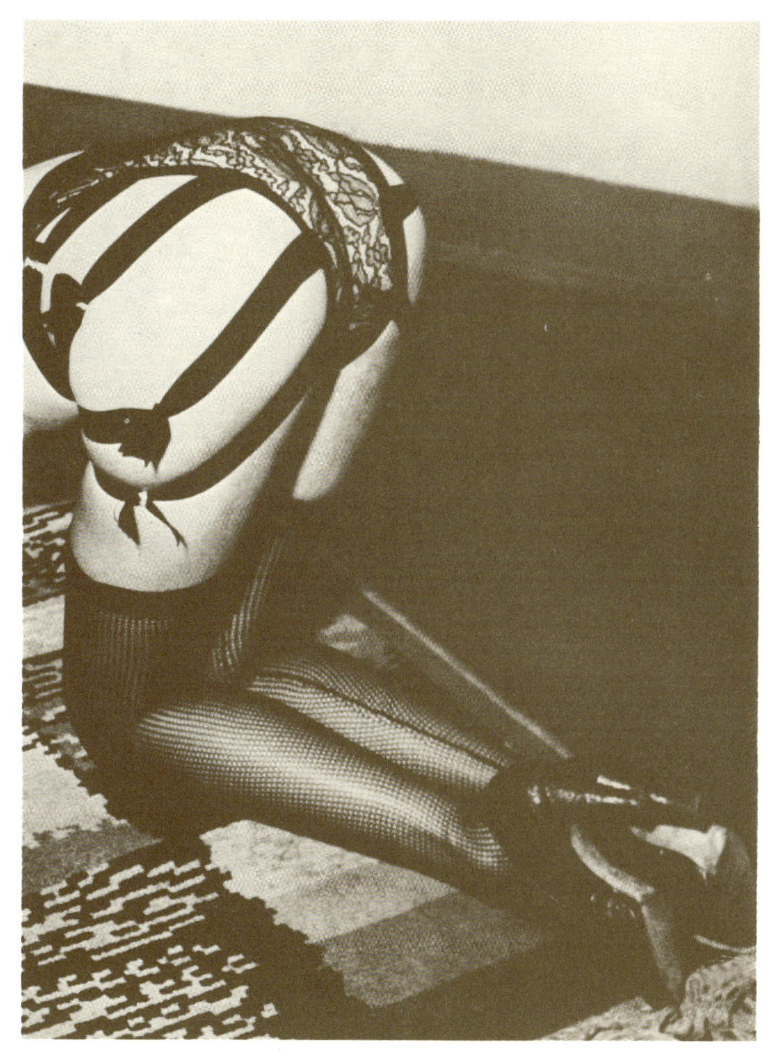

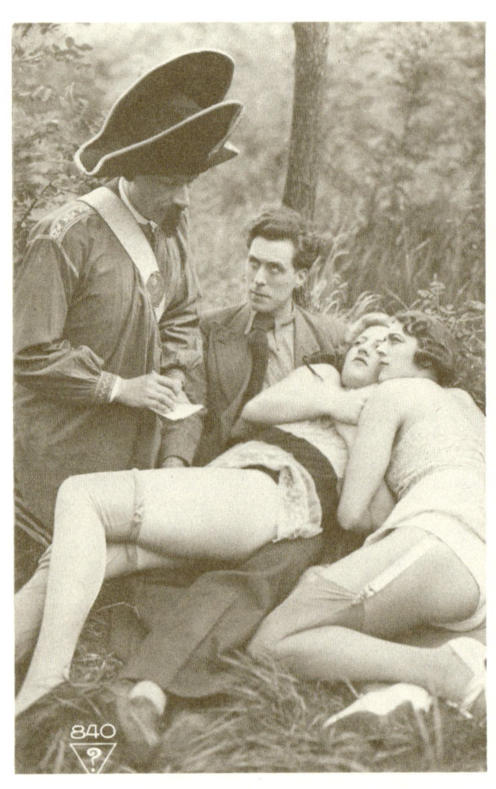
840

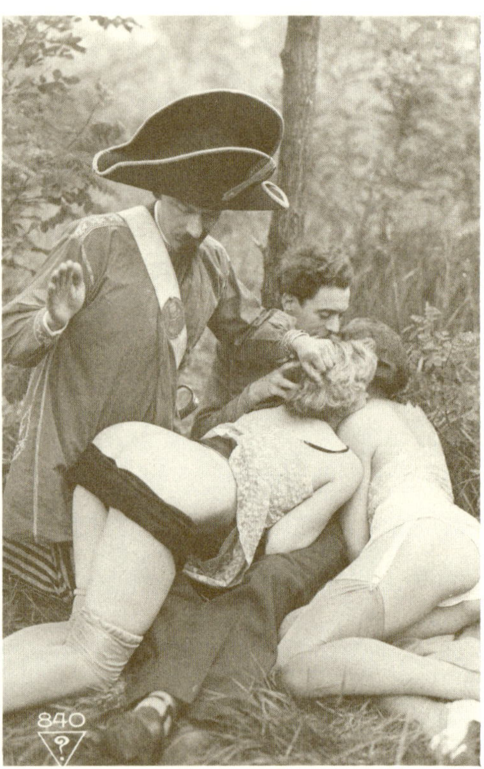
840

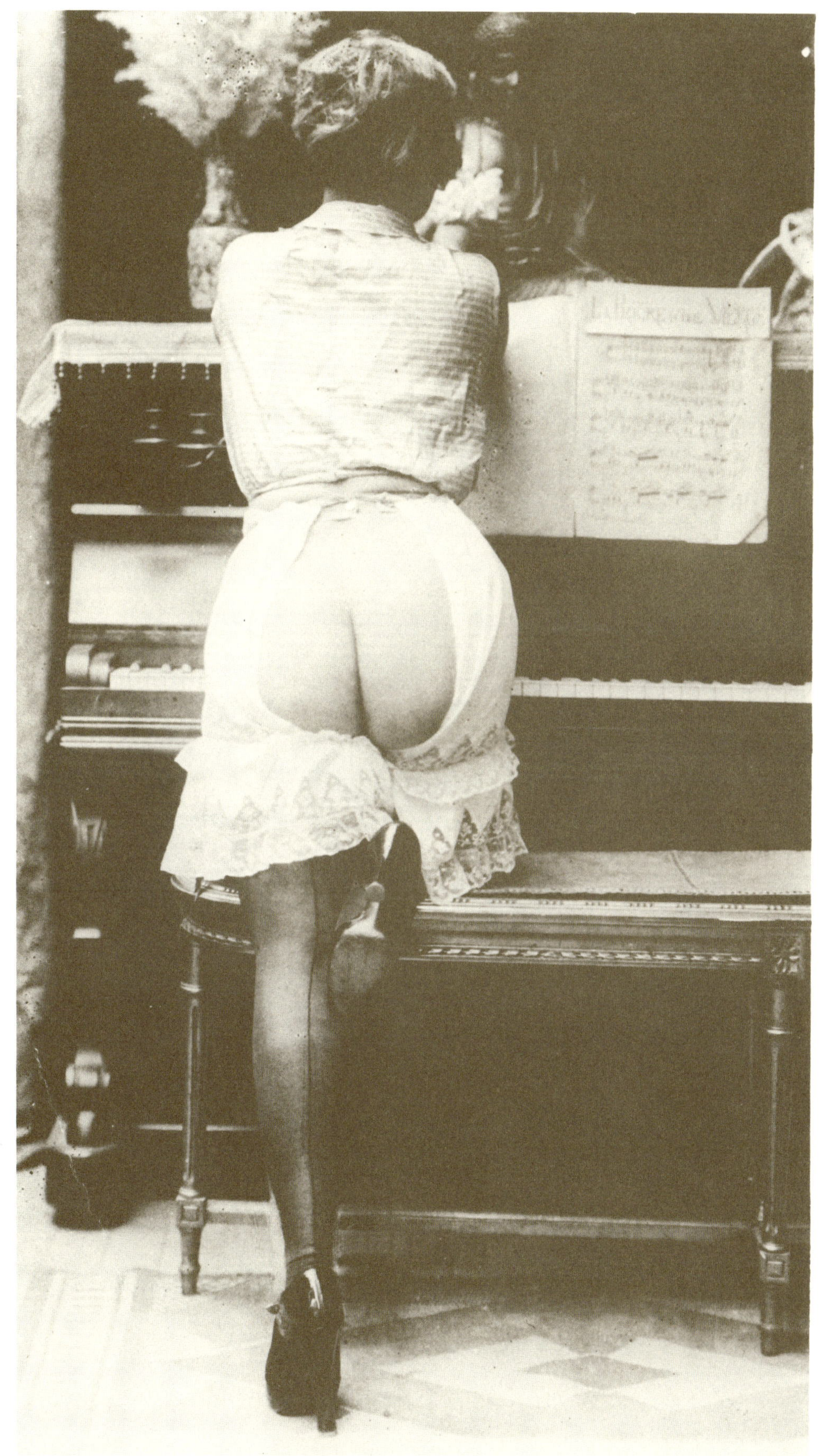

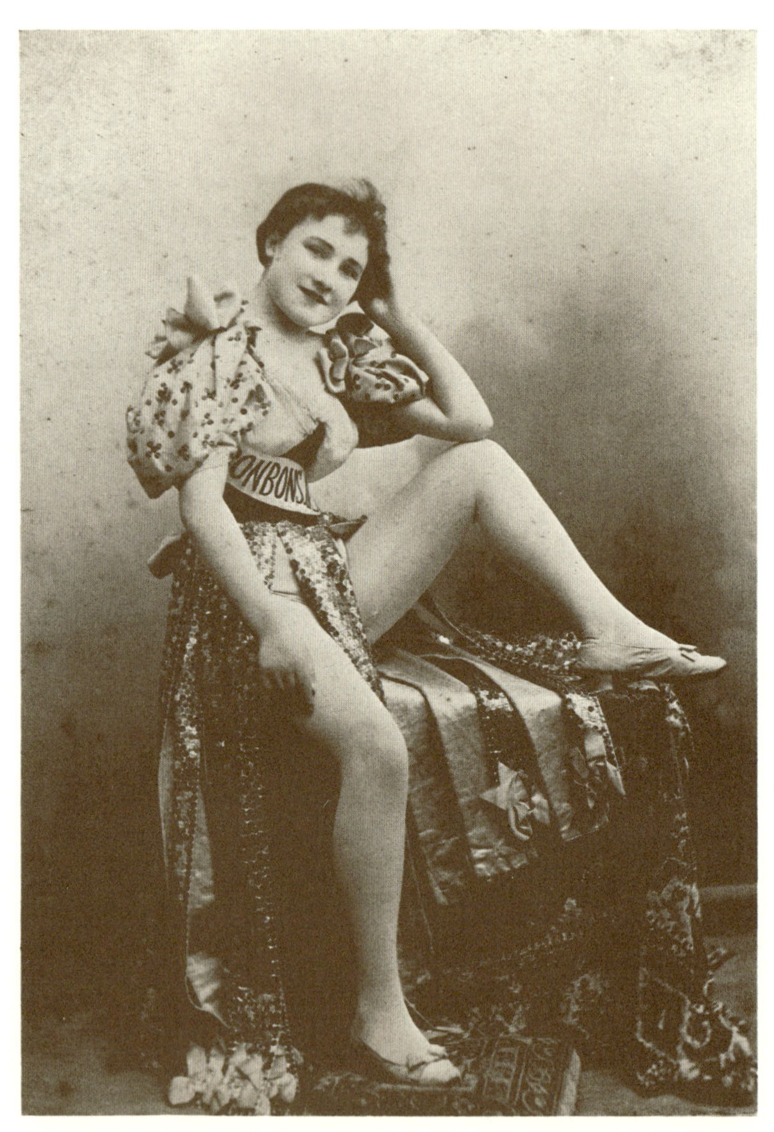
ONBONS

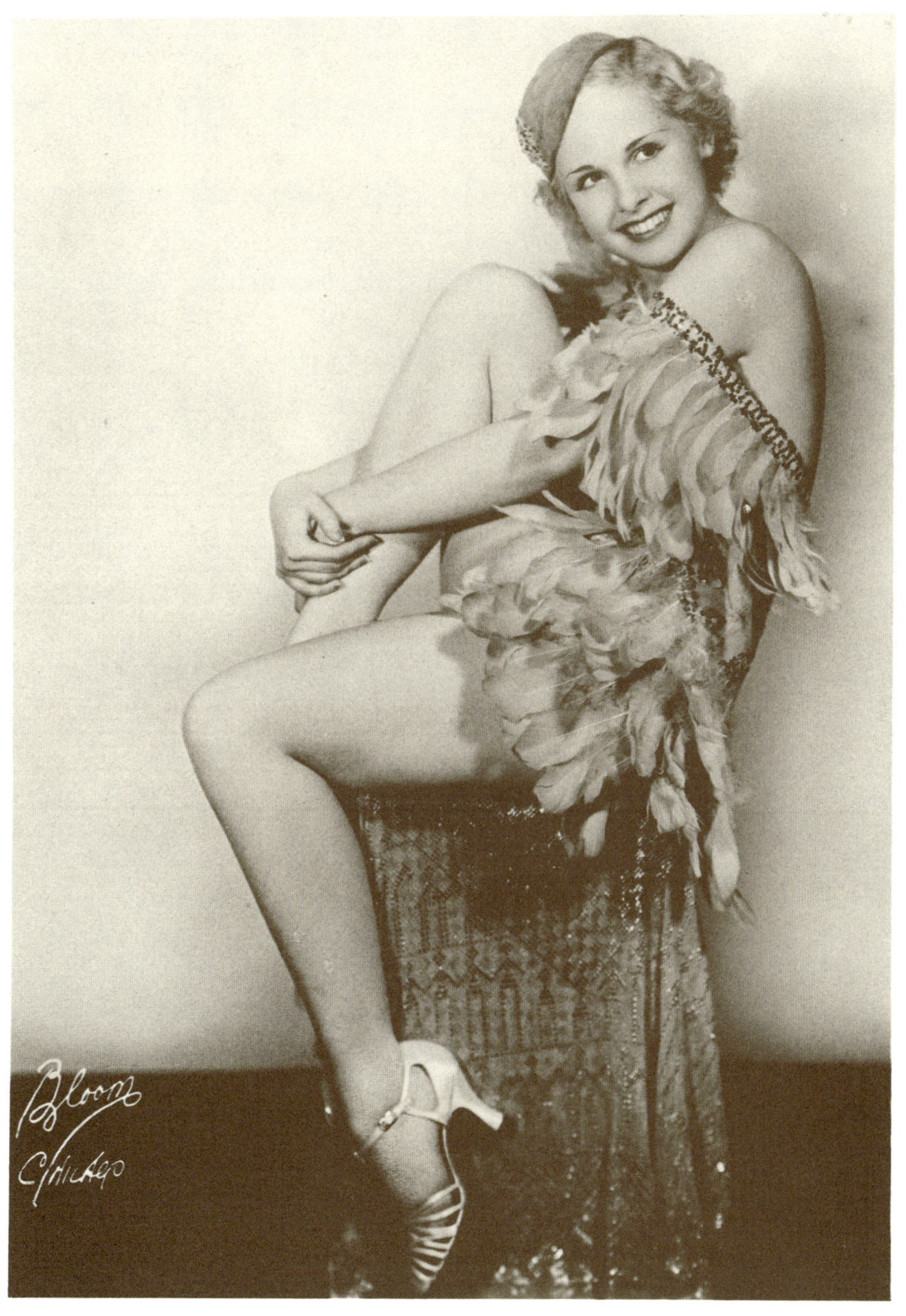
Bloom
Chicago

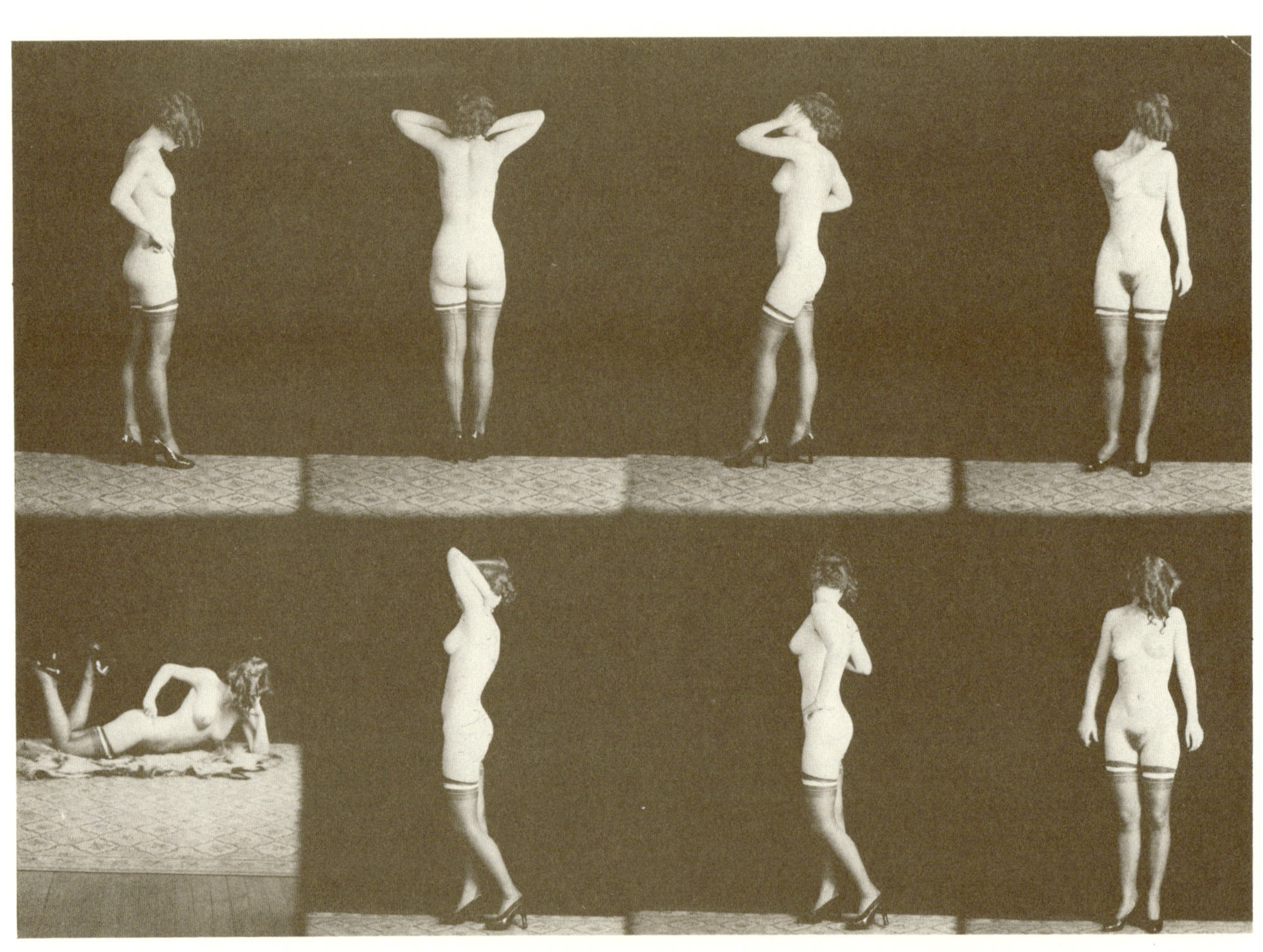

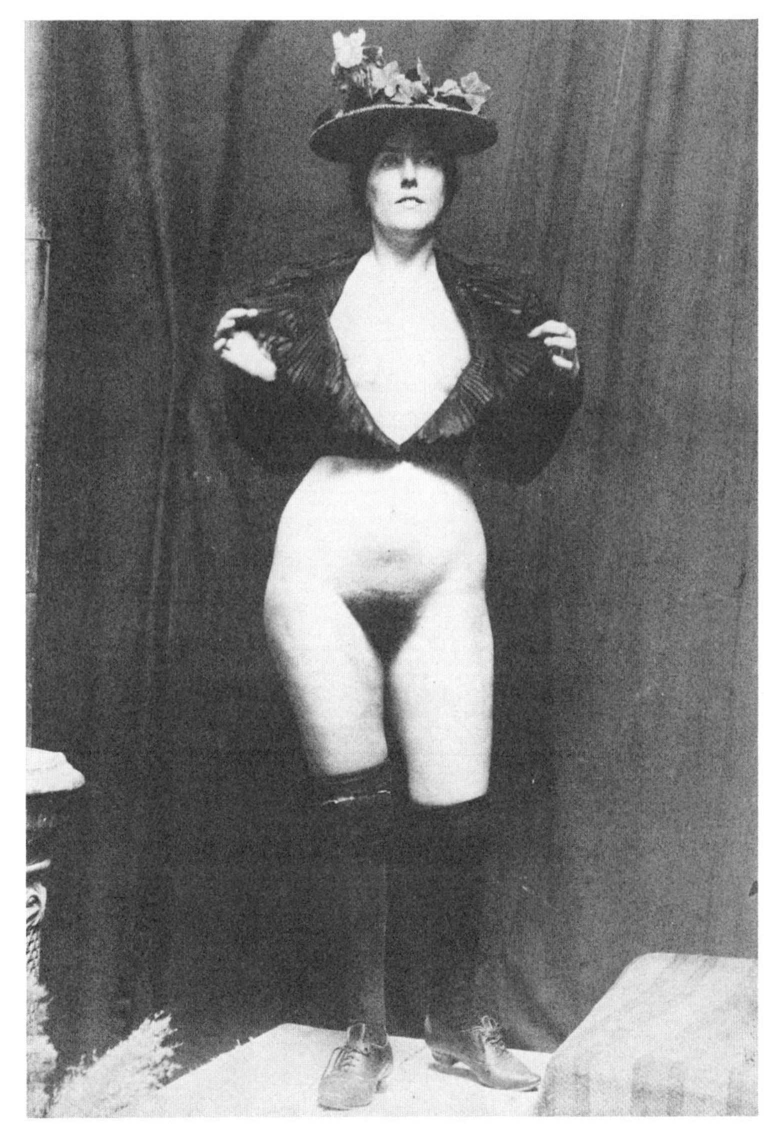

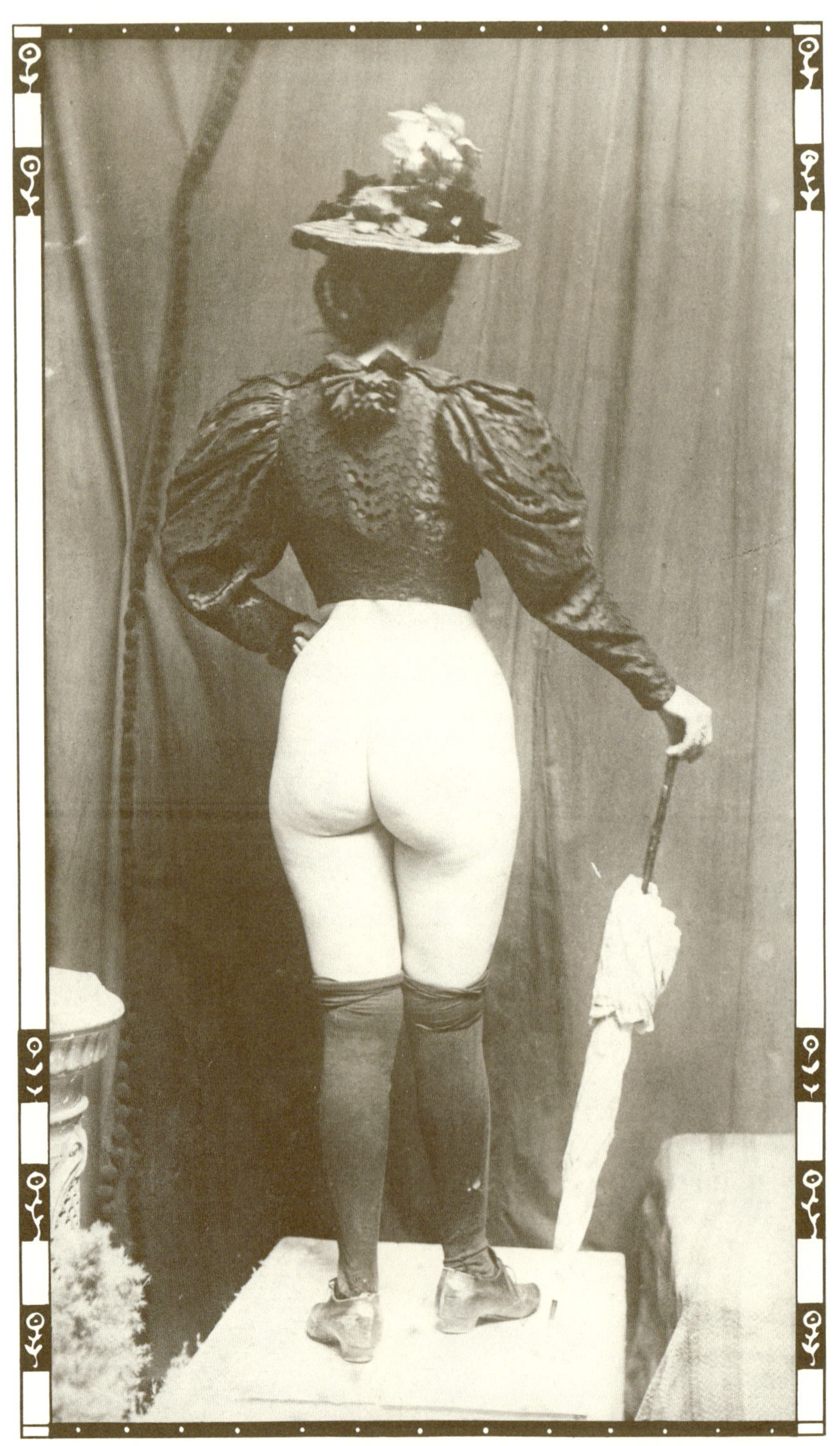

While it is impossible to document precisely the place of origin and date of every photograph in this book, the following represents a conscientious attempt at documenting the images in Velvet Eden. *—R.M.*

P. 1, France, circa 1930. P. 19, France, c. 1895. P. 20, France, c. 1895. P. 21, France, c. 1895. P. 22, France, c. 1895. P. 23, France, c. 1895. P. 24, France, 1925. P. 25, France, c. 1930. P. 26, United States, c. 1934. P. 27, United States, c. 1934. P. 28, France, c. 1900. P. 29, France, c. 1900. P. 30, France, 1930. P. 31, France, 1930. P. 32, France, 1930. P. 33, France, 1930. P. 34, France, c. 1925. P. 35, France, c. 1925. P. 36, France, c. 1895. P. 37, France, c. 1895. P. 38, Germany, 1930. P. 39, France, c. 1928. P. 40, France, c. 1925. P. 41, France, c. 1925. P. 42, France, c. 1925. P. 43, France, c. 1925. P. 44, France, c. 1925. P. 45, France, c. 1925. P. 46, Germany, 1930. P. 47, France, c. 1930. P. 48, France, 1925. P. 49, United States, c. 1940. P. 50, United States, c. 1940. P. 51, United States, c. 1940. P. 52, France, 1930. P. 53, France, c. 1930. P. 54, France, c. 1930. P. 55, France, c. 1930. P. 56, France, c. 1930. P. 57, France, c. 1930. P. 58, United States, 1934. P. 59, United States, 1934. P. 60, France, c. 1930. P. 61, France, c. 1900. P. 62, United States, 1938. P. 63, France, c. 1930. P. 64, France, c. 1930. P. 65, France, c. 1930. P. 66, United States, 1936. P. 67, France, 1925. P. 68, France, c. 1930. P. 69, France, c. 1930. P. 70, France, c. 1930. P. 71, France, c. 1930. P. 72, France, c. 1930. P. 73, France, c. 1930. P. 74, France, c. 1930. P. 75, France, c. 1930. P. 76, United States, 1940. P. 77, France, c. 1895. P. 78, United States, 1934. P. 79, United States, 1934. P. 80, France, c. 1930. P. 81, France, c. 1930. P. 82, France, c. 1930. P. 83, France, c. 1930. P. 84, France, c. 1930. P. 85, France, c. 1930. P. 86, United States, c. 1934. Sally Rand photographed by Palmer House Studios. P. 87, United States, c. 1934. Sally Rand photographed by Maurice Seymour. P. 88, France, c. 1930. P. 89, France, c. 1930. P. 90, France, c. 1930. P. 91, France, 1925. P. 92, France, c. 1920. P. 93, France, c. 1920. P. 94, France, c. 1930. P. 95, France, c. 1930. P. 96, France, c. 1930. P. 97, France, c. 1930. P. 98, France, c. 1930. P. 99, France, c. 1930. P. 100, United States, c. 1934. P. 101, France, 1925. P. 102, United States, 1940. P. 103, United States, 1940. P. 104, Germany, c. 1930. P. 105, France, c. 1925. P. 106, United States, 1940. P. 107, United States, 1940. P. 108, England, c. 1927. P. 109, France, c. 1925. P. 110, France, c. 1895. P. 111, France, 1920. P. 112, United States, C. 1932. P. 113, United States, c. 1920, Photograph of silent-screen actress. P. 114, France, c. 1925. P. 115, France, c. 1925. P. 116, France, c. 1925. P. 117, France, c. 1920. P. 118, France, c. 1895. P. 119, United States, 1936. Gypsy Rose Lee photographed by Maurice Seymour. P. 120, Germany, c. 1930. P. 121, United States, c. 1934. P. 122, France, c. 1890. P. 123, Germany, c. 1930. P. 124, France, c. 1930. P. 125, United States, c. 1938. P. 126, France, c. 1925. P. 127, France, c. 1925. P. 128, France, c. 1920. P. 129, France, c. 1920. P. 130, France, 1930. P. 131, France, c. 1925. P. 132, France, c. 1895. P. 133, France, c. 1895. P. 134, France, c. 1930. P. 135, France, c. 1930. P. 136, France, c. 1930. P. 137, France, 1925. P. 138, France, C. 1890. P. 139, United States, C. 1936. P. 140, United States, 1936. P. 141, France, c. 1900. P. 142, France, c. 1900.